THE MEDITATIONS

OF

DESCARTES

*TRANSLATED FROM THE LATIN AND COL-
LATED WITH THE FRENCH.*

The Meditations
AND
Selections from the Principles

René Descartes

translated by
John Veitch

with a preface,
copies of original title pages,
a bibliography, and an essay on
Descartes's philosophy
by L. Lévy-Bruhl, Maître de Conférences
in the Sorbonne

Open Court
La Salle, Illinois

OPEN COURT and the above logo are registered in the U.S. Patent and Trademark Office.

First published in 1901 by Open Court Publishing Company.

Reprinted in 1905, 1908, 1909, 1912, 1913, 1925, 1937, 1941, 1946, 1948, 1950, 1962, 1988.

Printed and bound in the United States of America.

René Descartes: The Meditations and Selections from the Principles
Translated by John Veitch

ISBN: 0-87548-043-8

PUBLISHERS' PREFACE.

An authorized reprint of Veitch's translation of Descartes' *Discourse on Method* has already been published as No. 38 of the Religion of Science Library. The present volume is a reprint of the remainder of Veitch's translations of Descartes' representative speculative treatises. The *Meditations on the First Philosophy* are translated entire, and the preface and the first part of the *Principles of Philosophy*, together with selections from the second, third and fourth parts of that work, corresponding to the extracts in the French edition of Garnier, are also given, as well as an appendix containing part of Descartes' reply to the *Second Objections* (*viz.*, his formal demonstrations of the existence of Deity), and Veitch's notes. The translations are based on the original Latin editions of the *Meditations* and *Principles*, published respectively in 1641 and 1644. Both works having been translated into French during Descartes' lifetime, and personally revised and corrected by him, the French text is evidently deserving of the same consideration as the Latin originals, and consequently, the additions and variations of the French version have also been given—the additions being put in square brackets in the text and the variations in the footnotes.

Dr. C. Güttler, of the University of Munich, has just published (Munich: C. H. Beck. 1901) a new critical and annotated edition of both the Latin and French texts of the *Meditations,* and students desirous of consulting the sources may be referred to this easily accessible book. Dr. Güttler made use of the copy of the original Latin edition (1641), preserved in the Bibliothèque Nationale at Paris, and of the copy of the original French translation by the Duc de Luynes (1647) found in the University Library at Göttingen. Literal copies of the title-pages of these original editions, as given in Dr. Güttler's work, are also reproduced in the present volume. The most recent French edition of the *Meditations* is that of Émile Thouverez (Paris: Belin Frères. 1898).

With a view to rendering the volume as complete and serviceable as possible, the publishers have added by way of a general introduction, Professor L. Lévy-Bruhl's essay on the philosophy of Descartes, which appeared in his *History of Modern Philosophy in France* (Chicago: The Open Court Publishing Co. 1899). A brief bibliography of Cartesian literature has also been appended.

It merely remains for us to add a few remarks as to the technical history of the *Meditations,* and to refer to the prevalent misconception that Descartes regarded his famous dictum, *Cogito, ergo sum,* as having the force of a syllogism.

The first draft of the *Meditations* was written in 1629 while Descartes was sojourning at a chateau of a noble family named Sjärdama, in Franeker, a small university town in Friesland. In a letter to Gibieuf, dated July 18, 1629, Descartes speaks of a small metaphysical tract on which he was engaged, and on April 15, 1630, he writes to Mersenne from Amsterdam that he had devoted the first nine months of his stay in Holland to meditation on the problem as to how the proofs of the truths of metaphysics might be rendered more evident than the demonstrations of geometry. The treatise did not see the light however, until 1641. In the meantime, the great work on *The World* was written (1633) and suppressed, and the *Discourse on Method* and the treatises on *Dioptrics, Meteors,* and *Geometry* (1637) appeared. It was to offset the criticisms which were aimed at these latter works by Fermat, Petit, De Roberval, Voëtius, Bourdin and others, that in 1639 Descartes took up the draft of the old tract prepared ten years before, to remodel it into an independent and systematic treatise on metaphysics. To forestall all possible animadversions, and to render his exposition explicit on all points, he submitted his manuscript before printing, to a number of learned men for examination and critical analysis. With the so-called *Objections,* which these critics supplied, and Descartes' answers, the book finally appeared on August 28, 1641. The authors of the *Objections* were: Caterus, a theologian of Louvain (First Objections); Mersenne, Desargues, and anonymous critics (Second and Sixth Objections); Hobbes, Arnauld and Gassendi (Third, Fourth and Fifth Objections). In later editions, other *Objections* were incorporated. The title *Meditationes* was chosen in contradistinction to the *Quaestiones* and *Disputationes* of scholastic literature.

* * *

PUBLISHERS' PREFACE.

The frequent misconception that Descartes regarded his famous *cogito, ergo sum,* as having the force of a syllogism also deserves brief mention. Descartes himself, although not always careful as to his mode of expression on this point, has explicitly anticipated the objection so often made to his reasoning. In *Meditation II.* (see pages 30-33) he omits the "therefore." In his reply to Gassendi's objection that *cogito ergo sum* implies *qui cogitat est,* a prejudgment, Descartes says:

"The term *pre-judgment* is here abused. Prejudgment there is none, when the *cogito ergo sum* is duly considered, because it then appears so evident to the mind that it cannot keep itself from believing it, the moment even it begins to think of it. But the principal mistake here is this, that the objector supposes that the cognition of particular propositions is always deduced from universals, according to the order of the syllogisms of logic. He thus shows that he is ignorant of the way in which truth is to be sought. For it is settled among philosophers, that in order to find it a beginning must always be made from particular notions, that afterwards the universal may be reached; although also reciprocally, universals being found, other particulars may thence be deduced." Again he says: "When we apprehend that we are thinking things, this is a first notion which is not drawn from any syllogism; and when some one says, *I think, hence I am,* or *I exist,* he does not conclude his existence from his thought as by force of some syllogism, but as a thing known of itself; he sees from this, that if he deduced it from a syllogism, he must beforehand have known this major, *All that which thinks is or exists.* Whereas, on the contrary, this is rather taught him, from the fact that he experiences in himself that it cannot be that he thinks if he does not exist. For it is the property of our mind to form general propositions from the knowledge of particulars."

In other places, also, Descartes has made the same distinct assertion.* Finally, Mr. C. S. Peirce, in THE OPEN COURT of June 15, 1893, cites a passage in a letter to Clerselier:

"Je pense, donc je suis, ne suppose pas la majeure, *Tout ce qui pense existe."*   T. J. McCORMACK.
La Salle, Ill., September, 1901.

(*See M. Cousin's edition, T. I., 247, 403; T. II., 74, 333.)

ESSAY ON DESCARTES.
BY PROF. L. LÉVY-BRUHL.

WITH Descartes a new period of modern philosophy begins. It is not, indeed, a beginning in a literal sense: there is no such thing in the history of ideas, nor elsewhere. Descartes, who came after the great scientific and philosophical illumination of the sixteenth century, had profited largely by it. He owed much to the Italian Renaissance, and not less to the Renaissance in France and in England. He was acquainted with the discoveries of contemporary men of science, such as Galileo, Torricelli, and Harvey. Even scholastic philosophy, which he was to combat, left a lasting impression upon his mind.

However, after we have considered all the influences, both of the past and of the present, which were exercised upon him, the originality of Descartes shines out all the more conspicuously, and we see the more clearly that he initiated a new philosophic method. Hegel called him a hero, and this hyperbole may in a certain sense be justified. Descartes had, indeed, no vocation for martyrdom. But nature had endowed him with that higher sort of courage which is love of truth and devotion to science; and if the name of hero is due the men whose exertions have laid open new paths for human thought, Descartes is undoubtedly entitled to the name.

The attitude of Descartes toward the philosophers who preceded him is remarkable,—he deliberately ignores them. Although well acquainted with their works, he builds his own system as if he knew nothing of them. He wishes to depend solely on his own method and reason. Not that he personally holds in contempt either the ancient or the modern philosophers. He is not so presumptuous as to believe that his mind is superior to theirs. He even acknowledges that many truths had been discovered before he created his method, but these truths he does not wish to accept on tradition. He is determined to discover them for himself. By means of his method he proposes to obtain these truths, no longer mixed pell-mell with the mass of doubtful or erroneous opinions, but set in their right places, and accompanied with their proofs. Thus only do they become valuable and useful. For a truth, when isolated, sporadic, and floating and unconnected with the truths that have gone before it, and consequently powerless to develop those that are to come after it, is of slight interest in itself. To acquire such a truth is not worth the trouble we must take in order to understand ancient books, and the time we lose in learning the ancient languages. All this time were better employed in training our reason to grasp the necessary concatenation of truths as deducible one from another.

This is already a first motive, and a quite sufficient one, for Descartes to dispense with erudition and to take no account of traditional doctrine. But he has another and more weighty one. He seeks not what is probable, but what is true. Now the first requisite in finding what is true he takes to be the casting aside of the philosophy taught in his time, which contented itself with probability and gave no satisfactory demonstrations. Therefore, though he occasionally retains the vocabulary of scholasticism (for instance in the greater part of his *Meditations*), though he even borrows some of his matter from it (for instance, in the ontological argument, in the theory of continuous creation), nevertheless Descartes broke distinctly and completely with the method and spirit of the philosophy which had been handed down from antiquity through the vicissitudes of the Middle Ages and the struggles of the Renaissance. Even what he seems to borrow from it, he really transforms. Cartesianism not only has a positive meaning, which we shall presently study, but it has to begin with a critical function, and proposes first of all to do away with a philosophical system which, appealing to substantial forms and occult causes, claimed to explain everything and could demonstrate nothing.

There is accordingly something more in his attitude to his predecessors than a mere protest against the authoritative method,—a protest which had already been raised by eloquent voices in the sixteenth century and even earlier. We have in it, in fact, a set determination to consider the generally accepted philosophy as null and void, and to replace it with another which shall owe nothing to the former. A bold undertaking, not merely of a reformative but of a revolutionary nature. In England, Bacon, while combating the Scholastic Philosophy in the matter of experimental method, nevertheless derived from it his conception of physical reality. Hobbes, however much he may have freed himself from traditional metaphysics, is nevertheless the heir of the later great English scholastics. In Germany likewise, the genius of Leibniz is one of conservatism as well as of innovation. He openly disapproves of Descartes's excessive severity toward scholasticism, of which, for his part, he preserves a great deal, in his doctrine as well as in his terminology. Therefore we see his successor Wolf restoring, so to speak, a new scholastic system based on the philosophy of Leibniz. It was this philosophy that Kant imbibed; and later on, after Kant's *Kritik*, a kind of new scholasticism appeared (in the school of Hegel for instance), indisputably related to that of the Middle Ages. Thus, in Germany, the thread of philosophical tradition was never entirely broken.

In France, owing to Descartes, the case was altogether different. The Cartesian philosophy aimed at nothing less than the utter destruction of its rival. It prevailed; and, as early as the latter part of the seventeenth century, the victory was complete. This was both favorable and unfavorable to the progress of French philosophy. Of course, it was no small advantage for the latter to free itself from the prestige of antiquity, from the tyranny of scholasticism, to regain its full independence, and to draw its inspiration freely from the spirit of the mathematical and physical sciences, the increasing power of which was a genuinely new element in the life of mankind. To this the success of Cartesianism, and the fact that its method persisted, even after the doctrine was discarded, bear sufficient testimony. But on the other hand, certain displeasing characteristics of French philosophy in the eighteenth century may, at least in some measure, have originated in this breaking with tradition. A taste for abstract and too simple solutions, a conviction that it is sufficient to argue soundly upon evident principles in order to discover the truth, even in the most complex problems of social life—in short, a lack of historical spirit, with which the French philosophy of that period has been reproached—all these faults are owing in some measure to the spirit of Cartesianism. Certain it is that Descartes and his followers, in their contest with tradition, failed to appreciate its value and necessary function.

Nothing is so significant in this respect as the way in which these writers speak of history. As it is not a science, it cannot possibly be the basis of a school. It may entertain us, but it cannot really teach us. It is even liable to beget false ideas, and to be an encouragement to extravagant undertakings. And, logically speaking, whatever rests on historical claims only is insufficiently justified. This last maxim may, in practice, have most serious consequences. Descartes foresaw the attempt that would be made to extend its application to political and social problems. He therefore openly disclaims beforehand this application, which he personally refuses to make. Yet if he wishes us to abstain from criticising existing institutions, it is in his case, as in Montaigne's, for reasons of utility alone. One can easily imagine circumstances in which considerations of utility would favor the other side. It is, then, a mere question of expediency.

This tendency to claim that reason alone ought to be the basis of opinion, because reason alone can demonstrate it to be true, and the consequent tendency to make free use of rational criticism, appear in the history which Descartes gives us of his mind. Of all that he learned at school, nothing satisfied him except mathematics. Hardly had he freed himself from the sway of his masters (the best, he says, there were then in Europe), when he deliberately set about forgetting their teaching. He speaks only with irony of the various sciences, or so-called sciences: medicine, law, philosophy, as they were taught in his day. He coolly turns his back on belles lettres, and holds history in contempt. Geometry alone found favor in his eyes; still he wondered greatly at its being used only as an object of amusement for the curious, and that "on so firm a basis nothing more lofty had been established." The ground was now cleared; Descartes could begin to build.

According to some, Descartes is first of all a man of science, and secondly a philosopher. According to others, the philosopher in him predominates over the man of science. In point of fact, philosophy and science were not separated in Descartes's view. He seeks to establish the system of truths accessible to man—a system which he conceived as unique, and which may be figured as an endless chain. And he seeks it in order to find the means of living as uprightly and happily as possible. Thus the end which Descartes has in view is a righteous and happy life: wherein he agrees with the philosophers of his time, and, we may also say, of all times.

In order to attain to this righteous and happy life, leaving out of account the teachings of religion, Descartes sees no sure way but the possession of truth or science. Now science, in its turn, rests on metaphysics, or primary philosophy, whence it derives its principles. Therefore Descartes proposes to be a metaphysician; but this he will be for the sake of science itself. Metaphysics is to him a road, but indeed a road of paramount importance, since all the rest depends upon the principles discovered therein. Besides, mathematics, physics, and other theoretical sciences are also roads, the terminal point lying in the applied sciences, to which they lead. "The whole of philosophy," says Descartes, in the Preface to the *Principes de la Philosophie,* "is like a tree, the roots of which are metaphysics; the trunk is the science of physics; and the branches shooting from that trunk are all the other sciences, which may be reduced to three main ones, viz., medicine, mechanics, and ethics, by which last I mean the highest and most perfect ethics, which, since it presupposes a complete knowledge of the other sciences, is the supreme degree of wisdom."

Thus if Descartes is careful to make a distinction between the sphere of action and that of knowledge, and if, before undertaking the long and difficult task of seeking after truth, he provides himself with a "provisional" ethics, which he unquestioningly accepts from authority and custom, he nevertheless proclaims the principles of action to be dependent upon knowledge. It is the business of reason not only to enlighten, but also to guide us. Descartes, believing in the future progress of mankind, considers it to be dependent on the development of the sciences. We even observe, in several passages, that the progress of ethics appears to him subordinate to that of mechanics and of medicine. But these in their turn depend for their advancement upon the establishment of a sound and rigorously demonstrated physical science. Thus, although science is not its own end, the fundamental problem of philosophy according to Descartes is finally reduced to the problem of the establishment of science.

Now there is no breach of continuity between metaphysics and physics; on the contrary, there is a natural and necessary transition from the one to the other. Descartes attempted to build up a system by means of which one could proceed uninterruptedly from the first principles of cognition and of being, in a word, from God, down to the most specific scientific proposition of physiology or of ethics, without one link missing in the chain. A bold conception, which dominates the whole system and is inseparable from the famous method of Descartes.

Up to this point mathematics alone appeared to Descartes worthy of being called a science. It differs from everything else he had learned in the perfect lucidity of its principles, in the rigorous demonstration of its propositions, and in the inevitable sequence of its truths. But to what does it owe these characteristics, if not to the method from which mathematicians make it a rule never to depart? Therefore, in order to establish the science or philosophy sought by Descartes, it was sufficient to find a method that should be to philosophy what the method of mathematical deduction is to arithmetic, algebra and geometry.

To apply to that universal science conceived by Descartes the method so effectively employed in the above-mentioned sciences would evidently be the simplest solution of the problem proposed. But this solution is impracticable. The mathematical method, as we see it practiced in "the analysis of the ancients and the algebra of the moderns" is a special method, limited to the study of figures in geometry, and confined in algebra to symbols and rules which hamper the mind. How could one pass from these processes, which are especially adapted to particular sciences, to the general method required by general science or philosophy? Descartes would undoubtedly never have conceived such an audacious hope, had not a great discovery of his set him on this track. He had invented analytical geometry, or the method of expressing by means of equations the properties of geometrical figures, or, inversely, of representing determinate equations by means of geometrical figures. In this way, Descartes substituted for the old methods, which were especially adapted to algebra and geometry as distinct branches, a general method, applicable to what he called the "universal mathematical science," viz., to the study of "the various ratios or proportions to be found between the objects of the mathematical sciences, hitherto regarded as distinct." Not only did this discovery mark a decisive epoch in the history of mathematics, which it provided with an instrument of incomparable simplicity and power, but it furthermore gave Descartes a right to hope for the philosophical method he was seeking. Ought not a last generalization to be possible, by means of which the method he had so happily discovered should become applicable, not only to the "universal mathematical science," but also to the systematic combination of all the truths which our finite minds may permit us to attain?

Thus was formed in Descartes's mind the method which he summed up in the *Discours de la Methode,* and which was destined in his plan to replace the useless and sterile ancient logic. It is inexpedient here to explain these rules minutely. We must, however, observe that the first one, "Never to accept a thing as true which I do not clearly know to be such," is not, properly speaking, a precept of method. Such precepts are set forth in a subsequent set of rules, where Descartes successively prescribes analysis for dividing difficulties into parts, and synthesis for constructing and expounding science. But the first rule is quite different. It does not lay down a process to be used in order to discover truth. It concerns method only in so far as method is not separated from science itself (and such indeed was Descartes's meaning). If such is the case, the first step of method—or of science—must be to determine accurately by what mark we can recognize what is to be regarded as true, and what is to be set aside as being only probable or dubious. This mark is what we call evidence. This first rule may have been suggested to Descartes, as the others were, by mathematics. Even as in his method he generalized the processes used for mathematical researches and demonstrations, so in this formula he laid down the regulating principle to which this science owes its perfection, and which was also to become the regulating principle of the new philosophy.

Thus the famous rule of "evidence" reaches far beyond the scope of a mere principle of method. Both from what it excludes and what it implies, it may be looked upon as the motto of the Cartesian philosophy. It rejects, to begin with, any knowledge grounded upon authority alone (excepting the truths of religion). Even though Aristotle and all his commentators were agreed on one opinion, this would be no proof of its being true; and should it really chance to be so, the authority of Aristotle would count for nothing towards establishing its standing in science. Nothing can be admitted in science but what is evident; i. e., nothing but what is so clear and plain as to leave no possible doubt, or is soundly deduced from principles which rest on such evidence. The whole system of scholasticism: metaphysics, logic, physics, thus stand irretrievably condemned *in toto*. The so-called moral sciences, which cannot attain to a degree of evidence comparable to that of mathematics, and which have to content themselves with more or less strong probability, are likewise rejected by the Cartesian formula; in fact, Descartes, as has already been observed, had but little esteem for history and erudition.

But what makes this rule of paramount importance is, that it establishes reason as supreme judge of what is false or true. Reason thus proclaims its own sovereign right to decide without appeal. What we are to think, to believe, and to do should be determined solely by evidence; and of that evidence reason alone is judge (except in the case of urgency compelling us to immediate action). It is true, reason being identical in all men, that such truth as becomes evident to one of them becomes so to all other men likewise. Therefore the assent given to evidence by one mind is by implication equivalent to the universal consent of mankind; so that the individual reason which distinguishes between true and false is precisely the universal feature in every man.

Nevertheless, Descartes felt the danger that lay in his formula. He foresaw the very serious misunderstandings to which it might give rise, and he endeavored to prevent these by taking multifarious precautions. First of all, the truths of religion are carefully set apart and withdrawn from the criticism of reason. They do not fall under its jurisdiction. It is not ours to examine them, but to believe them. According to Descartes, we must seek neither to adapt them to our reason, nor to adapt our reason to them. They belong to another domain. Then Descartes makes a distinction between the sphere of knowledge and that of conduct; he submits to provisional ethics, which is to be replaced by definitive ethics only when science is completed, that is to say, in a still remote future. Moreover, even in the province of speculative thought Descartes refrains from touching upon political and social questions. He censures "those blundering and restless humours" ever ready to propose unasked-for reforms. Thus, after moral and religious problems, political problems in their turn are cautiously set aside. Where, then, shall the absolute sovereignty of reason be exercised? In philosophy, in abstract sciences, in physics; in short, wherever men generally have no other interest but that of pure truth.

Well-meant precautions these were, no doubt, but vain precautions, too. Let reason rule supreme over this apparently limited province, and by degrees it will invade the others. If we allow it, as a principle, the right to decide without appeal between falsehood and truth, it soon will admit of no restrictions but those it sets of its own accord through the works of a Kant or of an Auguste Comte. In fact, French philosophy in the eighteenth century was in the main an endeavor to apply the spirit of the Cartesian method to the very objects: politics, ethics, religion, which Descartes had carefully set apart. By holding nothing as true until I have evidence of its being so, do I not in advance deprive all historical rights of the means of securing recognition; do I not thereby summon all privileges, institutions, beliefs, and fortunes to produce their title deeds before the bar of reason? By solemnly paying homage to Descartes, the "Assemblée Constituante" proved that the spirit of the Revolution was conscious of one of its chief sources.

Being now in possession of his method, did not Descartes have all that was necessary to construct his philosophic system with absolute mathematical certainty? No, for in mathematics the foundation principles: axioms and definitions, are so plain and evident that no reasonable mind will question them. But philosophy had until his time been wanting in such principles, and the object which Descartes has in view is precisely to establish them.

To attain this end, he first casts aside as false (at least provisionally) all the opinions which he has hitherto held as true, and which are only probable. In order to avoid tedious enumerations, he proposes to consider opinions from the point of view of their sources. "For instance," says he, "having sometimes found my senses deceitful, I will distrust all that they teach me. As I have sometimes erred with regard to very simple reasoning, I will distrust the results of even the most positive sciences. Lastly, I may suppose that an evil genius, who is all-powerful, takes delight in making me err, even when I believe I see the truth most plainly. Therefore, by a voluntary effort, which is always possible since I am free, I will suspend my judgment even in cases where the evidence seems to me irresistible.

"Is there any proposition which is not affected by this 'hyperbolical' doubt? There is one, and one only. Let my senses deceive me, let my reasonings be false, let an evil genius delude me concerning things which appear to me most certain; if I am mistaken, it is because I am—and this truth 'I think, therefore I am,' *cogito, ergo sum*, is so self-evident and so certain that the most extravagant doubt of skeptics is unable to shake it." Here, then, is the first principle of philosophy sought for by Descartes. And even as Archimedes asked only a standing-place to lift the world, so Descartes, having found a *quid inconcussum,* an indisputable proposition, set to work to erect his whole system upon this foundation.

However, if according to the custom of philosophers we distinguish the sphere of knowledge from that of existence, this proposition, or, as it is called, Descartes's *cogito,* is certainly first in the sphere of knowledge; for I may have doubts about whatever I may think, but about my thinking I can have no doubt, even in the very moment when I doubt. But in the sphere of existence the Absolute—that is, God—comes first. Therefore Descartes, as soon as he had established the *cogito,* turned to demonstrating the existence of God. He knows that he thinks, but he also knows that he doubts, and therefore that he is imperfect; for not knowing instead of knowing is an imperfection. He therefore has an idea of perfection. Whence comes this idea? Descartes examines all the conjectures which may be made as to its origin; he eliminates them one after another as inadequate until one only remains, viz., that the idea of perfection cannot have sprung from experience, that we could not have it if the all-perfect Being—that is, God—did not actually exist, and that therefore this idea is as "the stamp left by the workman upon his work."

Descartes was bound to demonstrate the existence of God at the very outset. Otherwise, the supposition of an evil genius, who was able to deceive him even when he conceived things with perfect clearness, would have cast suspicion upon all propositions but the *cogito*; the doubt which he himself had raised would have paralyzed him. In order to do away with such a supposition, Descartes at once proceeds to demonstrate the existence of an all-perfect God, who cannot possibly wish to deceive us. But is not this a syllogistic circle? If the plainest argument, in order to be accepted as valid, needs the guaranty of God, what will guarantee the argument intended to prove the existence of God?

A syllogistic circle, indeed, had not Descartes escaped from it with the help of the following reasons: God's guaranty is necessary, not for the sake of the evidence, which is quite sufficient in itself so long as it lasts (whereof the *cogito* is a proof); but in order to assure me of the truth of propositions which I remember having admitted as evident without remembering for what reasons. It is necessary, in short, wherever memory intervenes, but only in that case. Now if we have no need of memory to know that we think, neither do we need it to know that God exists. In spite of the syllogistic form which Descartes gave to the proof of the existence of God, this proof is rather intuitive than grounded on formal reasoning. In the act of conceiving the idea of the all-perfect Being, I *see* at the same time the impossibility of His not existing. The existence of all other things is looked upon as only possible; but the existence of God appears as evidently necessary, being comprised in the very notion of God. This is no argument, but rather an immediate apprehension. It is, as Malebranche said shortly afterward, a proof "from mere vision." The syllogistic circle therefore was only apparent. Descartes was right in establishing the existence of God immediately after the *cogito*. Henceforward he could in all confidence make use of the faculties given him by God, who never deceives. He only needed now to follow out his method carefully, and to link propositions together in the requisite order, in order to arrive infallibly at the truth.

Now, the requisite order is, to begin with things which are most general, simple and easy to grasp; that is, with the primary principles from which the other truths are to be deduced. Physics therefore is not to be studied until metaphysics is well grounded. Acting upon this precept, Descartes first established the existence of an absolute and perfect Being —that is, God; for the same reason he now proceeds to ascertain the essence of the soul and of the body. To reach this end his starting-point is again the *cogito*.

I think, I am; but what am I? A creature that thinks; that is to say, judges, remembers, feels, imagines and wills; a being whose existence is not linked to any place, nor dependent upon any material thing. Descartes has just got out of his universal doubt by means of the *cogito*. The only thing the existence of which he can maintain at this point is his own thought. Now, the existence of his thought does not appear to him to be necessarily linked to that of his body and dependent upon the latter. On the contrary, he may suppose that his body does not exist and that the perception of the external world and of his own members is an illusion. He is even unable for the present to reject this supposition; he cannot do so till later on, and even then with some difficulty. Nevertheless, since he thinks, he is certain he exists. But, conversely, let him for a moment suppose that he ceases to think; upon this supposition he ceases to exist, although all external bodies and his own body should remain real. Therefore, the cognition of his own being, which is his thought, by no means depends on material things, the existence of which is still problematic. Therefore his whole nature is to think.

"You suppose," some opponent said to Descartes, "that your own body does not exist, and you say that nevertheless you continue to think. But should your supposition prove true—that is to say, should your body and your brain be dissolved—can you affirm that *even then* you would continue to think?" To which Descartes answered: "I do not assert this—at least not now. My present object is not to demonstrate the immortality of the soul. This is a metaphysical question I am not now able to solve—for I know only one fact as yet, viz., that I think (and also that God exists). The whole question I am examining is merely: 'What am I?' Now it appears from what has been said that my existence is known to me as that of a being endowed with thought and endowed only with thought; for, whilst I am as certain as possible of the existence of my thought, the existence of anything else is still wholly doubtful to me. The existence of this thought may possibly be actually connected with that of the brain. I know nothing about that. I am not discussing that for the present. One thing is certain: I know myself as a thought, and I positively do not know myself as a brain."

This is one of the leading features of the philosophy of Descartes, and one which may enable us to measure his influence, by comparing what had been thought before him with what was thought after him. The *cogito* of Descartes displaced, so to speak, the axis of philosophy. To the ancients and to the scholastics (theology excepted) the thinking mind appeared inseparable from the universe, regarded as the object of its thought, just as the soul itself was conceived to be the "substantial form" of the living body. According to Descartes, on the contrary, the existence of the thinking mind, far from being dependent on any other existing thing, is the essential condition of every other existence conceivable to us; for if I am certain of the existence of anything but myself, with far better reason am I certain that I, who have that thought, am in existence. The only reality I cannot possibly question is that of my own thought.

Both the adversaries and the successors of Descartes started from this point. All the modern forms of idealism, so utterly different from the idealism of the ancients, have a common origin in the *cogito*. The tempered and prudent idealism of Locke, the Christian idealism of Malebranche, the skeptical idealism of Hume, the transcendental idealism of Kant, the absolute idealism of Fichte and many other doctrines derived from these, which have appeared in our century, are all more or less closely related to the foundation principle of the Cartesian philosophy. Moreover, the conception of nature in modern science must also be connected with it. For, as we shall see farther on, when Descartes set thought—that is, the soul—so distinctly apart from everything extraneous to itself, in so doing he made necessary a new conception of force and life in the material world.

Now, let us add to the Cartesian formula, "I am a thing which thinks," the following principle, "All that I conceive clearly and distinctly is true." Then, since I conceive clearly and distinctly that the nature of the body and that of the soul have no attributes in common, therefore it is true that these two natures or substances are separated one from the other. Not only is there no need of my having any notion of the body in order to comprehend the soul, but also the soul has no need of the body in order to exist.

Descartes, therefore, had a right to infer that "the soul is more easily known than the body." This does not mean that, according to his doctrine, psychology is an easier science than physics or physiology. Psychology as we conceive it has no place in the system of Descartes; there is at most a mere sketch of it in the *Passions de l' Ame*. But this maxim is metaphysical, not psychological. It means that there is no more evident knowledge than that which the soul has of itself, since there is none which it is more impossible to doubt; that the body, on the contrary, is known only representatively, and that, far from our being unable to doubt its existence, we cannot overcome such a doubt, when once raised, save by means of laborious and complicated reasonings.

In order to make all this clearer still, let us remember Descartes's oft-repeated caution to "cast off all the impressions of the senses and imagination and trust to reason alone." There are not two kinds of evidence: one which tells us that the sun shines, that honey is sweet, that lead is heavy; and another which informs us that if equals be added to equals the sums are equal. Only the latter proposition is self-evident; the former statements, in spite of any prepossession to the contrary, are not so. The impressions of the senses are vivid, but confused; we cannot account for them, and nothing can warrant them to be true. The water which is warm to me seems cold to you. Cold and heat, as well as all other qualities pertaining to bodies, with the exception of extension, are not inherent in them; they are relative to the sentient subject. Therefore, if we think we know bodies by what our senses teach us of them, we fall into error, as will happen every time when, through overhastiness or prejudice, we form a judgment before the evidence is complete. For can I not have in a dream all the perceptions I now have and be as firmly persuaded of their reality? But whether I am dreaming or waking it is true that two and two are four, and it is true that I, who think so, am in existence.

Thus, previous to philosophical reflection, nothing seems to us so well known as the body and its qualities, because we form images of them continually and without any difficulty; whereas it is not easy for us to realize what the soul is, seeing that it is not an object for the imagination to grasp. The first task of the philosopher consists precisely in disengaging himself from the false light of the senses and seeking the true light of reason. It is an effort akin to the one demanded by Plato, when he termed philosophy the science of the invisible, and recommended the study of mathematics as a preparatory training. The body and the organs of the senses, far from making us acquainted with what really is, are a hindrance to the proper activity of the mind. Even matter, which we fancy our hands, eyes, ears, etc., can apprehend immediately, we really know only by means of our understanding. For the latter alone can give us a distinct notion of it, viz., the notion of a thing measurable in length, breadth and depth.

The other qualities of bodies are not really inherent in them. "Look at this piece of wax; it has just been taken from the hive; it has not yet lost the sweetness of the honey it contained; it still retains something of the fragrance of the flowers from which it was gathered; its color, figure and size are apparent; it is hard, cold, easily handled, and if you strike it will give forth some sound. * * * But now, while I am speaking, somebody brings it near the fire; whatever taste remained in it is exhaled, the odor evaporates, its color changes, its shape is lost, its size increases, it becomes liquid, it is warmer, one can hardly handle it, and when we strike it, it will no longer give forth a sound." And yet the same wax is there. Therefore this wax was neither the honey-sweet flavor, nor the pleasant flowery smell, nor the whiteness, nor the form, nor the sound, but merely a body which, a short time before, was apparent to my senses under these forms, but now presents itself under other forms. Therefore all I can *conceive* clearly and distinctly about this body is its extension.

Descartes's definition of the soul is "a thing that thinks"; of the body, "a thing that has extension." This doctrine is strangely at variance with the metaphysics taught in his time. The scholastic philosophers, who on this point followed the teaching of Aristotle, regarded the soul as both the principle of life and the principle of thought. The same soul which in plants is purely nutritive, becomes locomotive, then sensitive in animals, and lastly, in man, rational. And though such a doctrine made the immortality of the soul a difficult thing to conceive, it was no cause of embarrassment to the schoolmen, for immortality to them was an object of faith, not of demonstration. There is neither a nutritive nor a locomotive soul, says Descartes. There is but one kind of soul, which is the thinking soul, for feeling is thinking. Nutrition and locomotion are explainable simply by the laws of mechanics. Animals, which do not think, do not feel either. They may be looked upon as automatons, and the perfection of some of their actions may be compared to the perfection of the workings of a clock. After this we can no longer suppose that the destiny of man after death is the same as that of flies and ants.

Scholastic physics likewise assumed the existence of forces and occult causes inherent in matter, and thought the specific nature of certain natural phenomena could not otherwise be accounted for. Here again Descartes adopts the reverse of their doctrine, rejecting *in toto* these assumed principles, forces and causes, which to him are but confused notions, hypotheses convenient to sluggish minds, explanations which explain nothing, but merely repeat the enunciation of the problem under another form. Given matter, that is, extension as considered by geometricians, he wants no other data than number, motion and duration. These are sufficient, he considers, to account for all the phenomena which take place in bodies either inorganic or living.

Thus Descartes's physical science is purely rational in character and in scrupulous accordance with the rule of his method which forbids him to "accept anything as true unless it appears by evidence to be so." It tends to assume a geometrical form, and all questions of physics are reduced, at least in principle, to problems of mechanics. "Give me matter and the laws of motion," says Descartes, "and I will build a universe exactly like the one that we behold, with skies, stars, sun and earth, and on the earth minerals, plants and animals; in short, everything that experience introduces to us, except the rational soul of man."

No doubt Descartes imagined all natural phenomena, and in particular those of animated beings, to be less complicated than they really are. His conceptions are those of a great mathematician, living at a time when physics and chemistry hardly existed and when biology did not exist at all. He thinks he can determine *a priori* the number of the fixed stars. He imagines he can describe accurately the formation of the fœtus. He hopes, by taking due care of the human machine and by repairing it when necessary, to protract the life of man indefinitely, to conquer disease and even death. Scientific men in our days are better acquainted with the difficulties of such problems and are consequently less pretentious. But the scientific ideal they aim at, though indefinitely removed from that which we are considering, has remained pretty much the same as Descartes conceived it: to discover the laws of every phenomenon by reducing them, as far as possible, to number and measure, and to discard every metaphysical hypothesis meant to explain any class of physical phenomena.

This geometrical conception of the material universe was repeatedly attacked by the successors of Descartes. Leibniz endeavored to prove that the Cartesian definition of matter was incompatible with the laws of motion. Leibniz is fond of connecting Democritus and Descartes, and is wont to quote them together. The parallel is an ingenious one, but should not be followed up too closely. No doubt Descartes, like Democritus, requires only matter and motion in order to explain the genesis of the physical universe. But, to say nothing of the very considerable differences between the explanation of Democritus and that of Descartes, can anyone forget that the physical science of Democritus and his metaphysics are all one and the same thing? Atoms and vacuum are to him the primal elements of all things, and, as was objected to him by Aristotle, he does not take the trouble even to explain the origin of motion. With Descartes, before physics is begun a complete metaphysical system has first been established, and it is from this that physics is to derive its principles: the primordial laws of phenomena (for instance, that light propagates itself in straight lines) are deduced from God's attributes. Moreover, Descartes is not compelled by his system, as Democritus is, to deny the existence of final causes. On the contrary, he maintains their existence. It is true that he forbids us to seek them out, but the reason is that, according to him, it would be highly presumptuous in us mortals to try to comprehend God's designs; the more so as God's liberty is absolute and infinite, and since, in consequence, His acts may be wholly unintelligible to our reason. And lastly, far from looking upon matter as self-existent, Descartes believes that bodies, as well as all other finite things, exist only by God's express will and constant help. Should this help cease for an instant all bodies would at once sink back into nothingness.

The mechanical character of Descartes's system, if mechanical it be, is therefore far removed from the materialism of Democritus. Descartes firmly maintained the reality of freewill, to which he ascribes an essential part in his theory of judgment and of error. It is only as physicist, not as philosopher, that Descartes may be termed mechanical. But in this sense nearly all men of science are so, too; for, to use F. A. Lange's striking expression: "Mechanism is an excellent formula for the science of nature."

But is not, however, the strictly deductive science conceived by Descartes very remote from the modern science of nature, which employs the experimental method with so much zeal and success? True, Descartes often thought deduction easy when it was difficult, and possible when it was impracticable. But this was a question of fact, not of principle. As this or that branch of science (at least, of physical science) is gradually brought nearer to perfection, we see it grow from the experimental into the rational. Such has long been the case with astronomy and celestial mechanics, and later, successively with optics, with acoustics, with hydrodynamics, with the theory of heat and electricity and other fields of physics, all so many confirmations of the Cartesian ideal.

Moreover, Descartes himself assigned an important rôle to the experimental method. Anecdotes depict him to us as rising very early, in Amsterdam, in order to choose in a butcher's shop the joints he wished "to anatomize at leisure"; or answering an inquirer who wished to see his library, "Here it is," at the same time pointing to a quarter of veal which he was busily dissecting. In the last years of his life he devoted only a few hours a year to mathematics, and not much more to metaphysics. He busied himself almost exclusively with experiments in physics and physiology. How could he have failed to appreciate the importance of a method which he was himself so assiduously putting into practice?

"Anticipating causes with effects," is Descartes's felicitous definition of experimenting. It clearly shows the functions he ascribed to it. Were there only one way in which a certain effect might be deduced from given causes, experimenting would be unnecessary. But natural phenomena are so complex, and the possible combinations of causes are so numerous, that we may nearly always explain in several ways the production of a given effect. Which is the right way? Experiment alone can decide. Let us make a distinction between science already developed and science which is developing. To expound a developed science the suitable method is deduction,—descent from causes to effects. But science which is developing cannot yet adopt this method; and to discover unknown laws, it must employ the experimental method, must anticipate causes with effects.

Descartes had written a *Traite du Monde* and was about to publish it, when the condemnation of Galileo for heresies concerning the motion of the earth altered his resolution. Being, above all, desirous to work in peace, and to postpone as long as he could a perhaps inevitable conflict with the theologians, he published only a few fragments of his physical theories, and put a summary sketch of it into the admirable fifth part of the *Discours de la Methode.* We must certainly deplore the loss of this great work, which would throw light upon many an obscure point in the Cartesian philosophy. But, after all, the essential part of the doctrine did not lie here, any more than in the well-known hypothesis of "vortices," which the Cartesian philosophers of the eighteenth century vainly tried to set up in opposition to the principle of universal gravitation discovered by Newton, and with which some physicists now partly agree in their theories of matter.

The main interest lies elsewhere, viz., in the perfect character of the science of nature, of which Descartes had such a clear and precise notion, even though he was far from being able to put it into practice save in a few points (for instance, by his discoveries in optics). It is said that the man who invented the plough still walks, invisible, beside the peasant who drives his own plough in our days. I might almost say that, in our laboratories, Descartes stands invisible and present, investigating with our scientific men the laws of phenomena.

If he had lived, would he have passed on from the sciences of life to the ethical and social sciences, as he had done already from mathematics to physics, and from physics to anatomy and physiology? This may be doubted. To say nothing of considerations of prudence, to which Descartes was most susceptible, he held in slight esteem the visionaries and political reformers of the sixteenth century, and would have been sorely vexed if any comparison had been drawn between their fancies and his own doctrines. On the other hand, he could not but find it extremely difficult to make social facts fall in with his method, since, as Auguste Comte very aptly observed, so long as biology is not sufficiently advanced, social science must needs be out of the question. Now, in the time of Descartes, biology was still unborn. Even ethics he does not seem to have taken into deep consideration. He borrows the rules of his provisional ethics from Montaigne and from the Stoics. Stoicism, modified in some respects, also forms the fundamental part of Descartes's moral letters to Princess Elizabeth. It is a peculiarity of French philosophy, that it has produced many moralists and few moral theorists. The reason for this we shall seek elsewhere. Certain it is that Descartes was not one of these theorists. Perhaps he believed that scientific ethics (ethics not grounded on religious authority) could not be established till the science of man was established, and the connection of the physical and the moral better known. To this knowledge he opened the way in his *Traite des Passions de l'Ame.*

All the precautions taken by Descartes, all his prudence, did not shield him from the attacks his philosophy was to bring upon him, as being "subtle, enticing, and bold." After hesitating a long while, the Jesuits, by whom he had been brought up at La Flèche, and among whom he had still some friends, declared themselves against his philosophy. The seventh series of *Objections,* by Father Bourdin, express the opinion of this society. Descartes wrote a vigorous reply. His quarrel with the Jesuits was one of his motives for not living in France. He established himself in Holland, where he lived a long while in undisturbed peace. But as his philosophy spread, attention was drawn to him, and as the universities of the country were beginning to quarrel about his theories, he felt that his life there would soon become unbearable. He therefore resolved to yield to the entreaties of Queen Christina, who earnestly urged him to come to Sweden. But he could not endure the severe climate of that country, and hardly six months had elapsed when he died of inflammation of the lungs. Later, his body was brought back to France.

The philosophy of Descartes was in accord with the leading tendencies of his time. The success which attended it from the moment it appeared is a proof of its opportuneness, and it is difficult to determine whether it formed, rather than expressed, the spirit of the age. Doubtless it did both. As has been said, the seventeenth century in France was pre-eminently the "age of reason."

> Aimez donc la raison ; que toujours vos écrits,
> Empruntent d'elle seule et leur lustre et leur prix,

said Boileau; yet perhaps, had it not been for the Cartesian philosophy, this taste for reason might not have asserted itself so earnestly and have been so perfectly conscious of its existence.

This philosophy of "clear ideas" prevailed in France in the second half of the seventeenth century, and from France its influence spread over all Europe. Though vigorously attacked in the eighteenth century, both as to its metaphysics and its physics, it nevertheless remained discernible even in the methods of its adversaries. Locke, Hume, and Condillac had not the same conception of evidence as Descartes; but their empiricism was as fond of clearness as his rationalism had been. Newton combated the hypothesis of "vortices," but he preserved the Cartesian notion of a mechanical explanation of physical phenomena. For a thorough-going and express negation of the Cartesian spirit we must go to the end of the eighteenth century. Then the German romantic writers spring up, and maintain that the philosophy of clear ideas is false from its very principle. According to them, reality is not clear, and the more satisfactory a doctrine is to the human understanding, the surer it is to reproduce only the surface of things, while the essence of them is mysterious, intangible and inexpressible. Whence it follows that religions, arts and literatures are spontaneous philosophies, incomparably deeper than the systems produced by the conscious labor of the understanding, even as the works of nature are artistically superior to the articles manufactured by man.

The philosophy of Descartes, to tell the truth, affords but little scope to sentiment, and still less to the imagination and to the hidden and unconscious activities of the mind. It places value on evidence alone, whose vivid, but glaring light, dispels the *chiaroscuro* so dear to romantic writers. This fixed and rigid purpose has its drawbacks, which were not long in making their appearance among the followers of Descartes.

But apart from the fact that in Descartes himself the rational effort was uncommonly sincere and vigorous, at the time when this philosophy appeared it was really necessary. It was a deliverer. It put an end to superannuated doctrines, the domination of which was still heavily felt. It cleared the ground, and set physics free, once for all, from the clogs of metaphysical hypotheses. Lastly, it formulated problems which needed formulation. Descartes wished to furnish science not only with a powerful and flexible instrument such as Bacon had already sought, but also with an unchanging and immovable basis. Thence sprang the "provisional doubt," with which his method bids him begin, which obliges him to test all previously acquired information, and which may be looked upon as the starting-point of all modern theories of knowledge. For this doubt, which affects successively perception, imagination, reasoning power, and stops only before the immediate self-intuition of thought, is itself a criticism of the faculty of knowledge. It studies it in its connection both with the outward object and with the very mind which is thinking; in short, it heralds Kant's *Critique of Pure Reason*.

An innovating and fruitful doctrine nearly always develops in various directions. The various minds that receive it gradually draw from it diverse and sometimes contradictory conclusions, most of which were overlooked and would often have been disapproved of by the founder of the system. This is perhaps even truer of Descartes than of any other philosopher. Being chiefly preoccupied with the method and structure of science, he did not hesitate to leave open, at least temporarily, many important questions which his method did not require him to solve immediately. Thus it happened that metaphysical systems very different from one another were soon founded on the Cartesian principles. Spinoza adopted the definition which Descartes had given of soul and matter, but in thought and extension he saw only two attributes of one and the same substance. Beside this pantheism, appeared the idealism of Malebranche, which proceeds no less directly from Descartes; for did not the latter say that "truth is the same thing as being?" And does not the theory of continued creation lead directly to that of occasional causes? Locke, who combated Descartes on the subject of innate ideas, without understanding him exactly, has on the other hand many points in common with him; the very idea of inventorying and examining the ideas in our minds is singularly akin to the critical examination of our knowledge which, in Descartes, precedes the *cogito*. And lastly, into the idealism of Leibniz the Cartesian element enters in large measure; for instance, the notion of sensation being but a dim intellection, which is the central point of Leibniz's theory of knowledge, had already been clearly stated by Descartes.

The philosophy of Descartes is therefore a sort of crossroad whence diverge the chief ways followed by modern thought. Still, outside of France, his method has not been followed without restrictions, and his philosophy has been accepted only to be immediately combined with other elements either traditional or modern. In France, the influence has been far deeper and more enduring. There, while the Cartesian philosophy may have lost its prestige rather quickly, the Cartesian spirit, owing, doubtless, to its close affinity with the very genius of the nation, has never disappeared, and we shall recognize its influence, not only throughout the whole eighteenth century and in the French Revolution, but in all the greatest thinkers of the nineteenth century.

CONTENTS.

	PAGE
Publishers' Preface	iii
Essay on the Philosophy of Descartes by Prof. L. Levy-Bruhl	vii
Title-pages of the original editions	xxxi

I.—THE MEDITATIONS.

Dedication	1
Preface	9
Synopsis of the Meditations	15

MEDITATION I.
Of the Things of which we may Doubt.................. 21

MEDITATION II.
Of the Nature of the Human Mind; and that it is more easily known than the Body...................... 29

MEDITATION III.
Of God; that he exists............................... 42

MEDITATION IV.
Of Truth and Error................................... 63

MEDITATION V.
Of the Essence of Material Things; and, again, of God: that he exists 75

MEDITATION VI.
Of the Existence of Material Things, and of the Real Distinction between the Mind and Body of Man...... 84

CONTENTS.

II.—THE PRINCIPLES OF PHILOSOPHY.

	PAGE
Preface	107
Dedication	126

Part I.
Of the Principles of Human Knowledge 130

Part II.
Of the Principles of Material Things. Sects. i. to xxv. . 175

Part III.
Of the Visible World. Sects. i. to iii. 192

Part IV.
Of the Earth. Sects. clxxxviii. to ccvii. 194

Appendix 215
Notes 224
Bibliography 249

THE MEDITATIONS

OF

DESCARTES

*TRANSLATED FROM THE LATIN AND COL-
LATED WITH THE FRENCH.*

Renati Des-Cartes Meditationes de Prima Philosophia

In qua dei existentia et animæ immortalitas demonstratur.

PARISIIS
Apud Michaelem Soly, viâ Jacobeâ, sub signo Phœnicis.
MDCXLI.

Cum Privilegio et Approbatione Doctorum.

Vignette: a phœnix with the inscription, „Aeternitati soli".

Renati Des-Cartes Meditationes de Prima Philosophia

In quibus Dei existentia, & animæ humanæ a corpore distinctio demonstratur.

His adjunctæ sunt variæ objectiones doctorum virorum in istas de Deo & anima demonstrationes.

Cum responsionibus Authoris.

Secunda editio septimis objectionibus antehac non visis aucta.

AMSTELODAMI,
Apud Ludovicum Elzevirium, 1642.

Vignette: Minerva beneath an olive tree: „Ne extra oleas·

LES
Meditations Metaphysiques de René Des=Cartes

TOUCHANT LA PREMIERE PHILOSOPHIE

dans lesquelles l'existence de Dieu, & la distinction réelle entre l'âme & le corps de l'homme, sont demonstrées.

Traduites du Latin de l'Auteur par
M. le D. D. L. N. S.

Et les objections faites contre ces Méditations par diverses personnes tres-doctes, avec les réponses de l'Auteur.

Traduites par Mr. C. L. R.

A PARIS.
Chez la Veuve JEAN CAMUSAT,
ET
PIERRE LE PETIT, rue S. Jacques,
à la Toyson d'Or.

M. DC. XLVII.
AVEC PRIVILEGE DU ROY.

Vignette: Jason with the golden fleece and the dragon: „Tegitet quos tangit inaurat".

TO

THE VERY SAGE AND ILLUSTRIOUS

THE

DEAN AND DOCTORS OF THE SACRED FACULTY OF THEOLOGY OF PARIS.

GENTLEMEN,

The motive which impels me to present this Treatise to you is so reasonable, and, when you shall learn its design, I am confident that you also will consider that there is ground so valid for your taking it under your protection, that I can in no way better recommend it to you than by briefly stating the end which I proposed to myself in it. I have always been of opinion that the two questions respecting God and the Soul were the chief of those that ought to be determined by help of Philosophy rather than of Theology; for although to us, the faithful, it be sufficient to hold as matters of faith, that the human soul does not perish with the body, and that God exists, it yet assuredly seems impossible ever to persuade infidels of the reality of any religion, or almost even any moral virtue, unless, first of all, those two things be proved to them by natural reason. And since in this life there are frequently greater rewards held out to vice than to virtue, few would prefer the right to the useful, if they were restrained neither by the fear of God nor the expectation of another life; and although it is quite true that the existence of God is to be believed since it is taught in the sacred Scriptures, and that, on the other hand, the sacred Scriptures are to be believed because they come from God (for since faith is a gift of God, the same Being who bestows grace to enable us to believe other things, can likewise impart of it to enable us to believe his own existence), nevertheless, this cannot be submitted to infidels, who would consider that the reasoning proceeded in a circle. And, indeed, I have observed that you, with all the other theologians, not only affirmed the sufficiency of natural reason for the proof of the existence of God, but also, that it may be inferred from sacred Scripture, that the knowledge of God is much clearer than of many created things, and that it is really so easy of acquisition as to leave those who do not possess it blameworthy. This is manifest from these words of the Book of Wisdom, chap. xiii., where it is said, *Howbeit they are not to be excused; for if their understanding was so great that they could discern the world and the creatures, why did they not rather find out the Lord thereof?* And in Romans, chap. i., it is said that they are *without excuse;* and again, in the same place, by these words,—*That which may be known of God is manifest in them*—we seem to be admonished that all which can be known of God may be made manifest by reasons obtained from no other source than the inspection of our own minds. I have, therefore, thought that it would not be unbecoming in me to inquire how and by what way, without going out of ourselves, God may be more easily and certainly known than the things of the world.

And as regards the Soul, although many have judged that its nature could not be easily discovered, and some have even ventured to say that human reason led to the conclusion that it perished with the body, and that the contrary opinion could be held through faith alone; nevertheless, since the Lateran Council, held under Leo X. (in session viii.), condemns these, and expressly enjoins Christian philosophers to refute their arguments, and establish the truth according to their ability, I have ventured to attempt it in this work. Moreover, I am aware that most of the irreligious deny the existence of God, and the distinctness of the human soul from the body, for no other reason than because these points, as they allege, have never as yet been demonstrated. Now, although I am by no means of their opinion, but, on the contrary, hold that almost all the proofs which have been adduced on these questions by great men, possess, when rightly understood, the force of demonstrations, and that it is next to impossible to discover new, yet there is, I apprehend, no more useful service to be performed in Philosophy, than if some one were, once for all, carefully to seek out the best of these reasons, and expound them so accurately and clearly that, for the future, it might be manifest to all that they are real demonstrations. And finally, since many persons were greatly desirous of this, who knew that I had cultivated a certain Method of resolving all kinds of difficulties in the sciences, which is not indeed new (there being nothing older than truth), but of which they were aware I had made successful use in other instances, I judged it to be my duty to make trial of it also on the present matter.

Now the sum of what I have been able to accomplish on the subject is contained in this treatise. Not that I here essayed to collect all the diverse reasons which might be adduced as proofs on this subject, for this does not seem to be necessary, unless on matters where no one proof of adequate certainty is to be had; but I treated the first and chief alone in such a manner that I should venture now to propose them as demonstrations of the highest certainty and evidence. And I will also add that they are such as to lead me to think that there is no way open to the mind of man by which proofs superior to them can ever be discovered; for the importance of the subject, and the glory of God, to which all this relates, constrain me to speak here somewhat more freely of myself than I have been accustomed to do. Nevertheless, whatever certitude and evidence I may find in these demonstrations, I cannot therefore persuade myself that they are level to the comprehension of all. But just as in geometry there are many of the demonstrations of Archimedes, Apollonius, Pappus, and others, which, though received by all as highly evident and certain (because indeed they manifestly contain nothing which, considered by itself, it is not very easy to understand, and no consequents that are inaccurately related to their antecedents), are nevertheless understood by a very limited number, because they are somewhat long, and demand the whole attention of the reader: so in the same way, although I consider the demonstrations of which I here make use, to be equal or even superior to the geometrical in certitude and evidence, I am afraid, nevertheless, that they will not be adequately understood by many, as well because they also are somewhat long and involved, as chiefly because they require the mind to be entirely free from prejudice, and able with ease to detach itself from the commerce of the senses. And, to speak the truth, the ability for metaphysical studies is less general than for those of geometry. And, besides, there is still this difference that, as in geometry, all are persuaded that nothing is usually advanced of which there is not a certain demonstration, those but partially versed in it err more frequently in assenting to what is false, from a desire of seeming to understand it, than in denying what is true. In philosophy, on the other hand, where it is believed that all is doubtful, few sincerely give themselves to the search after truth, and by far the greater number seek the reputation of bold thinkers by audaciously impugning such truths as are of the greatest moment.

Hence it is that, whatever force my reasonings may possess, yet because they belong to philosophy, I do not expect they will have much effect on the minds of men, unless you extend to them your patronage and approval. But since your Faculty is held in so great esteem by all, and since the name of SORBONNE is of such authority, that not only in matters of faith, but even also in what regards human philosophy, has the judgment of no other society, after the Sacred Councils, received so great deference, it being the universal conviction that it is impossible elsewhere to find greater perspicacity and solidity, or greater wisdom and integrity in giving judgment, I doubt not,—if you but condescend to pay so much regard to this Treatise as to be willing, in the first place, to correct it (for, mindful not only of my humanity, but chiefly also of my ignorance, I do not affirm that it is free from errors); in the second place, to supply what is wanting in it, to perfect what is incomplete, and to give more ample illustration where it is demanded, or at least to indicate these defects to myself that I may endeavour to remedy them; and, finally, when the reasonings contained in it, by which the existence of God and the distinction of the human soul from the body are established, shall have been brought to such degree of perspicuity as to be esteemed exact demonstrations, of which I am assured they admit, if you condescend to accord them the authority of your approbation, and render a public testimony of their truth and certainty,—I doubt not, I say, but that henceforward all the errors which have ever been entertained on these questions will very soon be effaced from the minds of men. For truth itself will readily lead the remainder of the ingenious and the learned to subscribe to your judgment; and your authority will cause the atheists, who are in general sciolists rather than ingenious or learned, to lay aside the spirit of contradiction, and lead them, perhaps, to do battle in their own persons for reasonings which they find considered demonstrations by all men of genius, lest they should seem not to understand them; and, finally, the rest of mankind will readily trust to so many testimonies, and there will no longer be any one who will venture to doubt either the existence of God or the real distinction of mind and body. It is for you, in your singular wisdom, to judge of the importance of the establishment of such beliefs, [who are cognisant of the disorders which doubt of these truths produces].* But it would not here become me to commend at greater length the cause of God and of religion to you, who have always proved the strongest support of the Catholic Church.

---

* The *square* brackets, here and throughout the volume, are used to mark additions to the original of the revised French translation.

PREFACE TO THE READER.

I HAVE already slightly touched upon the questions respecting the existence of God and the nature of the human soul, in the "Discourse on the Method of rightly conducting the Reason, and seeking truth in the Sciences," published in French in the year 1637; not, however, with the design of there treating of them fully, but only, as it were, in passing, that I might learn from the judgments of my readers in what way I should afterwards handle them: for these questions appeared to me to be of such moment as to be worthy of being considered more than once, and the path which I follow in discussing them is so little trodden, and so remote from the ordinary route, that I thought it would not be expedient to illustrate it at greater length in French, and in a discourse that might be read by all, lest even the more feeble minds should believe that this path might be entered upon by them.

But, as in the Discourse on Method, I had requested all who might find aught meriting censure in my writings, to do me the favour of pointing it out to me, I may state that no objections worthy of remark have been alleged against what I then said on these questions, except two, to which I will here briefly reply, before undertaking their more detailed discussion.

The first objection is that though, while the human mind reflects on itself, it does not perceive[1]* that it is any other than a thinking thing, it does not follow that its nature or essence consists only in its being a thing which thinks; so that the word *only* shall exclude all other things which might also perhaps be said to pertain to the nature of the mind.

To this objection I reply, that it was not my intention in that place to exclude these according to the order of truth in the matter (of which I did not then treat), but only according to the order of thought (perception); so that my meaning was, that I clearly apprehended nothing, so far as I was conscious, as belonging to my essence, except that I was a thinking thing, or a thing possessing in itself the faculty of thinking. But I will show hereafter how, from the consciousness that nothing besides thinking belongs to the essence of the mind, it follows that nothing else does in truth belong to it.

The second objection is that it does not follow, from my possessing the idea of a thing more perfect than I am, that the idea itself is more perfect than myself, and much less that what is represented by the idea exists.

But I reply that in the term *idea*[2] there is here something equivocal; for it may be taken either materially for an act of the understanding, and in this sense it cannot be said to be more perfect than I, or objectively, for the thing represented by that act, which, although it be not supposed to exist out of my understanding, may, nevertheless, be more perfect than my-

---

*The superior numerals in the text refer to the Notes at the end of this volume, where will be found some notices of the various terms that appeared to require comment.

self, by reason of its essence. But, in the sequel of this treatise I will show more amply how, from my possessing the idea of a thing more perfect than myself, it follows that this thing really exists.

Besides these two objections, I have seen, indeed, two treatises of sufficient length relating to the present matter. In these, however, my conclusions, much more than my premises, were impugned, and that by arguments borrowed from the commonplaces of the atheists. But, as arguments of this sort can make no impression on the minds of those who shall rightly understand my reasonings, and as the judgments of many are so irrational and weak that they are persuaded rather by the opinions on a subject that are first presented to them, however false and opposed to reason they may be, than by a true and solid, but subsequently received, refutation of them, I am unwilling here to reply to these strictures from a dread of being, in the first instance, obliged to state them.

I will only say, in general, that all which the atheists commonly allege in favour of the non-existence of God, arises continually from one or other of these two things, namely, either the ascription of human affections to Deity, or the undue attribution to our minds of so much vigour and wisdom that we may essay to determine and comprehend both what God can and ought to do; hence all that is alleged by them will occasion us no difficulty, provided only we keep in remembrance that our minds must be considered finite, while Deity is incomprehensible and infinite.

Now that I have once, in some measure, made proof of the opinions of men regarding my work, I again undertake to treat of God and the human soul, and at the same time to discuss the principles of the **entire First Philosophy**, without, however, expecting any commendation from the crowd for my endeavours, or a wide circle of readers. On the contrary, I would advise none to read this work, unless such as are able and willing to meditate with me in earnest, to detach their minds from commerce with the senses, and likewise to deliver themselves from all prejudice; and individuals of this character are, I well know, remarkably rare. But with regard to those who, without caring to comprehend the order and connection of the reasonings, shall study only detached clauses for the purpose of small but noisy criticism, as is the custom with many, I may say that such persons will not profit greatly by the reading of this treatise; and although perhaps they may find opportunity for cavilling in several places, they will yet hardly start any pressing objections, or such as shall be deserving of reply.

But since, indeed, I do not promise to satisfy others on all these subjects at first sight, nor arrogate so much to myself as to believe that I have been able to foresee all that may be the source of difficulty to each one, I shall expound, first of all, in the *Meditations*, those considerations by which I feel persuaded that I have arrived at a certain and evident knowledge of truth, in order that I may ascertain whether the reasonings which have prevailed with myself will also be effectual in convincing others. I will then reply to the objections of some men, illustrious for their genius and learning, to whom these Meditations were sent for criticism before they were committed to the press; for these objections are so numerous and varied that I venture to anticipate that nothing, at least nothing of any moment, will readily occur to any mind which has not been touched upon in them.

Hence it is that I earnestly entreat my readers not to come to any judgment on the questions raised in the Meditations until they have taken care to read the whole of the Objections, with the relative Replies.

SYNOPSIS OF THE SIX FOLLOWING MEDITATIONS.

IN the First Meditation I expound the grounds on which we may doubt in general of all things, and especially of material objects, so long, at least, as we have no other foundations for the sciences than those we have hitherto possessed. Now, although the utility of a doubt so general may not be manifest at first sight, it is nevertheless of the greatest, since it delivers us from all prejudice, and affords the easiest pathway by which the mind may withdraw itself from the senses; and, finally, makes it impossible for us to doubt wherever we afterwards discover truth.

In the Second, the mind which, in the exercise of the freedom peculiar to itself, supposes that no object is, of the existence of which it has even the slightest doubt, finds that, meanwhile, it must itself exist. And this point is likewise of the highest moment, for the mind is thus enabled easily to distinguish what pertains to itself, that is, to the intellectual nature, from what is to be referred to the body. But since some, perhaps, will expect, at this stage of our progress, a statement of the reasons which establish the doctrine of the immortality of the soul, I think it proper here to make such aware, that it was my aim to write nothing of which I could not give exact demonstration, and that I therefore felt myself obliged to adopt an order similar to that in use among the geometers, viz., to premise all upon which the proposition in question depends, before coming to any conclusion respecting it. Now, the first and chief pre-requisite for the knowledge of the immortality of the soul is our being able to form the clearest possible conception (*conceptus*—concept) of the soul itself, and such as shall be absolutely distinct from all our notions of body; and how this is to be accomplished is there shown. There is required, besides this, the assurance that all objects which we clearly and distinctly think are true (really exist) in that very mode in which we think them; and this could not be established previously to the Fourth Meditation. Farther, it is necessary, for the same purpose, that we possess a distinct conception of corporeal nature, which is given partly in the Second and partly in the Fifth and Sixth Meditations. And, finally, on these grounds, we are necessitated to conclude, that all those objects which are clearly and distinctly conceived to be diverse substances, as mind and body, are substances really reciprocally distinct; and this inference is made in the Sixth Meditation. The absolute distinction of mind and body is, besides, confirmed in this Second Meditation, by showing that we cannot conceive body unless as divisible; while, on the other hand, mind cannot be conceived unless as indivisible. For we are not able to conceive the half of a mind, as we can of any body, however small, so that the natures of these two substances are to be held, not only as diverse, but even in some measure as contraries. I have not, however, pursued this discussion further in the present treatise, as well for the reason that these considerations are sufficient to show that the destruction of the mind does not follow from the corruption of the body, and thus to afford to men the hope of a future life, as also because the premises from which it is competent for us to infer the immortality of the soul, involve an explication of the whole principles of Physics: in order to establish, in the first place, that generally all substances, that is, all things which can exist only in consequence of having been created by God, are in their own nature incorruptible, and can never cease to be, unless God himself, by refusing his concurrence to them, reduce them to nothing; and, in the second place, that body, taken generally, is a substance, and therefore can never perish, but that the human body, in as far as it differs from other bodies, is constituted only by a certain configuration of members, and by other accidents of this sort, while the human mind is not made up of accidents, but is a pure substance. For although all the accidents of the mind be changed—although, for example, it think certain things, will others, and perceive others, the mind itself does not vary with these changes; while, on the contrary, the human body is no longer the same if a change take place in the form of any of its parts: from which it follows that the body may, indeed, without difficulty perish, but that the mind is in its own nature immortal.

In the Third Meditation, I have unfolded at sufficient length, as appears to me, my chief argument for the existence of God. But yet, since I was there desirous to avoid the use of comparisons taken from material objects, that I might withdraw, as far as possible, the minds of my readers from the senses, numerous obscurities perhaps remain, which, however, will, I trust, be afterwards entirely removed in the Replies to the Objections: thus, among other things, it may be difficult to understand how the idea of a being absolutely perfect, which is found in our minds, possesses so much objective reality[3] [*i. e.*, participates by representation in so many degrees of being and perfection] that it must be held to arise from a cause absolutely perfect. This is illustrated in the Replies by the comparison of a highly perfect machine, the idea of which exists in the mind of some workman; for as the objective (*i. e.*, representative) perfection of this idea must have some cause, viz., either the science of the workman, or of some other person from whom he has received the idea, in the same way the idea of God, which is found in us, demands God himself for its cause.

In the Fourth, it is shown that all which we clearly and distinctly perceive (apprehend) is true; and, at the same time, is explained wherein consists the nature of error; points that require to be known as well for confirming the preceding truths, as for the better understanding of those that are to follow. But, meanwhile, it must be observed, that I do not at all there treat of Sin, that is, of error committed in the pursuit of good and evil, but of that sort alone which arises in the determination of the true and the false. Nor do I refer to matters of faith, or to the conduct of life, but only to what regards speculative truths, and such as are known by means of the natural light alone.

In the Fifth, besides the illustration of corporeal nature, taken generically, a new demonstration is given of the existence of God, not free, perhaps, any more than the former, from certain difficulties, but of these the solution will be found in the Replies to the Objections. I further show, in what sense it is true that the certitude of geometrical demonstrations themselves is dependent on the knowledge of God.

Finally, in the Sixth, the act of the understanding (*intellectio*) is distinguished from that of the imagination (*imaginatio*); the marks of this distinction are described; the human mind is shown to be really distinct from the body, and, nevertheless, to be so closely conjoined therewith, as together to form, as it were, a unity. The whole of the errors which arise from the senses are brought under review, while the means of avoiding them are pointed out; and, finally, all the grounds are adduced from which the existence of material objects may be inferred; not, however, because I deemed them of great utility in establishing what they prove, viz., that there is in reality a world, that men are possessed of bodies, and the like, the truth of which no one of sound mind ever seriously doubted; but because, from a close consideration of them, it is perceived that they are neither so strong nor clear as the reasonings which conduct us to the knowledge of our mind and of God; so that the latter are, of all which come under human knowledge, the most certain and manifest—a conclusion which it was my single aim in these Meditations to establish; on which account I here omit mention of the various other questions which, in the course of the discussion, I had occasion likewise to consider.

MEDITATIONS ON THE FIRST PHILOSOPHY,

IN WHICH

THE EXISTENCE OF GOD, AND THE REAL DISTINCTION OF MIND AND BODY, ARE DEMONSTRATED.

MEDITATION I.

OF THE THINGS OF WHICH WE MAY DOUBT.

SEVERAL years have now elapsed since I first became aware that I had accepted, even from my youth, many false opinions for true, and that consequently what I afterwards based on such principles was highly doubtful; and from that time I was convinced of the necessity of undertaking once in my life to rid myself of all the opinions I had adopted, and of commencing anew the work of building from the foundation, if I desired to establish a firm and abiding superstructure in the sciences. But as this enterprise appeared to me to be one of great magnitude, I waited until I had attained an age so mature as to leave me no hope that at any stage of life more advanced I should be better able to execute my design. On this account, I have delayed so long that I should henceforth consider I was doing wrong were I still to consume in deliberation any of the time that now remains for action. To-day, then, since I have opportunely freed my mind from all cares, [and am happily disturbed by no passions], and since I am in the secure possession of leisure in a peaceable retirement, I will at length apply myself earnestly and freely to the general overthrow of all my former opinions. But, to this end, it will not be necessary for me to show that the whole of these are false —a point, perhaps, which I shall never reach; but as even now my reason convinces me that I ought not the less carefully to withhold belief from what is not entirely certain and indubitable, than from what is manifestly false, it will be sufficient to justify the rejection of the whole if I shall find in each some ground for doubt. Nor for this purpose will it be necessary even to deal with each belief individually, which would be truly an endless labour; but, as the removal from below of the foundation necessarily involves the downfall of the whole edifice, I will at once approach the criticism of the principles on which all my former beliefs rested.

All that I have, up to this moment, accepted as possessed of the highest truth and certainty, I received either from or through the senses.[4] I observed, however, that these sometimes misled us; and it is the part of prudence not to place absolute confidence in that by which we have even once been deceived.

But it may be said, perhaps, that, although the senses occasionally mislead us respecting minute objects, and such as are so far removed from us as to be beyond the reach of close observation, there are yet many other of their informations (presentations), of the truth of which it is manifestly impossible to doubt; as for example, that I am in this place, seated by the fire, clothed in a winter dressing-gown, that I hold in my hands this piece of paper, with other intimations of the same nature. But how could I deny that I possess these hands and this body, and withal escape being classed with persons in a state of insanity, whose brains are so disordered and clouded by dark bilious vapours as to cause them pertinaciously to assert that they are monarchs when they are in the greatest poverty; or clothed [in gold] and purple when destitute of any covering; or that their head is made of clay, their body of glass, or that they are gourds? I should certainly be not less insane than they, were I to regulate my procedure according to examples so extravagant.

Though this be true, I must nevertheless here consider that I am a man, and that, consequently, I am in the habit of sleeping, and representing to myself in dreams those same things, or even sometimes others less probable, which the insane think are presented to them in their waking moments. How often have I dreamt that I was in these familiar circumstances,—that I was dressed, and occupied this place by the fire, when I was lying undressed in bed? At the present moment, however, I certainly look upon this paper with eyes wide awake; the head which I now move is not asleep; I extend this hand consciously and with express purpose, and I perceive it; the occurrences in sleep are not so distinct as all this. But I cannot forget that, at other times, I have been deceived in sleep by similar illusions; and, attentively considering those cases, I perceive so clearly that there exist no certain marks by which the state of waking can ever be distinguished from sleep, that I feel greatly astonished; and in amazement I almost persuade myself that I am now dreaming.

Let us suppose, then, that we are dreaming, and that all these particulars—namely, the opening of the eyes, the motion of the head, the forth-putting of the hands—are merely illusions; and even that we really possess neither an entire body nor hands such as we see. Nevertheless, it must be admitted at least that the objects which appear to us in sleep are, as it were, painted representations which could not have been formed unless in the likeness of realities; and, therefore, that those general objects, at all events,—namely, eyes, a head, hands, and an entire body—are not simply imaginary, but really existent. For, in truth, painters themselves, even when they study to represent sirens and satyrs by forms the most fantastic and extraordinary, cannot bestow upon them natures absolutely new, but can only make a certain medley of the members of different animals; or if they chance to imagine something so novel that nothing at all similar has ever been seen before, and such as is, therefore, purely fictitious and absolutely false, it is at least certain that the colours of which this is composed are real.

And on the same principle, although these general objects, viz. [a body], eyes, a head, hands, and the like, be imaginary, we are nevertheless absolutely necessitated to admit the reality at least of some other objects still more simple and universal than these, of which, just as of certain real colours, all those images

OF THE THINGS OF WHICH WE MAY DOUBT. 25

of things, whether true and real, or false and fantastic, that are found in our consciousness (*cogitatio*)[5], are formed.

To this class of objects seem to belong corporeal nature in general and its extension; the figure of extended things, their quantity or magnitude, and their number, as also the place in, and the time during, which they exist, and other things of the same sort. We will not, therefore, perhaps reason illegitimately if we conclude from this that Physics, Astronomy, Medicine, and all the other sciences that have for their end the consideration of composite objects, are indeed of a doubtful character; but that Arithmetic, Geometry, and the other sciences of the same class, which regard merely the simplest and most general objects, and scarcely inquire whether or not these are really existent, contain somewhat that is certain and indubitable: for whether I am awake or dreaming, it remains true that two and three make five, and that a square has but four sides; nor does it seem possible that truths so apparent can ever fall under a suspicion of falsity [or incertitude].

Nevertheless, the belief that there is a God who is all-powerful, and who created me, such as I am, has, for a long time, obtained steady possession of my mind. How, then, do I know that he has not arranged that there should be neither earth, nor sky, nor any extended thing, nor figure, nor magnitude, nor place, providing at the same time, however, for [the rise in me of the perceptions of all these objects, and] the persuasion that these do not exist otherwise than as I perceive them? And further, as I sometimes think that others are in error respecting matters of which they believe themselves to possess a perfect knowledge, how do I know that I am not also deceived each time I add together two and three, or number the sides of a square, or form some judgment still more simple, if more simple indeed can be imagined? But perhaps Deity has not been willing that I should be thus deceived, for He is said to be supremely good. If, however, it were repugnant to the goodness of Deity to have created me subject to constant deception, it would seem likewise to be contrary to his goodness to allow me to be occasionally deceived; and yet it is clear that this is permitted. Some, indeed, might perhaps be found who would be disposed rather to deny the existence of a Being so powerful than to believe that there is nothing certain. But let us for the present refrain from opposing this opinion, and grant that all which is here said of a Deity is fabulous: nevertheless in whatever way it be supposed that I reached the state in which I exist, whether by fate, or chance, or by an endless series of antecedents and consequents, or by any other means, it is clear (since to be deceived and to err is a certain defect) that the probability of my being so imperfect as to be the constant victim of deception, will be increased exactly in proportion as the power possessed by the cause, to which they assign my origin, is lessened. To these reasonings I have assuredly nothing to reply, but am constrained at last to avow that there is nothing of all that I formerly believed to be true of which it is impossible to doubt, and that not through thoughtlessness or levity, but from cogent and maturely considered reasons; so that henceforward, if I desire to discover anything certain, I ought not the less carefully

OF THE THINGS OF WHICH WE MAY DOUBT.

to refrain from assenting to those same opinions than to what might be shown to be manifestly false.

But it is not sufficient to have made these observations; care must be taken likewise to keep them in remembrance. For those old and customary opinions perpetually recur—long and familiar usage giving them the right of occupying my mind, even almost against my will, and subduing my belief; nor will I lose the habit of deferring to them and confiding in them so long as I shall consider them to be what in truth they are, viz., opinions to some extent doubtful, as I have already shown, but still highly probable, and such as it is much more reasonable to believe than deny. It is for this reason I am persuaded that I shall not be doing wrong, if, taking an opposite judgment of deliberate design, I become my own deceiver, by supposing, for a time, that all those opinions are entirely false and imaginary, until at length, having thus balanced my old by my new prejudices, my judgment shall no longer be turned aside by perverted usage from the path that may conduct to the perception of truth. For I am assured that, meanwhile, there will arise neither peril nor error from this course, and that I cannot for the present yield too much to distrust, since the end I now seek is not action but knowledge.

I will suppose, then, not that Deity, who is sovereignly good and the fountain of truth, but that some malignant demon, who is at once exceedingly potent and deceitful, has employed all his artifice to deceive me; I will suppose that the sky, the air, the earth, colours, figures, sounds, and all external things, are nothing better than the illusions of dreams, by means of which this being has laid snares for my credulity;

I will consider myself as without hands, eyes, flesh, blood, or any of the senses, and as falsely believing that I am possessed of these; I will continue resolutely fixed in this belief, and if indeed by this means it be not in my power to arrive at the knowledge of truth, I shall at least do what is in my power, viz., [suspend my judgment], and guard with settled purpose against giving my assent to what is false, and being imposed upon by this deceiver, whatever be his power and artifice.

But this undertaking is arduous, and a certain indolence insensibly leads me back to my ordinary course of life; and just as the captive, who, perchance, was enjoying in his dreams an imaginary liberty, when he begins to suspect that it is but a vision, dreads awakening, and conspires with the agreeable illusions that the deception may be prolonged; so I, of my own accord, fall back into the train of my former beliefs, and fear to arouse myself from my slumber, lest the time of laborious wakefulness that would succeed this quiet rest, in place of bringing any light of day, should prove inadequate to dispel the darkness that will arise from the difficulties that have now been raised.

MEDITATION II.

OF THE NATURE OF THE HUMAN MIND; AND THAT IT IS MORE EASILY KNOWN THAN THE BODY.

THE Meditation of yesterday has filled my mind with so many doubts, that it is no longer in my power to forget them. Nor do I see, meanwhile, any principle on which they can be resolved; and, just as if I had fallen all of a sudden into very deep water, I am so greatly disconcerted as to be unable either to plant my feet firmly on the bottom or sustain myself by swimming on the surface. I will, nevertheless, make an effort, and try anew the same path on which I had entered yesterday, that is, proceed by casting aside all that admits of the slightest doubt, not less than if I had discovered it to be absolutely false; and I will continue always in this track until I shall find something that is certain, or at least, if I can do nothing more, until I shall know with certainty that there is nothing certain. Archimedes, that he might transport the entire globe from the place it occupied to another, demanded only a point that was firm and immoveable; so also, I shall be entitled to entertain the highest expectations, if I am fortunate enough to discover only one thing that is certain and indubitable.

I suppose, accordingly, that all the things which I see are false (fictitious); I believe that none of those objects which my fallacious memory represents ever existed; I suppose that I possess no senses; I believe that body, figure, extension, motion, and place are merely fictions of my mind. What is there, then, that can be esteemed true? Perhaps this only, that there is absolutely nothing certain.

But how do I know that there is not something different altogether from the objects I have now enumerated, of which it is impossible to entertain the slightest doubt? Is there not a God, or some being, by whatever name I may designate him, who causes these thoughts to arise in my mind? But why suppose such a being, for it may be I myself am capable of producing them? Am I, then, at least not something? But I before denied that I possessed senses or a body; I hesitate, however, for what follows from that? Am I so dependent on the body and the senses that without these I cannot exist? But I had the persuasion that there was absolutely nothing in the world, that there was no sky and no earth, neither minds nor bodies; was I not, therefore, at the same time, persuaded that I did not exist? Far from it; I assuredly existed, since I was persuaded. But there is I know not what being, who is possessed at once of the highest power and the deepest cunning, who is constantly employing all his ingenuity in deceiving me. Doubtless, then, I exist, since I am deceived; and, let him deceive me as he may, he can never bring it about that I am nothing, so long as I shall be conscious that I am something. So that it must, in fine, be maintained, all things being maturely and carefully considered, that this proposition (*pronunciatum*) I am, I exist, is necessarily true each time it is expressed by me, or conceived in my mind.

But I do not yet know with sufficient clearness what

OF THE NATURE OF THE HUMAN MIND. 31

I am, though assured that I am; and hence, in the next place, I must take care, lest perchance I inconsiderately substitute some other object in room of what is properly myself, and thus wander from truth, even in that knowledge (cognition) which I hold to be of all others the most certain and evident. For this reason, I will now consider anew what I formerly believed myself to be, before I entered on the present train of thought; and of my previous opinion I will retrench all that can in the least be invalidated by the grounds of doubt I have adduced, in order that there may at length remain nothing but what is certain and indubitable. What then did I formerly think I was? Undoubtedly I judged that I was a man. But what is a man? Shall I say a rational animal? Assuredly not; for it would be necessary forthwith to inquire into what is meant by animal, and what by rational, and thus, from a single question, I should insensibly glide into others, and these more difficult than the first; nor do I now possess enough of leisure to warrant me in wasting my time amid subtleties of this sort. I prefer here to attend to the thoughts that sprung up of themselves in my mind, and were inspired by my own nature alone, when I applied myself to the consideration of what I was. In the first place, then, I thought that I possessed a countenance, hands, arms, and all the fabric of members that appears in a corpse, and which I called by the name of body. It further occurred to me that I was nourished, that I walked, perceived, and thought, and all those actions I referred to the soul; but what the soul itself was I either did not stay to consider, or, if I did, I imagined that it was something extremely rare and subtile, like wind, or flame, or ether, spread through my grosser parts. As regarded the body, I did not even doubt of its nature, but thought I distinctly knew it, and if I had wished to describe it according to the notions I then entertained, I should have explained myself in this manner: By body I understand all that can be terminated by a certain figure; that can be comprised in a certain place, and so fill a certain space as therefrom to exclude every other body; that can be perceived either by touch, sight, hearing, taste, or smell; that can be moved in different ways, not indeed of itself, but by something foreign to it by which it is touched [and from which it receives the impression]; for the power of self-motion, as likewise that of perceiving and thinking, I held as by no means pertaining to the nature of body; on the contrary, I was somewhat astonished to find such faculties existing in some bodies.

But [as to myself, what can I now say that I am], since I suppose there exists an extremely powerful, and, if I may so speak, malignant being, whose whole endeavours are directed towards deceiving me? Can I affirm that I possess any one of all those attributes of which I have lately spoken as belonging to the nature of body? After attentively considering them in my own mind, I find none of them that can properly be said to belong to myself. To recount them were idle and tedious. Let us pass, then, to the attributes of the soul. The first mentioned were the powers of nutrition and walking; but, if it be true that I have no body, it is true likewise that I am capable neither of walking nor of being nourished. Perception is another attribute of the soul; but perception too is impossible without the body: besides, I have frequently, during sleep, believed that I perceived objects which I afterwards observed I did not in reality perceive. Thinking is another attribute of the soul; and here I discover what properly belongs to myself. This alone is inseparable from me. I am—I exist: this is certain; but how often? As often as I think; for perhaps it would even happen, if I should wholly cease to think, that I should at the same time altogether cease to be. I now admit nothing that is not necessarily true: I am therefore, precisely speaking, only a thinking thing, that is, a mind (*mens sive animus*), understanding, or reason,—terms whose signification was before unknown to me. I am, however, a real thing, and really existent; but what thing? The answer was, a thinking thing. The question now arises, am I aught besides? I will stimulate my imagination with a view to discover whether I am not still something more than a thinking being. Now it is plain I am not the assemblage of members called the human body; I am not a thin and penetrating air diffused through all these members, or wind, or flame, or vapour, or breath, or any of all the things I can imagine; for I supposed that all these were not, and, without changing the supposition, I find that I still feel assured of my existence.

But it is true, perhaps, that those very things which I suppose to be non-existent, because they are unknown to me, are not in truth different from myself whom I know. This is a point I cannot determine, and do not now enter into any dispute regarding it. I can only judge of things that are known to me: I am conscious that I exist, and I who know that I exist inquire into what I am. It is, however, perfectly certain that the knowledge of my existence, thus precisely taken, is not dependent on things, the existence of which is as yet unknown to me: and consequently it is not dependent on any of the things I can feign in imagination. Moreover, the phrase itself, I frame an image (*effingo*), reminds me of my error; for I should in truth frame one if I were to imagine myself to be anything, since to imagine is nothing more than to contemplate the figure or image of a corporeal thing; but I already know that I exist, and that it is possible at the same time that all those images, and in general all that relates to the nature of body, are merely dreams [or chimeras]. From this I discover that it is not more reasonable to say, I will excite my imagination that I may know more distinctly what I am, than to express myself as follows: I am now awake, and perceive something real; but because my perception is not sufficiently clear, I will of express purpose go to sleep that my dreams may represent to me the object of my perception with more truth and clearness. And, therefore, I know that nothing of all that I can embrace in imagination belongs to the knowledge which I have of myself, and that there is need to recall with the utmost care the mind from this mode of thinking, that it may be able to know its own nature with perfect distinctness.

But what, then, am I? A thinking thing, it has been said. But what is a thinking thing? It is a thing that doubts, understands, [conceives], affirms, denies, wills, refuses, that imagines also, and perceives. Assuredly it is not little, if all these properties belong to my nature. But why should they not belong to it? Am I not that very being who now doubts of almost everything; who, for all that, understands and conceives certain things; who affirms one alone as true, and denies the others; who desires to know more of them, and does not wish to be deceived; who imagines many things, sometimes even despite his will; and is likewise percipient of many, as if through the medium of the senses. Is there nothing of all this as true as that I am, even although I should be always dreaming, and although he who gave me being employed all his ingenuity to deceive me? Is there also any one of these attributes that can be properly distinguished from my thought, or that can be said to be separate from myself? For it is of itself so evident that it is I who doubt, I who understand, and I who desire, that it is here unnecessary to add anything by way of rendering it more clear. And I am as certainly the same being who imagines; for, although it may be (as I before supposed) that nothing I imagine is true, still the power of imagination does not cease really to exist in me and to form part of my thought. In fine, I am the same being who perceives, that is, who apprehends certain objects as by the organs of sense, since, in truth, I see light, hear a noise, and feel heat. But it will be said that these presentations are false, and that I am dreaming. Let it be so. At all events it is certain that I seem to see light, hear a noise, and feel heat; this cannot be false, and this is what in me is properly called perceiving (*sentire*), which is nothing else than thinking. From this I begin to know what I am with somewhat greater clearness and distinctness than heretofore.

But, nevertheless, it still seems to me, and I cannot help believing, that corporeal things, whose images are formed by thought, [which fall under the senses], and are examined by the same, are known with much greater distinctness than that I know not what part of myself which is not imaginable; although, in truth, it may seem strange to say that I know and comprehend with greater distinctness things whose existence appears to me doubtful, that are unknown, and do not belong to me, than others of whose reality I am persuaded, that are known to me, and appertain to my proper nature; in a word, than myself. But I see clearly what is the state of the case. My mind is apt to wander, and will not yet submit to be restrained within the limits of truth. Let us therefore leave the mind to itself once more, and, according to it every kind of liberty, [permit it to consider the objects that appear to it from without], in order that, having afterwards withdrawn it from these gently and opportunely, [and fixed it on the consideration of its being and the properties it finds in itself], it may then be the more easily controlled.

Let us now accordingly consider the objects that are commonly thought to be [the most easily, and likewise] the most distinctly known, viz., the bodies we touch and see; not, indeed, bodies in general, for these general notions are usually somewhat more confused, but one body in particular. Take, for example, this piece of wax; it is quite fresh, having been but recently taken from the bee-hive; it has not yet lost the sweetness of the honey it contained; it still retains somewhat of the odour of the flowers from which it was gathered; its colour, figure, size, are apparent (to the sight); it is hard, cold, easily handled; and sounds when struck upon with the finger. In fine, all that contributes to make a body as distinctly known as possible, is found in the one before us. But, while I am speaking, let it be placed near the fire—what remained of the taste exhales, the smell evaporates, the colour changes, its figure is destroyed, its size increases, it becomes liquid, it grows hot, it can hardly be handled, and, although struck upon, it emits no sound. Does the same wax still remain after this change? It must be admitted that it does remain; no one doubts it, or judges otherwise. What, then, was it I knew with so much distinctness in the piece of wax? Assuredly, it could be nothing of all that I observed by means of the senses, since all the things that fell under taste, smell, sight, touch, and hearing are changed, and yet the same wax remains. It was perhaps what I now think, viz., that this wax was neither the sweetness of honey, the pleasant odour of flowers, the whiteness, the figure, nor the sound, but only a body that a little before appeared to me conspicuous under these forms, and which is now perceived under others. But, to speak precisely, what is it that I imagine when I think of it in this way? Let it be attentively considered, and, retrenching all that does not belong to the wax, let us see what remains. There certainly remains nothing, except something extended, flexible, and movable. But what is meant by flexible and movable? Is it not that I imagine that the piece of wax, being round, is capable of becoming square, or of passing from a square into a triangular figure? Assuredly such is not the case, because I conceive that it admits of an infinity of similar changes; and I am, mor⟨e⟩ to compass this infinity by imagination quently this conception which I have of t⟨he⟩

the product of the faculty of imagination. But what now is this extension? Is it not also unknown? for it becomes greater when the wax is melted, greater when it is boiled, and greater still when the heat increases; and I should not conceive [clearly and] according to truth, the wax as it is, if I did not suppose that the piece we are considering admitted even of a wider variety of extension than I ever imagined. I must, therefore, admit that I cannot even comprehend by imagination what the piece of wax is, and that it is the mind alone (*mens*, Lat., *entendement*, F.) which perceives it. I speak of one piece in particular; for, as to wax in general, this is still more evident. But what is the piece of wax that can be perceived only by the [understanding or] mind? It is certainly the same which I see, touch, imagine; and, in fine, it is the same which, from the beginning, I believed it to be. But (and this it is of moment to observe) the perception of it is neither an act of sight, of touch, nor of imagination, and never was either of these, though it might formerly seem so, but is simply an intuition (*inspectio*) of the mind, which may be imperfect and confused, as it formerly was, or very clear and distinct, as it is at present, according as the attention is more or less directed to the elements which it contains, and of which it is composed.

But, meanwhile, I feel greatly astonished when I observe [the weakness of my mind, and] its proneness to error. For although, without at all giving expression to what I think, I consider all this in my own mind, words yet occasionally impede my progress, and I am almost led into error by the terms of ordinary language. We say, for example, that we see the same

OF THE NATURE OF THE HUMAN MIND. 39

wax when it is before us, and not that we judge it to be the same from its retaining the same colour and figure: whence I should forthwith be disposed to conclude that the wax is known by the act of sight, and not by the intuition of the mind alone, were it not for the analogous instance of human beings passing on in the street below, as observed from a window. In this case I do not fail to say that I see the men themselves, just as I say that I see the wax; and yet what do I see from the window beyond hats and cloaks that might cover artificial machines, whose motions might be determined by springs? But I judge that there are human beings from these appearances, and thus I comprehend, by the faculty of judgment alone which is in the mind, what I believed I saw with my eyes.

The man who makes it his aim to rise to knowledge superior to the common, ought to be ashamed to seek occasions of doubting from the vulgar forms of speech: instead, therefore, of doing this, I shall proceed with the matter in hand, and inquire whether I had a clearer and more perfect perception of the piece of wax when I first saw it, and when I thought I knew it by means of the external sense itself, or, at all events, by the common sense (*sensus communis*), as it is called, that is, by the imaginative faculty; or whether I rather apprehend it more clearly at present, after having examined with greater care, both what it is, and in what way it can be known. It would certainly be ridiculous to entertain any doubt on this point. For what, in that first perception, was there distinct? What did I perceive which any animal might not have perceived? But when I distinguish the wax from its exterior forms, and when, as if I had stripped it of its vestments, I consider it quite naked, it is certain, although some error may still be found in my judgment, that I cannot, nevertheless, thus apprehend it without possessing a human mind.

But, finally, what shall I say of the mind itself, that is, of myself? for as yet I do not admit that I am anything but mind. What, then! I who seem to possess so distinct an apprehension of the piece of wax,—do I not know myself, both with greater truth and certitude, and also much more distinctly and clearly? For if I judge that the wax exists because I see it, it assuredly follows, much more evidently, that I myself am or exist, for the same reason: for it is possible that what I see may not in truth be wax, and that I do not even possess eyes with which to see anything; but it cannot be that when I see, or, which comes to the same thing, when I think I see, I myself who think am nothing. So likewise, if I judge that the wax exists because I touch it, it will still also follow that I am; and if I determine that my imagination, or any other cause, whatever it be, persuades me of the existence of the wax, I will still draw the same conclusion. And what is here remarked of the piece of wax, is applicable to all the other things that are external to me. And further, if the [notion or] perception of wax appeared to me more precise and distinct, after that not only sight and touch, but many other causes besides, rendered it manifest to my apprehension, with how much greater distinctness must I now know myself, since all the reasons that contribute to the knowledge of the nature of wax, or of any body whatever, manifest still better the nature of my mind? And there are besides so many other things in the mind itself

OF THE NATURE OF THE HUMAN MIND. 41

that contribute to the illustration of its nature, that those dependent on the body, to which I have here referred, scarcely merit to be taken into account.

But, in conclusion, I find I have insensibly reverted to the point I desired; for, since it is now manifest to me that bodies themselves are not properly perceived by the senses nor by the faculty of imagination, but by the intellect alone; and since they are not perceived because they are seen and touched, but only because they are understood [or rightly comprehended by thought], I readily discover that there is nothing more easily or clearly apprehended than my own mind. But because it is difficult to rid one's self so promptly of an opinion to which one has been long accustomed, it will be desirable to tarry for some time at this stage, that, by long continued meditation, I may more deeply impress upon my memory this new knowledge.

MEDITATION III.

OF GOD: THAT HE EXISTS.

I WILL now close my eyes, I will stop my ears, I will turn away my senses from their objects, I will even efface from my consciousness all the images of corporeal things; or at least, because this can hardly be accomplished, I will consider them as empty and false; and thus, holding converse only with myself, and closely examining my nature, I will endeavour to obtain by degrees a more intimate and familiar knowledge of myself. I am a thinking (conscious) thing, that is, a being who doubts, affirms, denies, knows a few objects, and is ignorant of many,—[who loves, hates], wills, refuses,—who imagines likewise, and perceives; for, as I before remarked, although the things which I perceive or imagine are perhaps nothing at all apart from me [and in themselves], I am nevertheless assured that those modes of consciousness which I call perceptions and imaginations, in as far only as they are modes of consciousness, exist in me. And in the little I have said I think I have summed up all that I really know, or at least all that up to this time I was aware I knew. Now, as I am endeavouring to extend my knowledge more widely, I will use circumspection, and consider with care whether I can still discover in myself anything further which I have not yet hitherto observed. I am certain that I am a thinking thing; but do I not there-

OF GOD: THAT HE EXISTS.

fore likewise know what is required to render me certain of a truth? In this first knowledge, doubtless, there is nothing that gives me assurance of its truth except the clear and distinct perception of what I affirm, which would not indeed be sufficient to give me the assurance that what I say is true, if it could ever happen that anything I thus clearly and distinctly perceived should prove false; and accordingly it seems to me that I may now take as a general rule, that all that is very clearly and distinctly apprehended (conceived) is true.

Nevertheless I before received and admitted many things as wholly certain and manifest, which yet I afterwards found to be doubtful. What, then, were those? They were the earth, the sky, the stars, and all the other objects which I was in the habit of perceiving by the senses. But what was it that I clearly [and distinctly] perceived in them? Nothing more than that the ideas and the thoughts of those objects were presented to my mind. And even now I do not deny that these ideas are found in my mind. But there was yet another thing which I affirmed, and which, from having been accustomed to believe it, I thought I clearly perceived, although, in truth, I did not perceive it at all; I mean the existence of objects external to me, from which those ideas proceeded, and to which they had a perfect resemblance; and it was here I was mistaken, or if I judged correctly, this assuredly was not to be traced to any knowledge I possessed (the force of my perception, Lat.).

But when I considered any matter in arithmetic and geometry, that was very simple and easy, as, for example, that two and three added together make five, and things of this sort, did I not view them with at least sufficient clearness to warrant me in affirming their truth? Indeed, if I afterwards judged that we ought to doubt of these things, it was for no other reason than because it occurred to me that a God might perhaps have given me such a nature as that I should be deceived, even respecting the matters that appeared to me the most evidently true. But as often as this preconceived opinion of the sovereign power of a God presents itself to my mind, I am constrained to admit that it is easy for him, if he wishes it, to cause me to err, even in matters where I think I possess the highest evidence; and, on the other hand, as often as I direct my attention to things which I think I apprehend with great clearness, I am so persuaded of their truth that I naturally break out into expressions such as these: Deceive me who may, no one will yet ever be able to bring it about that I am not, so long as I shall be conscious that I am, or at any future time cause it to be true that I have never been, it being now true that I am, or make two and three more or less than five, in supposing which, and other like absurdities, I discover a manifest contradiction.

And in truth, as I have no ground for believing that Deity is deceitful, and as, indeed, I have not even considered the reasons by which the existence of a Deity of any kind is established, the ground of doubt that rests only on this supposition is very slight, and, so to speak, metaphysical. But, that I may be able wholly to remove it, I must inquire whether there is a God, as soon as an opportunity of doing so shall present itself; and if I find that there is a God, I must examine likewise whether he can be a deceiver; for, without the knowledge of these two truths, I do not see that I can ever be certain of anything. And that I may be enabled to examine this without interrupting the order of meditation I have proposed to myself [which is, to pass by degrees from the notions that I shall find first in my mind to those I shall afterwards discover in it], it is necessary at this stage to divide all my thoughts into certain classes, and to consider in which of these classes truth and error are, strictly speaking, to be found.

Of my thoughts some are, as it were, images of things, and to these alone properly belongs the name *idea;* as when I think [represent to my mind] a man, a chimera, the sky, an angel, or God. Others, again, have certain other forms; as when I will, fear, affirm, or deny, I always, indeed, apprehend something as the object of my thought, but I also embrace in thought something more than the representation of the object; and of this class of thoughts some are called volitions or affections, and others judgments.

Now, with respect to ideas, if these are considered only in themselves, and are not referred to any object beyond them, they cannot, properly speaking, be false; for, whether I imagine a goat or a chimera, it is not less true that I imagine the one than the other. Nor need we fear that falsity may exist in the will or affections; for, although I may desire objects that are wrong, and even that never existed, it is still true that I desire them. There thus only remain our judgments, in which we must take diligent heed that we be not deceived. But the chief and most ordinary error that arises in them consists in judging that the ideas which are in us are like or conformed to the things that are external to us; for assuredly, if we but considered the ideas themselves as certain modes of our thought (consciousness), without referring them to anything beyond, they would hardly afford any occasion of error.

But, among these ideas, some appear to me to be innate[6], others adventitious, and others to be made by myself (factitious); for, as I have the power of conceiving what is called a thing, or a truth, or a thought, it seems to me that I hold this power from no other source than my own nature; but if I now hear a noise, if I see the sun, or if I feel heat, I have all along judged that these sensations proceeded from certain objects existing out of myself; and, in fine, it appears to me that sirens, hippogryphs, and the like, are inventions of my own mind. But I may even perhaps come to be of opinion that all my ideas are of the class which I call adventitious, or that they are all innate, or that they are all factitious, for I have not yet clearly discovered their true origin; and what I have here principally to do is to consider, with reference to those that appear to come from certain objects without me, what grounds there are for thinking them like these objects.

The first of these grounds is that it seems to me I am so taught by nature; and the second that I am conscious that those ideas are not dependent on my will, and therefore not on myself, for they are frequently presented to me against my will,—as at present, whether I will or not, I feel heat; and I am thus persuaded that this sensation or idea (*sensum vel ideam*) of heat is produced in me by something different from myself, viz., by the heat of the fire by which I sit. And it is very reasonable to suppose that this object impresses me with its own likeness rather than any other thing.

But I must consider whether these reasons are sufficiently strong and convincing. When I speak of being taught by nature in this matter, I understand by the word nature only a certain spontaneous impetus that impels me to believe in a resemblance between ideas and their objects, and not a natural light that affords a knowledge of its truth. But these two things are widely different; for what the natural light shows to be true can be in no degree doubtful, as, for example, that I am because I doubt, and other truths of the like kind: inasmuch as I possess no other faculty whereby to distinguish truth from error, which can teach me the falsity of what the natural light declares to be true, and which is equally trustworthy; but with respect to [seemingly] natural impulses, I have observed, when the question related to the choice of right or wrong in action, that they frequently led me to take the worse part; nor do I see that I have any better ground for following them in what relates to truth and error. Then, with respect to the other reason, which is that because these ideas do not depend on my will, they must arise from objects existing without me, I do not find it more convincing than the former; for, just as those natural impulses, of which I have lately spoken, are found in me, notwithstanding that they are not always in harmony with my will, so likewise it may be that I possess some power not sufficiently known to myself capable of producing ideas without the aid of external objects, and, indeed, it has always hitherto appeared to me that they are formed during sleep, by some power of this nature, without the aid of aught external. And, in fine, although I should grant that they proceeded from those objects, it is not a necessary consequence that they must be like them. On the contrary, I have observed, in a number of instances, that there was a great difference between the object and its idea. Thus, for example, I find in my mind two wholly diverse ideas of the sun; the one, by which it appears to me extremely small, draws its origin from the senses, and should be placed in the class of adventitious ideas; the other, by which it seems to be many times larger than the whole earth, is taken up on astronomical grounds, that is, elicited from certain notions born with me, or is framed by myself in some other manner. These two ideas cannot certainly both resemble the same sun; and reason teaches me that the one which seems to have immediately emanated from it is the most unlike. And these things sufficiently prove that hitherto it has not been from a certain and deliberate judgment, but only from a sort of blind impulse, that I believed in the existence of certain things different from myself, which, by the organs of sense, or by whatever other means it might be, conveyed their ideas or images into my mind [and impressed it with their likenesses].

But there is still another way of inquiring whether, of the objects whose ideas are in my mind, there are any that exist out of me. If ideas are taken in so far only as they are certain modes of consciousness, I do not remark any difference or inequality among them, and all seem, in the same manner, to proceed from myself; but, considering them as images, of which one represents one thing and another a different, it is evident that a great diversity obtains among them. For, without doubt, those that represent substances are something more, and contain in themselves, so to speak, more objective reality [that is, participate by representation in higher degrees of being or perfection], than those that represent only modes or accidents; and again, the idea by which I conceive a God [sovereign], eternal, infinite, [immutable], all-knowing, all-powerful, and the creator of all things that are out of himself,—this, I say, has certainly in it more objective reality than those ideas by which finite substances are represented.

Now, it is manifest by the natural light that there must at least be as much reality in the efficient and total cause as in its effect; for whence can the effect draw its reality if not from its cause? and how could the cause communicate to it this reality unless it possessed it in itself? And hence it follows, not only that what is cannot be produced by what is not, but likewise that the more perfect,—in other words, that which contains in itself more reality,—cannot be the effect of the less perfect: and this is not only evidently true of those effects, whose reality is actual or formal, but likewise of ideas, whose reality is only considered as objective. Thus, for example, the stone that is not yet in existence, not only cannot now commence to be, unless it be produced by that which possesses in itself, formally or eminently[7], all that enters into its composition, [in other words, by that which contains in itself the same properties that are in the stone, or others superior to them]; and heat can only be produced in a subject that was before devoid of it, by a cause that is of an order [degree or kind], at least as perfect as heat; and so of the others. But further, even the idea of the heat, or of the stone, cannot exist in me unless it be put there by a cause that contains, at least, as much reality as I conceive existent in the heat or in the stone: for, although that cause may not transmit into my idea anything of its actual or formal reality, we ought not on this account to imagine that it is less real; but we ought to consider that, [as every idea is a work of the mind], its nature is such as of itself to demand no other formal reality than that which it borrows from our consciousness, of which it is but a mode, [that is, a manner or way of thinking]. But in order that an idea may contain this objective reality rather than that, it must doubtless derive it from some cause in which is found at least as much formal reality as the idea contains of objective; for, if we suppose that there is found in an idea anything which was not in its cause, it must of course derive this from nothing. But, however imperfect may be the mode of existence by which a thing is objectively [or by representation] in the understanding by its idea, we certainly cannot, for all that, allege that this mode of existence is nothing, nor, consequently, that the idea owes its origin to nothing. Nor must it be imagined that, since the reality which is considered in these ideas is only objective, the same reality need not be formally (actually) in the causes of these ideas, but only objectively: for, just as the mode of existing objectively belongs to ideas by their peculiar nature, so likewise the mode of existing formally appertains to the causes of these ideas (at least to the first and principal), by their peculiar nature. And although an idea may give rise to another idea, this regress can-

OF GOD: THAT HE EXISTS.

not, nevertheless, be infinite; we must in the end reach a first idea, the cause of which is, as it were, the archetype in which all the reality [or perfection] that is found objectively [or by representation] in these ideas is contained formally [and in act]. I am thus clearly taught by the natural light that ideas exist in me as pictures or images, which may in truth readily fall short of the perfection of the objects from which they are taken, but can never contain anything greater or more perfect.

And in proportion to the time and care with which I examine all those matters, the conviction of their truth brightens and becomes distinct. But, to sum up, what conclusion shall I draw from it all? It is this;—if the objective reality [or perfection] of any one of my ideas be such as clearly to convince me, that this same reality exists in me neither formally nor eminently, and if, as follows from this, I myself cannot be the cause of it, it is a necessary consequence that I am not alone in the world, but that there is besides myself some other being who exists as the cause of that idea; while, on the contrary, if no such idea be found in my mind, I shall have no sufficient ground of assurance of the existence of any other being besides myself; for, after a most careful search, I have, up to this moment, been unable to discover any other ground.

But, among these my ideas, besides that which represents myself, respecting which there can be here no difficulty, there is one that represents a God; others that represent corporeal and inanimate things; others angels; others animals; and, finally, there are some that represent men like myself. But with respect to the ideas that represent other men, or animals, or angels, I can easily suppose that they were formed by the mingling and composition of the other ideas which I have of myself, of corporeal things, and of God, although there were, apart from myself, neither men, animals, nor angels. And with regard to the ideas of corporeal objects, I never discovered in them anything so great or excellent which I myself did not appear capable of originating; for, by considering these ideas closely and scrutinising them individually, in the same way that I yesterday examined the idea of wax, I find that there is but little in them that is clearly and distinctly perceived. As belonging to the class of things that are clearly apprehended, I recognise the following, viz., magnitude or extension in length, breadth, and depth; figure, which results from the termination of extension; situation, which bodies of diverse figures preserve with reference to each other; and motion or the change of situation; to which may be added substance, duration, and number. But with regard to light, colours, sounds, odours, tastes, heat, cold, and the other tactile qualities, they are thought with so much obscurity and confusion, that I cannot determine even whether they are true or false; in other words, whether or not the ideas I have of these qualities are in truth the ideas of real objects. For although I before remarked that it is only in judgments that formal falsity, or falsity properly so called, can be met with, there may nevertheless be found in ideas a certain material falsity, which arises when they represent what is nothing as if it were something. Thus, for example, the ideas I have of cold and heat are so far from being clear and distinct, that I am unable from them to discover whether cold is only the privation of heat, or heat the privation of cold; or whether they are not real qualities: and since, ideas being as it were images, there can be none that does not seem to us to represent some object, the idea which represents cold as something real and positive will not improperly be called false, if it be correct to say that cold is nothing but a privation of heat; and so in other cases. To ideas of this kind, indeed, it is not necessary that I should assign any author besides myself: for if they are false, that is, represent objects that are unreal, the natural light teaches me that they proceed from nothing; in other words, that they are in me only because something is wanting to the perfection of my nature; but if these ideas are true, yet because they exhibit to me so little reality that I cannot even distinguish the object represented from non-being, I do not see why I should not be the author of them.

With reference to those ideas of corporeal things that are clear and distinct, there are some which, as appears to me, might have been taken from the idea I have of myself, as those of substance, duration, number, and the like. For when I think that a stone is a substance, or a thing capable of existing of itself, and that I am likewise a substance, although I conceive that I am a thinking and non-extended thing, and that the stone, on the contrary, is extended and unconscious, there being thus the greatest diversity between the two concepts,—yet these two ideas seem to have this in common that they both represent substances. In the same way, when I think of myself as now existing, and recollect besides that I existed some time ago, and when I am conscious of various thoughts whose number I know, I then acquire the ideas of duration and number, which I can afterwards transfer to as many objects as I please. With respect to the other qualities that go to make up the ideas of corporeal objects, viz., extension, figure, situation, and motion, it is true that they are not formally in me, since I am merely a thinking being; but because they are only certain modes of substance, and because I myself am a substance, it seems possible that they may be contained in me eminently.

There only remains, therefore, the idea of God, in which I must consider whether there is anything that cannot be supposed to originate with myself. By the name God, I understand a substance infinite, [eternal, immutable], independent, all-knowing, all-powerful, and by which I myself, and every other thing that exists, if any such there be, were created. But these properties are so great and excellent, that the more attentively I consider them the less I feel persuaded that the idea I have of them owes its origin to myself alone. And thus it is absolutely necessary to conclude, from all that I have before said, that God exists: for though the idea of substance be in my mind owing to this, that I myself am a substance, I should not, however, have the idea of an infinite substance, seeing I am a finite being, unless it were given me by some substance in reality infinite.

And I must not imagine that I do not apprehend the infinite by a true idea, but only by the negation of the finite, in the same way that I comprehend repose and darkness by the negation of motion and light: since, on the contrary, I clearly perceive that there is more reality in the infinite substance than in the finite, and therefore that in some way I possess the perception (notion) of the infinite before that of the finite, that is, the perception of God before that of myself, for how could I know that I doubt, desire, or that something is wanting to me, and that I am not wholly perfect, if I possessed no idea of a being more perfect than myself, by comparison of which I knew the deficiencies of my nature?

And it cannot be said that this idea of God is perhaps materially false, and consequently that it may have arisen from nothing, [in other words, that it may exist in me from my imperfection], as I before said of the ideas of heat and cold, and the like: for, on the contrary, as this idea is very clear and distinct, and contains in itself more objective reality than any other, there can be no one of itself more true, or less open to the suspicion of falsity.

The idea, I say, of a being supremely perfect, and infinite, is in the highest degree true; for although, perhaps, we may imagine that such a being does not exist, we cannot, nevertheless, suppose that his idea represents nothing real, as I have already said of the idea of cold. It is likewise clear and distinct in the highest degree, since whatever the mind clearly and distinctly conceives as real or true, and as implying any perfection, is contained entire in this idea. And this is true, nevertheless, although I do not comprehend the infinite, and although there may be in God an infinity of things that I cannot comprehend, nor perhaps even compass by thought in any way; for it is of the nature of the infinite that it should not be comprehended by the finite; and it is enough that I rightly understand this, and judge that all which I clearly perceive, and in which I know there is some perfection, and perhaps also an infinity of properties of which I am ignorant, are formally or eminently in God, in order that the idea I have of him may become the most true, clear, and distinct of all the ideas in my mind.

But perhaps I am something more than I suppose myself to be, and it may be that all those perfections which I attribute to God, in some way exist potentially in me, although they do not yet show themselves, and are not reduced to act. Indeed, I am already conscious that my knowledge is being increased [and perfected] by degrees; and I see nothing to prevent it from thus gradually increasing to infinity, nor any reason why, after such increase and perfection, I should not be able thereby to acquire all the other perfections of the Divine nature; nor, in fine, why the power I possess of acquiring those perfections, if it really now exist in me, should not be sufficient to produce the ideas of them. Yet, on looking more closely into the matter, I discover that this cannot be; for, in the first place, although it were true that my knowledge daily acquired new degrees of perfection, and although there were potentially in my nature much that was not as yet actually in it, still all these excellences make not the slightest approach to the idea I have of the Deity, in whom there is no perfection merely potentially [but all actually] existent; for it is even an unmistakeable token of imperfection in my knowledge, that it is augmented by degrees. Further, although my knowledge increase more and more, nevertheless I am not, therefore, induced to think that it will ever be actually infinite, since it can never reach that point beyond which it shall be incapable of further increase. But I conceive God as actually infinite, so that nothing can be added to his perfection. And, in fine, I readily perceive that the objective being of an idea cannot be produced by a being that is merely potentially existent, which, properly speaking, is nothing, but only by a being existing formally or actually.

And, truly, I see nothing in all that I have now said which it is not easy for any one, who shall carefully consider it, to discern by the natural light; but when I allow my attention in some degree to relax, the vision of my mind being obscured, and, as it were, blinded by the images of sensible objects, I do not readily remember the reason why the idea of a being more perfect than myself, must of necessity have proceeded from a being in reality more perfect. On this account I am here desirous to inquire further, whether I, who possess this idea of God, could exist supposing there were no God. And I ask, from whom could I, in that case, derive my existence? Perhaps from myself, or from my parents, or from some other causes less perfect than God; for anything more perfect, or even equal to God, cannot be thought or imagined. But if I [were independent of every other existence, and] were myself the author of my being, I should doubt of nothing, I should desire nothing, and, in fine, no perfection would be awanting to me; for I should have bestowed upon myself every perfection of which I possess the idea, and I should thus be God. And it must not be imagined that what is now wanting to me is perhaps of more difficult acquisition than that of which I am already possessed; for, on the contrary, it is quite manifest that it was a matter of much higher difficulty that I, a thinking being, should arise from nothing, than it would be for me to acquire the knowledge of many things of which I am ignorant, and which are merely the accidents of a thinking substance; and certainly, if I possessed of myself the greater perfection of which I have now spoken, [in other words, if I were the author of my own existence], I would not at least have denied to myself things that may be more easily obtained, [as that infinite variety of knowledge of which I am at present destitute]. I could not, indeed, have denied to myself any property which I perceive is contained in the idea of God, because there is none of these that seems to me to be more difficult to make or acquire; and if there were any that should happen to be more difficult to acquire, they would certainly appear so to me (supposing that I myself were the source of the other things I possess), because I should discover in them a limit to my power. And though I were to suppose that I always was as I now am, I should not, on this ground, escape the force of these reasonings, since it would not follow, even on this supposition, that no author of my existence needed to be sought after. For the whole time of my life may be divided into an infinity of parts, each of which is in no way dependent on any other; and, accordingly, because I was in existence a short time ago, it does not follow that I must now exist, unless in this moment some cause create me anew as it were,—that is, conserve me. In truth, it is perfectly clear and evident to all who will attentively consider the nature of duration, that the conservation of a substance, in each moment of its duration, requires the same power and act that would be necessary to create it, supposing it were not yet in existence; so that it is manifestly a dictate of the natural light that conservation and creation differ merely in respect of our mode of thinking [and not in reality]. All that is here required, therefore, is that I interrogate myself to discover whether I possess any power by means of which I can bring it about that I, who now am, shall exist a moment afterwards; for, since I am merely a thinking thing (or since, at least, the precise question, in the meantime, is only of that part of myself), if such a power resided in me, I should, without doubt, be conscious of it; but I am conscious of no such power, and thereby I manifestly know that I am dependent upon some being different from myself.

But perhaps the being upon whom I am dependent, is not God, and I have been produced either by my parents, or by some causes less perfect than Deity. This cannot be: for, as I before said, it is perfectly evident that there must at least be as much reality in the cause as in its effect; and accordingly, since I am a thinking thing, and possess in myself an idea of God, whatever in the end be the cause of my existence, it must of necessity be admitted that it is likewise a thinking being, and that it possesses in itself the idea and all the perfections I attribute to Deity. Then it may again be inquired whether this cause owes its origin and existence to itself, or to some other cause. For if it be self-existent, it follows, from what I have before laid down, that this cause is God; for, since it possesses the perfection of self-existence, it must likewise, without doubt, have the power of actually possessing every perfection of which it has the idea,—in other words, all the perfections I conceive to belong to God. But if it owe its existence to another cause than itself, we demand again, for a similar reason, whether this second cause exists of itself or through some other, until, from stage to stage, we at length arrive at an ultimate cause, which will be God. And it is quite manifest that in this matter there can be no infinite regress of causes, seeing that the question raised respects not so much the cause which once produced me, as that by which I am at this present moment conserved.

Nor can it be supposed that several causes concurred in my production, and that from one I received the idea of one of the perfections I attribute to Deity, and from another the idea of some other, and thus that all those perfections are indeed found somewhere in the universe, but do not all exist together in a single being who is God; for, on the contrary, the unity, the simplicity or inseparability of all the properties of Deity, is one of the chief perfections I conceive him to possess; and the idea of this unity of all the perfections of Deity could certainly not be put into my mind by any cause from which I did not likewise receive the ideas of all the other perfections; for no power could enable me to embrace them in an inseparable unity, without at the same time giving me the knowledge of what they were [and of their existence in a particular mode].

Finally, with regard to my parents [from whom it appears I sprung], although all that I believed respecting them be true, it does not, nevertheless, follow that I am conserved by them, or even that I was produced by them, in so far as I am a thinking being. All that, at the most, they contributed to my origin was the giving of certain dispositions (modifications) to the matter in which I have hitherto judged that I or my mind, which is what alone I now consider to be myself, is enclosed; and thus there can here be no difficulty with respect to them, and it is absolutely necessary to con-

OF GOD: THAT HE EXISTS.

clude from this alone that I am, and possess the idea of a being absolutely perfect, that is, of God, that his existence is most clearly demonstrated.

There remains only the inquiry as to the way in which I received this idea from God; for I have not drawn it from the senses, nor is it even presented to me unexpectedly, as is usual with the ideas of sensible objects, when these are presented or appear to be presented to the external organs of the senses; it is not even a pure production or fiction of my mind, for it is not in my power to take from or add to it; and consequently there but remains the alternative that it is innate, in the same way as is the idea of myself. And, in truth, it is not to be wondered at that God, at my creation, implanted this idea in me, that it might serve, as it were, for the mark of the workman impressed on his work; and it is not also necessary that the mark should be something different from the work itself; but considering only that God is my creator, it is highly probable that he in some way fashioned me after his own image and likeness, and that I perceive this likeness, in which is contained the idea of God, by the same faculty by which I apprehend myself,—in other words, when I make myself the object of reflection, I not only find that I am an incomplete, [imperfect] and dependent being, and one who unceasingly aspires after something better and greater than he is; but, at the same time, I am assured likewise that he upon whom I am dependent possesses in himself all the goods after which I aspire, [and the ideas of which I find in my mind], and that not merely indefinitely and potentially, but infinitely and actually, and that he is thus God. And the whole force of the argument of which I have here availed myself to establish the existence of **God**, consists in this, that I perceive I could not possibly be of such a nature as I am, and yet have in my mind the idea of a God, if God did not in reality exist,—this same God, I say, whose idea is in my mind—that is, a being who possesses all those lofty perfections, of which the mind may have some slight conception, without, however, being able fully to comprehend them— and who is wholly superior to all defect,[and has nothing that marks imperfection] : whence it is sufficiently manifest that he cannot be a deceiver, since it is a dictate of the natural light that all fraud and deception spring from some defect.

But before I examine this with more attention, and pass on to the consideration of other truths that may be evolved out of it, I think it proper to remain here for some time in the contemplation of God himself— that I may ponder at leisure his marvellous attributes —and behold, admire, and adore the beauty of this light so unspeakably great, as far, at least, as the strength of my mind, which is to some degree dazzled by the sight, will permit. For just as we learn by faith that the supreme felicity of another life consists in the contemplation of the Divine majesty alone, so even now we learn from experience that a like meditation, though incomparably less perfect, is the source of the highest satisfaction of which we are susceptible in this life.

MEDITATION IV.

OF TRUTH AND ERROR.

I HAVE been habituated these bygone days to detach my mind from the senses, and I have accurately observed that there is exceedingly little which is known with certainty respecting corporeal objects,—that we know much more of the human mind, and still more of God himself. I am thus able now without difficulty to abstract my mind from the contemplation of [sensible of] imaginable objects, and apply it to those which, as disengaged from all matter, are purely intelligible. And certainly the idea I have of the human mind in so far as it is a thinking thing, and not extended in length, breadth, and depth, and participating in none of the properties of body, is incomparably more distinct than the idea of any corporeal object; and when I consider that I doubt, in other words, that I am an incomplete and dependent being, the idea of a complete and independent being, that is to say of God, occurs to my mind with so much clearness and distinctness, —and from the fact alone that this idea is found in me, or that I who possess it exist, the conclusions that God exists, and that my own existence, each moment of its continuance, is absolutely dependent upon him, are so manifest,—as to lead me to believe it impossible that the human mind can know anything with more clearness and certitude. And now I seem to discover a path that will conduct us from the contemplation of the true God, in whom are contained all the treasures of science and wisdom, to the knowledge of the other things in the universe.

For, in the first place, I discover that it is impossible for him ever to deceive me, for in all fraud and deceit there is a certain imperfection: and although it may seem that the ability to deceive is a mark of subtlety or power, yet the will testifies without doubt of malice and weakness; and such, accordingly, cannot be found in God. In the next place, I am conscious that I possess a certain faculty of judging [or discerning truth from error], which I doubtless received from God, along with whatever else is mine; and since it is impossible that he should will to deceive me, it is likewise certain that he has not given me a faculty that will ever lead me into error, provided I use it aright.

And there would remain no doubt on this head, did it not seem to follow from this, that I can never therefore be deceived; for if all I possess be from God, and if he planted in me no faculty that is deceitful, it seems to follow that I can never fall into error. Accordingly, it is true that when I think only of God (when I look upon myself as coming from God, Fr.), and turn wholly to him, I discover [in myself] no cause of error or falsity: but immediately thereafter, recurring to myself, experience assures me that I am nevertheless subject to innumerable errors. When I come to inquire into the cause of these, I observe that there is not only present to my consciousness a real and positive idea of God, or of a being supremely perfect, but also, so to speak, a certain negative idea of nothing,— in other words, of that which is at an infinite distance from every sort of perfection, and that I am, as it were,

OF TRUTH AND ERROR. 65

a mean between God and nothing, or placed in such a way between absolute existence and non-existence, that there is in truth nothing in me to lead me into error, in so far as an absolute being is my creator; but that, on the other hand, as I thus likewise participate in some degree of nothing or of non-being, in other words, as I am not myself the supreme Being, and as I am wanting in many perfections, it is not surprising I should fall into error. And I hence discern that error, so far as error is not something real, which depends for its existence on God, but is simply defect; and therefore that, in order to fall into it, it is not necessary God should have given me a faculty expressly for this end, but that my being deceived arises from the circumstance that the power which God has given me of discerning truth from error is not infinite.

Nevertheless this is not yet quite satisfactory; for error is not a pure negation, [in other words, it is not the simple deficiency or want of some knowledge which is not due], but the privation or want of some knowledge which it would seem I ought to possess. But, on considering the nature of God, it seems impossible that he should have planted in his creature any faculty not perfect in its kind, that is, wanting in some perfection due to it: for if it be true, that in proportion to the skill of the maker the perfection of his work is greater, what thing can have been produced by the supreme Creator of the universe that is not absolutely perfect in all its parts? And assuredly there is no doubt that God could have created me such as that I should never be deceived; it is certain, likewise, that he always wills what is best; is it better, then, that I should be capable of being deceived than that I should not?

Considering this more attentively, the first thing that occurs to me is the reflection that I must not be surprised if I am not always capable of comprehending the reasons why God acts as he does; nor must I doubt of his existence because I find, perhaps, that there are several other things besides the present respecting which I understand neither why nor how they were created by him; for, knowing already that my nature is extremely weak and limited, and that the nature of God, on the other hand, is immense, incomprehensible, and infinite, I have no longer any difficulty in discerning that there is an infinity of things in his power whose causes transcend the grasp of my mind: and this consideration alone is sufficient to convince me, that the whole class of final causes is of no avail in physical [or natural] things; for it appears to me that I cannot, without exposing myself to the charge of temerity, seek to discover the [impenetrable] ends of Deity.

It further occurs to me that we must not consider only one creature apart from the others, if we wish to determine the perfection of the works of Deity, but generally all his creatures together; for the same object that might perhaps, with some show of reason, be deemed highly imperfect if it were alone in the world, may for all that be the most perfect possible, considered as forming part of the whole universe: and although, as it was my purpose to doubt of everything, I only as yet know with certainty my own existence and that of God, nevertheless, after having remarked the infinite power of Deity, I cannot deny that he may have produced many other objects, or at least that he is able to produce them, so that I may occupy a place in the relation of a part to the great whole of his creatures.

Whereupon, regarding myself more closely, and considering what my errors are (which alone testify to the existence of imperfection in me), I observe that these depend on the concurrence of two causes, viz., the faculty of cognition which I possess, and that of election or the power of free choice,—in other words, the understanding and the will. For by the understanding alone, I [neither affirm nor deny anything, but] merely apprehend (*percipio*) the ideas regarding which I may form a judgment; nor is any error, properly so called, found in it thus accurately taken. And although there are perhaps innumerable objects in the world of which I have no idea in my understanding, it cannot, on that account, be said that I am deprived of those ideas [as of something that is due to my nature], but simply that I do not possess them, because, in truth, there is no ground to prove that Deity ought to have endowed me with a larger faculty of cognition than he has actually bestowed upon me; and however skilful a workman I suppose him to be, I have no reason, on that account, to think that it was obligatory on him to give to each of his works all the perfections he is able to bestow upon some. Nor, moreover, can I complain that God has not given me freedom of choice, or a will sufficiently ample and perfect, since, in truth, I am conscious of will so ample and extended as to be superior to all limits. And what appears to me here to be highly remarkable is that, of all the other properties I possess, there is none so great and perfect as that I do not clearly discern it could be still greater and more perfect. For, to take an example, if

I consider the faculty of understanding which I possess, I find that it is of very small extent, and greatly limited, and at the same time I form the idea of another faculty of the same nature, much more ample and even infinite; and seeing that I can frame the idea of it, I discover, from this circumstance alone, that it pertains to the nature of God. In the same way, if I examine the faculty of memory or imagination, or any other faculty I possess, I find none that is not small and circumscribed, and in God immense [and infinite]. It is the faculty of will only, or freedom of choice, which I experience to be so great that I am unable to conceive the idea of another that shall be more ample and extended; so that it is chiefly my will which leads me to discern that I bear a certain image and similitude of Deity. For although the faculty of will is incomparably greater in God than in myself, as well in respect of the knowledge and power that are conjoined with it, and that render it stronger and more efficacious, as in respect of the object, since in him it extends to a greater number of things, it does not, nevertheless, appear to me greater, considered in itself formally and precisely: for the power of will consists only in this, that we are able to do or not to do the same thing (that is, to affirm or deny, to pursue or shun it), or rather in this alone, that in affirming or denying, pursuing or shunning, what is proposed to us by the understanding, we so act that we are not conscious of being determined to a particular action by any external force. For, to the possession of freedom, it is not necessary that I be alike indifferent towards each of two contraries; but, on the contrary, the more I am inclined towards the one, whether because I clearly know that in it there is the reason of truth and goodness, or because God thus internally disposes my thought, the more freely do I choose and embrace it; and assuredly divine grace and natural knowledge, very far from diminishing liberty, rather augment and fortify it. But the indifference of which I am conscious when I am not impelled to one side rather than to another for want of a reason, is the lowest grade of liberty, and manifests defect or negation of knowledge rather than perfection of will; for if I always clearly knew what was true and good, I should never have any difficulty in determining what judgment I ought to come to, and what choice I ought to make, and I should thus be entirely free without ever being indifferent.

From all this I discover, however, that neither the power of willing, which I have received from God, is of itself the source of my errors, for it is exceedingly ample and perfect in its kind; nor even the power of understanding, for as I conceive no object unless by means of the faculty that God bestowed upon me, all that I conceive is doubtless rightly conceived by me, and it is impossible for me to be deceived in it.

Whence, then, spring my errors? They arise from this cause alone, that I do not restrain the will, which is of much wider range than the understanding, within the same limits, but extend it even to things I do not understand, and as the will is of itself indifferent to such, it readily falls into error and sin by choosing the false in room of the true, and evil instead of good.

For example, when I lately considered whether aught really existed in the world, and found that because I considered this question, it very manifestly followed that I myself existed, I could not but judge that what I so clearly conceived was true, not that I was forced to this judgment by any external cause, but simply because great clearness of the understanding was succeeded by strong inclination in the will; and I believed this the more freely and spontaneously in proportion as I was less indifferent with respect to it. But now I not only know that I exist, in so far as I am a thinking being, but there is likewise presented to my mind a certain idea of corporeal nature; hence I am in doubt as to whether the thinking nature which is in me, or rather which I myself am, is different from that corporeal nature, or whether both are merely one and the same thing, and I here suppose that I am as yet ignorant of any reason that would determine me to adopt the one belief in preference to the other: whence it happens that it is a matter of perfect indifference to me which of the two suppositions I affirm or deny, or whether I form any judgment at all in the matter.

This indifference, moreover, extends not only to things of which the understanding has no knowledge at all, but in general also to all those which it does not discover with perfect clearness at the moment the will is deliberating upon them; for, however probable the conjectures may be that dispose me to form a judgment in a particular matter, the simple knowledge that these are merely conjectures, and not certain and indubitable reasons, is sufficient to lead me to form one that is directly the opposite. Of this I lately had abundant experience, when I laid aside as false all that I had before held for true, on the single ground that I could in some degree doubt of it. But if I abstain from judging of a thing when I do not conceive it with suf-

OF TRUTH AND ERROR.

ficient clearness and distinctness, it is plain that I act rightly, and am not deceived; but if I resolve to deny or affirm, I then do not make a right use of my free will; and if I affirm what is false, it is evident that I am deceived: moreover, even although I judge according to truth, I stumble upon it by chance, and do not therefore escape the imputation of a wrong use of my freedom; for it is a dictate of the natural light, that the knowledge of the understanding ought always to precede the determination of the will.

And it is this wrong use of the freedom of the will in which is found the privation that constitutes the form of error. Privation, I say, is found in the act, in so far as it proceeds from myself, but it does not exist in the faculty which I received from God, nor even in the act, in so far as it depends on him; for I have assuredly no reason to complain that God has not given me a greater power of intelligence or more perfect natural light than he has actually bestowed, since it is of the nature of a finite understanding not to comprehend many things, and of the nature of a created understanding to be finite; on the contrary, I have every reason to render thanks to God, who owed me nothing, for having given me all the perfections I possess, and I should be far from thinking that he has unjustly deprived me of, or kept back, the other perfections which he has not bestowed upon me.

I have no reason, moreover, to complain because he has given me a will more ample than my understanding, since, as the will consists only of a single element, and that indivisible, it would appear that this faculty is of such a nature that nothing could be taken from it [without destroying it]; and certainly, the more extensive it is, the more cause I have to thank the goodness of him who bestowed it upon me.

And, finally, I ought not also to complain that God concurs with me in forming the acts of this will, or the judgments in which I am deceived, because those acts are wholly true and good, in so far as they depend on God; and the ability to form them is a higher degree of perfection in my nature than the want of it would be. With regard to privation, in which alone consists the formal reason of error and sin, this does not require the concurrence of Deity, because it is not a thing [or existence], and if it be referred to God as to its cause, it ought not to be called privation, but negation, [according to the signification of these words in the schools]. For in truth it is no imperfection in Deity that he has accorded to me the power of giving or withholding my assent from certain things of which he has not put a clear and distinct knowledge in my understanding; but it is doubtless an imperfection in me that I do not use my freedom aright, and readily give my judgment on matters which I only obscurely and confusedly conceive.

I perceive, nevertheless, that it was easy for Deity so to have constituted me as that I should never be deceived, although I still remained free and possessed of a limited knowledge, viz., by implanting in my understanding a clear and distinct knowledge of all the objects respecting which I should ever have to deliberate; or simply by so deeply engraving on my memory the resolution to judge of nothing without previously possessing a clear and distinct conception of it, that I should never forget it. And I easily understand that, in so far as I consider myself as a single whole, without reference to any other being in the universe, I should have been much more perfect than I now am, had Deity created me superior to error; but I cannot therefore deny that it is not somehow a greater perfection in the universe, that certain of its parts are not exempt from defect, as others are, than if they were all perfectly alike.

And I have no right to complain because God, who placed me in the world, was not willing that I should sustain that character which of all others is the chief and most perfect; I have even good reason to remain satisfied on the ground that, if he has not given me the perfection of being superior to error by the first means I have pointed out above, which depends on a clear and evident knowledge of all the matters regarding which I can deliberate, he has at least left in my power the other means, which is, firmly to retain the resolution never to judge where the truth is not clearly known to me: for, although I am conscious of the weakness of not being able to keep my mind continually fixed on the same thought, I can nevertheless, by attentive and oft-repeated meditation, impress it so strongly on my memory that I shall never fail to recollect it as often as I require it, and I can acquire in this way the habitude of not erring; and since it is in being superior to error that the highest and chief perfection of man consists, I deem that I have not gained little by this day's meditation, in having discovered the source of error and falsity.

And certainly this can be no other than what I have now explained: for as often as I so restrain my will within the limits of my knowledge, that it forms no judgment except regarding objects which are clearly and distinctly represented to it by the understanding, I can never be deceived; because every clear and distinct conception is doubtless something, and as such cannot owe its origin to nothing, but must of necessity have God for its author—God, I say, who, as supremely perfect, cannot, without a contradiction, be the cause of any error; and consequently it is necessary to conclude that every such conception [or judgment] is true. Nor have I merely learned to-day what I must avoid to escape error, but also what I must do to arrive at the knowledge of truth; for I will assuredly reach truth if I only fix my attention sufficiently on all the things I conceive perfectly, and separate these from others which I conceive more confusedly and obscurely: to which for the future I shall give diligent heed.

MEDITATION V.

OF THE ESSENCE OF MATERIAL THINGS; AND, AGAIN, OF GOD; THAT HE EXISTS.

SEVERAL other questions remain for consideration respecting the attributes of God and my own nature or mind. I will, however, on some other occasion perhaps resume the investigation of these. Meanwhile, as I have discovered what must be done and what avoided to arrive at the knowledge of truth, what I have chiefly to do is to essay to emerge from the state of doubt in which I have for some time been, and to discover whether anything can be known with certainty regarding material objects. But before considering whether such objects as I conceive exist without me, I must examine their ideas in so far as these are to be found in my consciousness, and discover which of them are distinct and which confused.

In the first place, I distinctly imagine that quantity which the philosophers commonly call continuous, or the extension in length, breadth, and depth that is in this quantity, or rather in the object to which it is attributed. Further, I can enumerate in it many diverse parts, and attribute to each of these all sorts of sizes, figures, situations, and local motions; and, in fine, I can assign to each of these motions all degrees of duration. And I not only distinctly know these things when I thus consider them in general; but besides, by a little attention, I discover innumerable particulars respecting figures, numbers, motion, and the like, which are so evidently true, and so accordant with my nature, that when I now discover them I do not so much appear to learn anything new, as to call to remembrance what I before knew, or for the first time to remark what was before in my mind, but to which I had not hitherto directed my attention. And what I here find of most importance is, that I discover in my mind innumerable ideas of certain objects, which cannot be esteemed pure negations, although perhaps they possess no reality beyond my thought, and which are not framed by me though it may be in my power to think, or not to think them, but possess true and immutable natures of their own. As, for example, when I imagine a triangle, although there is not perhaps and never was in any place in the universe apart from my thought one such figure, it remains true nevertheless that this figure possesses a certain determinate nature, form, or essence, which is immutable and eternal, and not framed by me, nor in any degree dependent on my thought; as appears from the circumstance, that diverse properties of the triangle may be demonstrated, viz., that its three angles are equal to two right, that its greatest side is subtended by its greatest angle, and the like, which, whether I will or not, I now clearly discern to belong to it, although before I did not at all think of them, when, for the first time, I imagined a triangle, and which accordingly cannot be said to have been invented by me. Nor is it a valid objection to allege, that perhaps this idea of a triangle came into my mind by the medium of the senses, through my having seen bodies of a triangular figure; for I am able to form in thought an innumerable variety of

OF THE ESSENCE OF MATERIAL THINGS. 77

figures with regard to which it cannot be supposed that they were ever objects of sense, and I can nevertheless demonstrate diverse properties of their nature no less than of the triangle, all of which are assuredly true since I clearly conceive them: and they are therefore something, and not mere negations; for it is highly evident that all that is true is something, [truth being identical with existence]; and I have already fully shown the truth of the principle, that whatever is clearly and distinctly known is true. And although this had not been demonstrated, yet the nature of my mind is such as to compel me to assent to what I clearly conceive while I so conceive it; and I recollect that even when I still strongly adhered to the objects of sense, I reckoned among the number of the most certain truths those I clearly conceived relating to figures, numbers, and other matters that pertain to arithmetic and geometry, and in general to the pure mathematics.

But now if because I can draw from my thought the idea of an object, it follows that all I clearly and distinctly apprehend to pertain to this object, does in truth belong to it, may I not from this derive an argument for the existence of God? It is certain that I no less find the idea of a God in my consciousness, that is, the idea of a being supremely perfect, than that of any figure or number whatever: and I know with not less clearness and distinctness that an [actual and] eternal existence pertains to his nature than that all which is demonstrable of any figure or number really belongs to the nature of that figure or number; and, therefore, although all the conclusions of the preceding Meditations were false, the existence of God would pass with me for a truth at least as certain as I ever judged any truth of mathematics to be, although indeed such a doctrine may at first sight appear to contain more sophistry than truth. For, as I have been accustomed in every other matter to distinguish between existence and essence, I easily believe that the existence can be separated from the essence of God, and that thus God may be conceived as not actually existing. But, nevertheless, when I think of it more attentively, it appears that the existence can no more be separated from the essence of God, than the idea of a mountain from that of a valley, or the equality of its three angles to two right angles, from the essence of a [rectilineal] triangle; so that it is not less impossible to conceive a God, that is, a being supremely perfect, to whom existence is awanting, or who is devoid of a certain perfection, than to conceive a mountain without a valley.

But though, in truth, I cannot conceive a God unless as existing, any more than I can a mountain without a valley, yet, just as it does not follow that there is any mountain in the world merely because I conceive a mountain with a valley, so likewise, though I conceive God as existing, it does not seem to follow on that account that God exists; for my thought imposes no necessity on things; and as I may imagine a winged horse, though there be none such, so I could perhaps attribute existence to God, though no God existed. But the cases are not analogous, and a fallacy lurks under the semblance of this objection: for because I cannot conceive a mountain without a valley, it does not follow that there is any mountain or valley in existence, but simply that the mountain or valley, whether they do or do not exist, are inseparable from each other; whereas, on the other hand, because I cannot conceive God unless as existing, it follows that existence is inseparable from him, and therefore that he really exists: not that this is brought about by my thought, or that it imposes any necessity on things, but, on the contrary, the necessity which lies in the thing itself, that is, the necessity of the existence of God, determines me to think in this way: for it is not in my power to conceive a God without existence, that is, a being supremely perfect, and yet devoid of an absolute perfection, as I am free to imagine a horse with or without wings.

Nor must it be alleged here as an objection, that it is in truth necessary to admit that God exists, after having supposed him to possess all perfections, since existence is one of them, but that my original supposition was not necessary; just as it is not necessary to think that all quadrilateral figures can be inscribed in the circle, since, if I supposed this, I should be constrained to admit that the rhombus, being a figure of four sides, can be therein inscribed, which, however, is manifestly false. This objection is, I say, incompetent; for although it may not be necessary that I shall at any time entertain the notion of Deity, yet each time I happen to think of a first and sovereign being, and to draw, so to speak, the idea of him from the storehouse of the mind, I am necessitated to attribute to him all kinds of perfections, though I may not then enumerate them all, nor think of each of them in particular. And this necessity is sufficient, as soon as I discover that existence is a perfection, to cause me to infer the existence of this first and sovereign being: just as it is not necessary that I should ever imagine any triangle, but whenever I am desirous of considering a rectilineal figure composed of only three angles, it is absolutely necessary to attribute those properties to it from which it is correctly inferred that its three angles are not greater than two right angles, although perhaps I may not then advert to this relation in particular. But when I consider what figures are capable of being inscribed in the circle, it is by no means necessary to hold that all quadrilateral figures are of this number; on the contrary, I cannot even imagine such to be the case, so long as I shall be unwilling to accept in thought aught that I do not clearly and distinctly conceive: and consequently there is a vast difference between false suppositions, as is the one in question, and the true ideas that were born with me, the first and chief of which is the idea of God. For indeed I discern on many grounds that this idea is not factitious, depending simply on my thought, but that it is the representation of a true and immutable nature: in the first place, because I can conceive no other being, except God, to whose essence existence [necessarily] pertains; in the second, because it is impossible to conceive two or more gods of this kind; and it being supposed that one such God exists, I clearly see that he must have existed from all eternity, and will exist to all eternity; and finally, because I apprehend many other properties in God, none of which I can either diminish or change.

But, indeed, whatever mode of probation I in the end adopt, it always returns to this, that it is only the things I clearly and distinctly conceive which have the power of completely persuading me. And although, of the objects I conceive in this manner, some, indeed, are obvious to every one, while others are only discovered after close and careful investigation; nevertheless, after they are once discovered, the latter are not esteemed less certain than the former. Thus, for example, to take the case of a right-angled triangle, although it is not so manifest at first that the square of the base is equal to the squares of the other two sides, as that the base is opposite to the greatest angle; nevertheless, after it is once apprehended, we are as firmly persuaded of the truth of the former as of the latter. And, with respect to God, if I were not pre-occupied by prejudices, and my thought beset on all sides by the continual presence of the images of sensible objects, I should know nothing sooner or more easily than the fact of his being. For is there any truth more clear than the existence of a Supreme Being, or of God, seeing it is to his essence alone that [necessary and eternal] existence pertains? And although the right conception of this truth has cost me much close thinking, nevertheless at present I feel not only as assured of it as of what I deem most certain, but I remark further that the certitude of all other truths is so absolutely dependent on it, that without this knowledge it is impossible ever to know anything perfectly.

For although I am of such a nature as to be unable, while I possess a very clear and distinct apprehension of a matter, to resist the conviction of its truth, yet because my constitution is also such as to incapacitate me from keeping my mind continually fixed on the same object, and as I frequently recollect a past judgment without at the same time being able to recall the grounds of it, it may happen meanwhile that other reasons are presented to me which would readily cause me to change my opinion, if I did not know that God existed; and thus I should possess no true and certain knowledge, but merely vague and vacillating opinions. Thus, for example, when I consider the nature of the [rectilineal] triangle, it most clearly appears to me, who have been instructed in the principles of geometry, that its three angles are equal to two right angles, and I find it impossible to believe otherwise, while I apply my mind to the demonstration; but as soon as I cease from attending to the process of proof, although I still remember that I had a clear comprehension of it, yet I may readily come to doubt of the truth demonstrated, if I do not know that there is a God: for I may persuade myself that I have been so constituted by nature as to be sometimes deceived, even in matters which I think I apprehend with the greatest evidence and certitude, especially when I recollect that I frequently considered many things to be true and certain which other reasons afterwards constrained me to reckon as wholly false.

But after I have discovered that God exists, seeing I also at the same time observed that all things depend on him, and that he is no deceiver, and thence inferred that all which I clearly and distinctly perceive is of necessity true: although I no longer attend to the grounds of a judgment, no opposite reason can be alleged sufficient to lead me to doubt of its truth, provided only I remember that I once possessed a clear and distinct comprehension of it. My knowledge of it thus becomes true and certain. And this same knowledge extends likewise to whatever I remember to have formerly demonstrated, as the truths of geometry and the like: for what can be alleged against them to lead me to doubt of them? Will it be that my nature is

OF THE ESSENCE OF MATERIAL THINGS.

such that I may be frequently deceived? But I already know that I cannot be deceived in judgments of the grounds of which I possess a clear knowledge. Will it be that I formerly deemed things to be true and certain which I afterwards discovered to be false? But I had no clear and distinct knowledge of any of those things, and, being as yet ignorant of the rule by which I am assured of the truth of a judgment, I was led to give my assent to them on grounds which I afterwards discovered were less strong than at the time I imagined them to be. What further objection, then, is there? Will it be said that perhaps I am dreaming (an objection I lately myself raised), or that all the thoughts of which I am now conscious have no more truth than the reveries of my dreams? But although, in truth, I should be dreaming, the rule still holds that all which is clearly presented to my intellect is indisputably true.

And thus I very clearly see that the certitude and truth of all science depends on the knowledge alone of the true God, insomuch that, before I knew him, I could have no perfect knowledge of any other thing. And now that I know him, I possess the means of acquiring a perfect knowledge respecting innumerable matters, as well relative to God himself and other intellectual objects as to corporeal nature, in so far as it is the object of pure mathematics [which do not consider whether it exists or not].

MEDITATION VI.

OF THE EXISTENCE OF MATERIAL THINGS, AND OF THE REAL DISTINCTION BETWEEN THE MIND AND BODY OF MAN.

THERE now only remains the inquiry as to whether material things exist. With regard to this question, I at least know with certainty that such things may exist, in as far as they constitute the object of the pure mathematics, since, regarding them in this aspect, I can conceive them clearly and distinctly. For there can be no doubt that God possesses the power of producing all the objects I am able distinctly to conceive, and I never considered anything impossible to him, unless when I experienced a contradiction in the attempt to conceive it aright. Further, the faculty of imagination which I possess, and of which I am conscious that I make use when I apply myself to the consideration of material things, is sufficient to persuade me of their existence: for, when I attentively consider what imagination is, I find that it is simply a certain application of the cognitive faculty (*facultas cognoscitiva*) to a body which is immediately present to it, and which therefore exists.

And to render this quite clear, I remark, in the first place, the difference that subsists between imagination and pure intellection [or conception]. For example, when I imagine a triangle I not only conceive (*intelligo*) that it is a figure comprehended by three lines,

OF THE EXISTENCE OF MATERIAL THINGS. 85

but at the same time also I look upon (*intueor*) these three lines as present by the power and internal application of my mind (*acie mentis*), and this is what I call imagining. But if I desire to think of a chiliogon, I indeed rightly conceive that it is a figure composed of a thousand sides, as easily as I conceive that a triangle is a figure composed of only three sides; but I cannot imagine the thousand sides of a chiliogon as I do the three sides of a triangle, nor, so to speak, view them as present [with the eyes of my mind]. And although, in accordance with the habit I have of always imagining something when I think of corporeal things, it may happen that, in conceiving a chiliogon, I confusedly represent some figure to myself, yet it is quite evident that this is not a chiliogon, since it in no wise differs from that which I would represent to myself, if I were to think of a myriogon, or any other figure of many sides; nor would this representation be of any use in discovering and unfolding the properties that constitute the difference between a chiliogon and other polygons. But if the question turns on a pentagon, it is quite true that I can conceive its figure, as well as that of a chiliogon, without the aid of imagination; but I can likewise imagine it by applying the attention of my mind to its five sides, and at the same time to the area which they contain. Thus I observe that a special effort of mind is necessary to the act of imagination, which is not required to conceiving or understanding (*ad intelligendum*); and this special exertion of mind clearly shows the difference between imagination and pure intellection (*imaginatio et intellectio pura*). I remark, besides, that this power of imagination which I possess, in as far as it differs from the power of conceiving, is in no way necessary to my [nature or] essence, that is, to the essence of my mind; for although I did not possess it, I should still remain the same that I now am, from which it seems we may conclude that it depends on something different from the mind. And I easily understand that, if some body exists, with which my mind is so conjoined and united as to be able, as it were, to consider it when it chooses, it may thus imagine corporeal objects; so that this mode of thinking differs from pure intellection only in this respect, that the mind in conceiving turns in some way upon itself, and considers some one of the ideas it possesses within itself; but in imagining it turns towards the body, and contemplates in it some object conformed to the idea which it either of itself conceived or apprehended by sense. I easily understand, I say, that imagination may be thus formed, if it is true that there are bodies; and because I find no other obvious mode of explaining it, I thence, with probability, conjecture that they exist, but only with probability; and although I carefully examine all things, nevertheless I do not find that, from the distinct idea of corporeal nature I have in my imagination, I can necessarily infer the existence of any body.

But I am accustomed to imagine many other objects besides that corporeal nature which is the object of the pure mathematics, as, for example, colours, sounds, tastes, pain, and the like, although with less distinctness; and, inasmuch as I perceive these objects much better by the senses, through the medium of which and of memory, they seem to have reached the imagination, I believe that, in order the more advantageously to examine them, it is proper I should at the same time

OF THE EXISTENCE OF MATERIAL THINGS. 87

examine what sense-perception is, and inquire whether from those ideas that are apprehended by this mode of thinking (consciousness), I cannot obtain a certain proof of the existence of corporeal objects.

And, in the first place, I will recall to my mind the things I have hitherto held as true, because perceived by the senses, and the foundations upon which my belief in their truth rested; I will, in the second place, examine the reasons that afterwards constrained me to doubt of them; and, finally, I will consider what of them I ought now to believe.

Firstly, then, I perceived that I had a head, hands, feet, and other members composing that body which I considered as part, or perhaps even as a whole, of myself. I perceived further, that that body was placed among many others, by which it was capable of being affected in diverse ways, both beneficial and hurtful; and what was beneficial I remarked by a certain sensation of pleasure, and what was hurtful by a sensation of pain. And, besides this pleasure and pain, I was likewise conscious of hunger, thirst, and other appetites, as well as certain corporeal inclinations towards joy, sadness, anger, and similar passions. And, out of myself, besides the extension, figure, and motions of bodies, I likewise perceived in them hardness, heat, and the other tactile qualities, and, in addition, light, colours, odours, tastes, and sounds, the variety of which gave me the means of distinguishing the sky, the earth, the sea, and generally all the other bodies, from one another. And certainly, considering the ideas of all these qualities, which were presented to my mind, and which alone I properly and immediately perceived, it was not without reason that I thought I perceived certain objects wholly different from my thought, namely, bodies from which those ideas proceeded; for I was conscious that the ideas were presented to me without my consent being required, so that I could not perceive any object, however desirous I might be, unless it were present to the organ of sense; and it was wholly out of my power not to perceive it when it was thus present. And because the ideas I perceived by the senses were much more lively and clear, and even, in their own way, more distinct than any of those I could of myself frame by meditation, or which I found impressed on my memory, it seemed that they could not have proceeded from myself, and must therefore have been caused in me by some other objects; and as of those objects I had no knowledge beyond what the ideas themselves gave me, nothing was so likely to occur to my mind as the supposition that the objects were similar to the ideas which they caused. And because I recollected also that I had formerly trusted to the senses, rather than to reason, and that the ideas which I myself formed were not so clear as those I perceived by sense, and that they were even for the most part composed of parts of the latter, I was readily persuaded that I had no idea in my intellect which had not formerly passed through the senses. Nor was I altogether wrong in likewise believing that that body which, by a special right, I called my own, pertained to me more properly and strictly than any of the others; for in truth, I could never be separated from it as from other bodies: I felt in it and on account of it all my appetites and affections, and in fine I was affected in its parts by pain and the titillation of pleasure, and not in the parts of the other bodies that were separated from it. But when I inquired into the reason why, from this I know not what sensation of pain, sadness of mind should follow, and why from the sensation of pleasure joy should arise, or why this indescribable twitching of the stomach, which I call hunger, should put me in mind of taking food, and the parchedness of the throat of drink, and so in other cases, I was unable to give any explanation, unless that I was so taught by nature; for there is assuredly no affinity, at least none that I am able to comprehend, between this irritation of the stomach and the desire of food, any more than between the perception of an object that causes pain and the consciousness of sadness which springs from the perception. And in the same way it seemed to me that all the other judgments I had formed regarding the objects of sense, were dictates of nature; because I remarked that those judgments were formed in me, before I had leisure to weigh and consider the reasons that might constrain me to form them.

But, afterwards, a wide experience by degrees sapped the faith I had reposed in my senses; for I frequently observed that towers, which at a distance seemed round, appeared square when more closely viewed, and that colossal figures, raised on the summits of these towers, looked like small statues, when viewed from the bottom of them; and, in other instances without number, I also discovered error in judgments founded on the external senses; and not only in those founded on the external, but even in those that rested on the internal senses; for is there aught more internal than pain? and yet I have sometimes been informed by parties whose arm or leg had been amputated, that they still occasionally seemed to feel pain in that part of the body which they had lost,—a circumstance that led me to think that I could not be quite certain even that any one of my members was affected when I felt pain in it. And to these grounds of doubt I shortly afterwards also added two others of very wide generality: the first of them was that I believed I never perceived anything when awake which I could not occasionally think I also perceived when asleep, and as I do not believe that the ideas I seem to perceive in my sleep proceed from objects external to me, I did not any more observe any ground for believing this of such as I seem to perceive when awake; the second was that since I was as yet ignorant of the author of my being, or at least supposed myself to be so, I saw nothing to prevent my having been so constituted by nature as that I should be deceived even in matters that appeared to me to possess the greatest truth. And, with respect to the grounds on which I had before been persuaded of the existence of sensible objects, I had no great difficulty in finding suitable answers to them; for as nature seemed to incline me to many things from which reason made me averse, I thought that I ought not to confide much in its teachings. And although the perceptions of the senses were not dependent on my will, I did not think that I ought on that ground to conclude that they proceeded from things different from myself, since perhaps there might be found in me some faculty, though hitherto unknown to me, which produced them.

But now that I begin to know myself better, and to discover more clearly the author of my being, I do not, indeed, think that I ought rashly to admit all which the senses seem to teach, nor, on the other hand, is it my

OF THE EXISTENCE OF MATERIAL THINGS.

conviction that I ought to doubt in general of their teachings.

And, firstly, because I know that all which I clearly and distinctly conceive can be produced by God exactly as I conceive it, it is sufficient that I am able clearly and distinctly to conceive one thing apart from another, in order to be certain that the one is different from the other, seeing they may at least be made to exist separately, by the omnipotence of God; and it matters not by what power this separation is made, in order to be compelled to judge them different; and, therefore, merely because I know with certitude that I exist, and because, in the meantime, I do not observe that aught necessarily belongs to my nature or essence beyond my being a thinking thing, I rightly conclude that my essence consists only in my being a thinking thing, [or a substance whose whole essence or nature is merely thinking]. And although I may, or rather, as I will shortly say, although I certainly do possess a body with which I am very closely conjoined; nevertheless, because, on the one hand, I have a clear and distinct idea of myself, in as far as I am only a thinking and unextended thing, and as, on the other hand, I possess a distinct idea of body, in as far as it is only an extended and unthinking thing, it is certain that I, [that is, my mind, by which I am what I am], is entirely and truly distinct from my body, and may exist without it.

Moreover, I find in myself diverse faculties of thinking that have each their special mode: for example, I find I possess the faculties of imagining and perceiving, without which I can indeed clearly and distinctly conceive myself as entire, but I cannot reciprocally conceive them without conceiving myself, that is to say, without an intelligent substance in which they reside, for [in the notion we have of them, or to use the terms of the schools] in their formal concept, they comprise some sort of intellection; whence I perceive that they are distinct from myself as modes are from things. I remark likewise certain other faculties, as the power of changing place, of assuming diverse figures, and the like, that cannot be conceived and cannot therefore exist, any more than the preceding, apart from a substance in which they inhere. It is very evident, however, that these faculties, if they really exist, must belong to some corporeal or extended substance, since in their clear and distinct concept there is contained some sort of extension, but no intellection at all. Farther, I cannot doubt but that there is in me a certain passive faculty of perception, that is, of receiving and taking knowledge of the ideas of sensible things; but this would be useless to me, if there did not also exist in me, or in some other thing, another active faculty capable of forming and producing those ideas. But this active faculty cannot be in me [in as far as I am but a thinking thing], seeing that it does not presuppose thought, and also that those ideas are frequently produced in my mind without my contributing to it in any way, and even frequently contrary to my will. This faculty must therefore exist in some substance different from me, in which all the objective reality of the ideas that are produced by this faculty, is contained formally or eminently, as I before remarked; and this substance is either a body, that is to say, a corporeal nature in which is contained formally [and in effect] all that is objectively [and by representation] in those ideas; or it is God himself, or some other creature, of

OF THE EXISTENCE OF MATERIAL THINGS. 93

a rank superior to body, in which the same is contained eminently. But as God is no deceiver, it is manifest that he does not of himself and immediately communicate those ideas to me, nor even by the intervention of any creature in which their objective reality is not formally, but only eminently, contained. For as he has given me no faculty whereby I can discover this to be the case, but, on the contrary, a very strong inclination to believe that those ideas arise from corporeal objects, I do not see how he could be vindicated from the charge of deceit, if in truth they proceeded from any other source, or were produced by other causes than corporeal things: and accordingly it must be concluded, that corporeal objects exist. Nevertheless they are not perhaps exactly such as we perceive by the senses, for their comprehension by the senses is, in many instances, very obscure and confused; but it is at least necessary to admit that all which I clearly and distinctly conceive as in them, that is, generally speaking, all that is comprehended in the object of speculative geometry, really exists external to me.

But with respect to other things which are either only particular, as, for example, that the sun is of such a size and figure, etc., or are conceived with less clearness and distinctness, as light, sound, pain, and the like, although they are highly dubious and uncertain, nevertheless on the ground alone that God is no deceiver, and that consequently he has permitted no falsity in my opinions which he has not likewise given me a faculty of correcting, I think I may with safety conclude that I possess in myself the means of arriving at the truth. And, in the first place, it cannot be doubted that in each of the dictates of nature there is some truth: for by nature, considered in general, I now understand nothing more than God himself, or the order and disposition established by God in created things; and by my nature in particular I understand the assemblage of all that God has given me.

But there is nothing which that nature teaches me more expressly [or more sensibly] than that I have a body which is ill affected when I feel pain, and stands in need of food and drink when I experience the sensations of hunger and thirst, etc. And therefore I ought not to doubt but that there is some truth in these informations.

Nature likewise teaches me by these sensations of pain, hunger, thirst, etc., that I am not only lodged in my body as a pilot in a vessel, but that I am besides so intimately conjoined, and as it were intermixed with it, that my mind and body compose a certain unity. For if this were not the case, I should not feel pain when my body is hurt, seeing I am merely a thinking thing, but should perceive the wound by the understanding alone, just as a pilot perceives by sight when any part of his vessel is damaged; and when my body has need of food or drink, I should have a clear knowledge of this, and not be made aware of it by the confused sensations of hunger and thirst: for, in truth, all these sensations of hunger, thirst, pain, etc., are nothing more than certain confused modes of thinking, arising from the union and apparent fusion of mind and body.

Besides this, nature teaches me that my own body is surrounded by many other bodies, some of which I have to seek after, and others to shun. And indeed, as I perceive different sorts of colours, sounds, odours, tastes, heat, hardness, etc., I safely conclude that there

OF THE EXISTENCE OF MATERIAL THINGS. 95

are in the bodies from which the diverse perceptions of the senses proceed, certain varieties corresponding to them, although, perhaps, not in reality like them; and since, among these diverse perceptions of the senses, some are agreeable, and others disagreeable, there can be no doubt that my body, or rather my entire self, in as far as I am composed of body and mind, may be variously affected, both beneficially and hurtfully, by surrounding bodies.

But there are many other beliefs which, though seemingly the teaching of nature, are not in reality so, but which obtained a place in my mind through a habit of judging inconsiderately of things. It may thus easily happen that such judgments shall contain error: thus, for example, the opinion I have that all space in which there is nothing to affect [or make an impression on] my senses is void; that in a hot body there is something in every respect similar to the idea of heat in my mind; that in a white or green body there is the same whiteness or greenness which I perceive; that in a bitter or sweet body there is the same taste, and so in other instances; that the stars, towers, and all distant bodies, are of the same size and figure as they appear to our eyes, etc. But that I may avoid everything like indistinctness of conception, I must accurately define what I properly understand by being taught by nature. For nature is here taken in a narrower sense than when it signifies the sum of all the things which God has given me; seeing that in that meaning the notion comprehends much that belongs only to the mind [to which I am not here to be understood as referring when I use the term nature]; as, for example, the notion I have of the truth, that what is done cannot be undone, and all the other truths I discern by the natural light [without the aid of the body]; and seeing that it comprehends likewise much besides that belongs only to body, and is not here any more contained under the name nature, as the quality of heaviness, and the like, of which I do not speak,—the term being reserved exclusively to designate the things which God has given to me as a being composed of mind and body. But nature, taking the term in the sense explained, teaches me to shun what causes in me the sensation of pain, and to pursue what affords me the sensation of pleasure, and other things of this sort; but I do not discover that it teaches me, in addition to this, from these diverse perceptions of the senses, to draw any conclusions respecting external objects without a previous [careful and mature] consideration of them by the mind; for it is, as appears to me, the office of the mind alone, and not of the composite whole of mind and body, to discern the truth in those matters Thus, although the impression a star makes on my eye is not larger than that from the flame of a candle, I do not, nevertheless, experience any real or positive impulse determining me to believe that the star is not greater than the flame; the true account of the matter being merely that I have so judged from my youth without any rational ground. And, though on approaching the fire I feel heat, and even pain on approaching it too closely, I have, however, from this no ground for holding that something resembling the heat I feel is in the fire, any more than that there is something similar to the pain; all that I have ground for believing is, that there is something in it, whatever it may be, which excites in me those sensations of heat or pain. So also, although there are spaces in which I find nothing to excite and affect my senses, I must not therefore conclude that those spaces contain in them no body; for I see that in this, as in many other similar matters, I have been accustomed to pervert the order of nature, because these perceptions of the senses, although given me by nature merely to signify to my mind what things are beneficial and hurtful to the composite whole of which it is a part, and being sufficiently clear and distinct for that purpose, are nevertheless used by me as infallible rules by which to determine immediately the essence of the bodies that exist out of me, of which they can of course afford me only the most obscure and confused knowledge.

But I have already sufficiently considered how it happens that, notwithstanding the supreme goodness of God, there is falsity in my judgments. A difficulty, however, here presents itself, respecting the things which I am taught by nature must be pursued or avoided, and also respecting the internal sensations in which I seem to have occasionally detected error, [and thus to be directly deceived by nature] : thus, for example, I may be so deceived by the agreeable taste of some viand with which poison has been mixed, as to be induced to take the poison. In this case, however, nature may be excused, for it simply leads me to desire the viand for its agreeable taste, and not the poison, which is unknown to it; and thus we can infer nothing from this circumstance beyond that our nature is not omniscient; at which there is assuredly no ground for surprise, since, man being of a finite nature, his knowledge must likewise be of limited perfection. But we also not unfrequently err in that to which we are directly impelled by nature, as is the case with invalids who desire drink or food that would be hurtful to them. It will here, perhaps, be alleged that the reason why such persons are deceived is that their nature is corrupted; but this leaves the difficulty untouched, for a sick man is not less really the creature of God than a man who is in full health; and therefore it is as repugnant to the goodness of God that the nature of the former should be deceitful as it is for that of the latter to be so. And, as a clock, composed of wheels and counter weights, observes not the less accurately all the laws of nature when it is ill made, and points out the hours incorrectly, than when it satisfies the desire of the maker in every respect; so likewise if the body of man be considered as a kind of machine, so made up and composed of bones, nerves, muscles, veins, blood, and skin, that although there were in it no mind, it would still exhibit the same motions which it at present manifests involuntarily, and therefore without the aid of the mind, [and simply by the dispositions of its organs], I easily discern that it would also be as natural for such a body, supposing it dropsical, for example, to experience the parchedness of the throat that is usually accompanied in the mind by the sensation of thirst, and to be disposed by this parchedness to move its nerves and its other parts in the way required for drinking, and thus increase its malady and do itself harm, as it is natural for it, when it is not indisposed to be stimulated to drink for its good by a similar cause; and although looking to the use for which a clock was destined by its maker, I may say that it is deflected from its proper nature when it incorrectly indicates the hours, and on the same principle, considering the machine of the human body as having been formed by God for the sake of the motions which it usually manifests, although I may likewise have ground for thinking that it does not follow the order of its nature when the throat is parched and drink does not tend to its preservation, nevertheless I yet plainly discern that this latter acceptation of the term nature is very different from the other; for this is nothing more than a certain denomination, depending entirely on my thought, and hence called extrinsic, by which I compare a sick man and an imperfectly constructed clock with the idea I have of a man in good health and a well made clock; while by the other acceptation of nature is understood something which is truly found in things, and therefore possessed of some truth.

But certainly, although in respect of a dropsical body, it is only by way of exterior denomination that we say its nature is corrupted, when, without requiring drink, the throat is parched; yet, in respect of the composite whole, that is, of the mind in its union with the body, it is not a pure denomination, but really an error of nature, for it to feel thirst when drink would be hurtful to it: and, accordingly, it still remains to be considered why it is that the goodness of God does not prevent the nature of man thus taken from being fallacious.

To commence this examination accordingly, I here remark, in the first place, that there is a vast difference between mind and body, in respect that body, from its nature, is always divisible, and that mind is entirely indivisible. For in truth, when I consider the mind, that is, when I consider myself in so far only as I am a thinking thing, I can distinguish in myself no parts, but I very clearly discern that I am somewhat absolutely one and entire; and although the whole mind seems to be united to the whole body, yet, when a foot, an arm, or any other part is cut off, I am conscious that nothing has been taken from my mind; nor can the faculties of willing, perceiving, conceiving, etc., properly be called its parts, for it is the same mind that is exercised [all entire] in willing, in perceiving, and in conceiving, etc. But quite the opposite holds in corporeal or extended things; for I cannot imagine any one of them [how small soever it may be], which I cannot easily sunder in thought, and which, therefore, I do not know to be divisible. This would be sufficient to teach me that the mind or soul of man is entirely different from the body, if I had not already been apprised of it on other grounds.

I remark, in the next place, that the mind does not immediately receive the impression from all the parts of the body, but only from the brain, or perhaps even from one small part of it, viz., that in which the common sense (*sensus communis*) is said to be, which as often as it is affected in the same way, gives rise to the same perception in the mind, although meanwhile the other parts of the body may be diversely disposed, as is proved by innumerable experiments, which it is unnecessary here to enumerate.

I remark, besides, that the nature of body is such that none of its parts can be moved by another part a little removed from the other, which cannot likewise be moved in the same way by any one of the parts that lie between those two, although the most remote part does not act at all. As, for example, in the cord A, B, C, D, [which is in tension], if its last part D, be pulled, the first part A, will not be moved in a different way than it would be were one of the intermediate parts B or C to be pulled, and the last part D meanwhile to remain fixed. And in the same way, when I feel pain in the foot, the science of physics teaches me that this sensation is experienced by means of the nerves dispersed over the foot, which, extending like cords from it to the brain, when they are contracted in the foot, contract at the same time the inmost parts of the brain in which they have their origin, and excite in these parts a certain motion appointed by nature to cause in the mind a sensation of pain, as if existing in the foot: but as these nerves must pass through the tibia, the leg, the loins, the back, and neck, in order to reach the brain, it may happen that although their extremities in the foot are not affected, but only certain of their parts that pass through the loins or neck, the same movements, nevertheless, are excited in the brain by this motion as would have been caused there by a hurt received in the foot, and hence the mind will necessarily feel pain in the foot, just as if it had been hurt; and the same is true of all the other perceptions of our senses.

I remark, finally, that as each of the movements that are made in the part of the brain by which the mind is immediately affected, impresses it with but a single sensation, the most likely supposition in the circumstances is, that this movement causes the mind to experience, among all the sensations which it is capable of impressing upon it, that one which is the best fitted, and generally the most useful for the preservation of the human body when it is in full health. But experience shows us that all the perceptions which nature has given us are of such a kind as I have mentioned; and accordingly, there is nothing found in them that does not manifest the power and goodness of God. Thus, for example, when the nerves of the foot are violently or more than usually shaken, the motion passing through the medulla of the spine to the innermost parts of the brain affords a sign to the mind on which it experiences a sensation, viz., of pain, as if it were in the foot, by which the mind is admonished and excited to do its utmost to remove the cause of it as dangerous and hurtful to the foot. It is true that God could have so constituted the nature of man as that the same motion in the brain would have informed the mind of something altogether different: the motion might, for example, have been the occasion on which the mind became conscious of itself, in so far as it is in the brain, or in so far as it is in some place intermediate between the foot and the brain, or, finally, the occasion on which it perceived some other object quite different, whatever that might be; but nothing of all this would have so well contributed to the preservation of the body as that which the mind actually feels. In the same way, when we stand in need of drink, there arises from this want a certain parchedness in the throat that moves its nerves, and by means of them the internal parts of the brain; and this movement affects the mind with the sensation of thirst, because there is nothing on that occasion which is more useful for us than to be made aware that we have need of drink for the preservation of our health; and so in other instances.

Whence it is quite manifest that, notwithstanding the sovereign goodness of God, the nature of man, in so far as it is composed of mind and body, cannot but be sometimes fallacious. For, if there is any cause which excites, not in the foot, but in some one of the parts of the nerves that stretch from the foot to the brain, or even in the brain itself, the same movement that is ordinarily created when the foot is ill affected, pain will be felt, as it were, in the foot, and the sense will thus be naturally deceived; for as the same movement in the brain can but impress the mind with the same sensation, and as this sensation is much more frequently excited by a cause which hurts the foot than by one acting in a different quarter, it is reasonable that it should lead the mind to feel pain in the foot rather than in any other part of the body. And if it sometimes happens that the parchedness of the throat does not arise, as is usual, from drink being necessary for the health of the body, but from quite the opposite cause, as is the case with the dropsical, yet it is much better that it should be deceitful in that instance, than if, on the contrary, it were continually fallacious when the body is well-disposed; and the same holds true in other cases.

And certainly this consideration is of great service, not only in enabling me to recognize the errors to which my nature is liable, but likewise in rendering it more easy to avoid or correct them: for, knowing that all my senses more usually indicate to me what is true than what is false, in matters relating to the advantage of the body, and being able almost always to make use of more than a single sense in examining the same object, and besides this, being able to use my memory in connecting present with past knowledge, and my understanding which has already discovered all the causes of my errors, I ought no longer to fear that falsity maybe met with in what is daily presented to me by the senses. And I ought to reject all the doubts of those bygone days, as hyperbolical and ridiculous, especially the general uncertainty respecting sleep, which I could not distinguish from the waking state: for I now find a very marked difference between the two states, in respect that our memory can never connect our dreams with each other and with the course of life, in the way it is in the habit of doing with events that occur when we are awake. And, in truth, if some one, when I am awake, appeared to me all of a sudden and as suddenly disappeared, as do the images I see in sleep, so that I could not observe either whence he came or whither he went, I should not without reason esteem it either a spectre or phantom formed in my brain, rather than a real man. But when I perceive objects with regard to which I can distinctly determine both the place whence they come, and that in which they are, and the time at which they appear to me, and when, without interruption, I can connect the perception I have of them with the whole of the other parts of my life, I am perfectly sure that what I thus perceive occurs while I am awake and not during sleep. And I ought not in the least degree to doubt of the truth of those presentations, if, after having called together all my senses, my memory, and my understanding for the purpose of examining them, no deliverance is given by any one of these faculties which is repugnant to that of any other: for since God is no deceiver, it necessarily follows that I am not herein deceived. But because the necessities of action frequently oblige us to come to a determination before we have had leisure for so careful an examination, it must be confessed that the life of man is frequently obnoxious to error with respect to individual objects; and we must, in conclusion, acknowledge the weakness of our nature.

SELECTIONS

FROM

THE PRINCIPLES OF PHILOSOPHY

OF

DESCARTES

*TRANSLATED FROM THE LATIN AND COLLATED
WITH THE FRENCH*

LETTER OF THE AUTHOR

TO THE
FRENCH TRANSLATOR OF THE PRINCIPLES OF PHILO-
SOPHY SERVING FOR A PREFACE.

Sir,—The version of my principles which you have been at pains to make, is so elegant and finished as to lead me to expect that the work will be more generally read in French than in Latin, and better understood. The only apprehension I entertain is lest the title should deter some who have not been brought up to letters, or with whom philosophy is in bad repute, because the kind they were taught has proved unsatisfactory; and this makes me think that it will be useful to add a preface to it for the purpose of showing what the *matter* of the work is, what *end* I had in view in writing it, and what *utility* may be derived from it. But although it might be my part to write a preface of this nature, seeing I ought to know those particulars better than any other person, I cannot nevertheless prevail upon myself to do anything more than merely to give a summary of the chief points that fall, as I think, to be discussed in it: and I leave it to your discretion to present to the public such part of them as you shall judge proper.

I should have desired, in the first place, to explain in it what philosophy is, by commencing with the most common matters, as, for example, that the word *philosophy* signifies the study of wisdom, and that by wisdom is to be understood not merely prudence in the management of affairs, but a perfect knowledge of all that man can know, as well for the conduct of his life as for the preservation of his health and the discovery of all the arts, and that knowledge to subserve these ends must necessarily be deduced from first causes; so that in order to study the acquisition of it (which is properly called philosophizing), we must commence with the investigation of those first causes which are called *Principles*. Now these principles must possess *two conditions:* in the first place, they must be so clear and evident that the human mind, when it attentively considers them, cannot doubt of their truth; in the second place, the knowledge of other things must be so dependent on them as that though the principles themselves may indeed be known apart from what depends on them, the latter cannot nevertheless be known apart from the former. It will accordingly be necessary thereafter to endeavour so to deduce from those principles the knowledge of the things that depend on them, as that there may be nothing in the whole series of deductions which is not perfectly manifest. God is in truth the only being who is absolutely wise, that is, who possesses a perfect knowledge of all things; but we may say that men are more or less wise as their knowledge of the most important truths is greater or less. And I am confident that there is nothing, in what I have now said, in which all the learned do not concur.

I should, in the next place, have proposed to consider the utility of philosophy, and at the same time have shown that, since it embraces all that the human mind can know, we ought to believe that it is by it we are distinguished from savages and barbarians, and that the civilisation and culture of a nation is regulated by the degree in which true philosophy flourishes in it, and, accordingly, that to contain true philosophers is the highest privilege a state can enjoy. Besides this, I should have shown that, as regards individuals, it is not only useful for each man to have intercourse with those who apply themselves to this study, but that it is incomparably better he should himself direct his attention to it; just as it is doubtless to be preferred that a man should make use of his own eyes to direct his steps, and enjoy by means of the same the beauties of colour and light, than that he should blindly follow the guidance of another; though the latter course is certainly better than to have the eyes closed with no guide except one's self. But to live without philosophizing is in truth the same as keeping the eyes closed without attempting to open them; and the pleasure of seeing all that sight discloses is not to be compared with the satisfaction afforded by the discoveries of philosophy. And, finally, this study is more imperatively requisite for the regulation of our manners, and for conducting us through life, than is the use of our eyes for directing our steps. The brutes, which have only their bodies to conserve, are continually occupied in seeking sources of nourishment; but men, of whom the chief part is the mind, ought to make the search after wisdom their principal care, for wisdom is the true nourishment of the mind; and I feel assured, moreover, that there are very many who would not fail in the search, if they would but hope for success in it, and knew the degree of their capabilities for it. There is no mind, how ignoble soever it be, which remains so firmly bound up in the objects of the senses, as not sometime or other to turn itself away from them in the aspiration after some higher good, although not knowing frequently wherein that good consists. The greatest favourites of fortune—those who have health, honours, and riches in abundance—are not more exempt from aspirations of this nature than others; nay, I am persuaded that these are the persons who sigh the most deeply after another good greater and more perfect still than any they already possess. But the supreme good, considered by natural reason without the light of faith, is nothing more than the knowledge of truth through its first causes, in other words, the wisdom of which philosophy is the study. And, as all these particulars are indisputably true, all that is required to gain assent to their truth is that they be well stated.

But as one is restrained from assenting to these doctrines by experience, which shows that they who make pretensions to philosophy are often less wise and reasonable than others who never applied themselves to the study, I should have here shortly explained wherein consists all the science we now possess, and what are the degrees of wisdom at which we have arrived. The first degree contains only notions so clear of themselves that they can be acquired without meditation; the second comprehends all that the experience of the senses dictates; the third, that which the conversation of other men teaches us; to which may be added as the fourth, the reading, not of all books, but especially of such as have been written by persons capable of conveying proper instruction, for it is a species of conversation we hold with their authors. And it seems to me that all the wisdom we in ordinary possess is acquired only in these four ways; for I do not class divine revelation among them, because it does not conduct us by degrees, but elevates us at once to an infallible faith.

There have been, indeed, in all ages great minds who endeavoured to find a fifth road to wisdom, incomparably more sure and elevated than the other four. The path they essayed was the search of first causes and true principles, from which might be deduced the reasons of all that can be known by man; and it is to them the appellation of philosophers has been more especially accorded. I am not aware that there is any one of them up to the present who has succeeded in this enterprise. The first and chief whose writings we possess are Plato and Aristotle, between whom there was no difference, except that the former, following in the footsteps of his master, Socrates, ingenuously confessed that he had never yet been able to find anything certain, and that he was contented to write what seemed to him probable, imagining, for this end, certain principles by which he endeavoured to account for the other things. Aristotle, on the other hand, characterised by less candour, although for twenty years the disciple of Plato, and with no principles beyond those of his master, completely reversed his mode of putting them, and proposed as true and certain what it is probable he himself never esteemed as such. But these two men had acquired much judgment and wisdom by the four preceding means, qualities which raised their authority very high, so much so that those who succeeded them were willing rather to acquiesce in their opinions, than to seek better for themselves. The chief question among their disciples, however, was as to whether we ought to doubt of all things or hold some as certain,—a dispute which led them on both sides into extravagant errors; for a part of those who were for doubt, extended it even to the actions of life, to the neglect of the most ordinary rules required for its conduct; those, on the other hand, who maintained the doctrine of certainty, supposing that it must depend upon the senses, trusted entirely to them. To such an extent was this carried by Epicurus, that it is said he ventured to affirm, contrary to all the reasonings of the astronomers, that the sun is no larger than it appears.

It is a fault we may remark in most disputes, that, as truth is the mean between the two opinions that are upheld, each disputant departs from it in proportion to the degree in which he possesses the spirit of contradiction. But the error of those who leant too much to the side of doubt, was not followed for any length of time, and that of the opposite party has been to some extent corrected by the doctrine that the senses are deceitful in many instances. Nevertheless, I do not know that this error was wholly removed by showing that certitude is not in the senses, but in the understanding alone when it has clear perceptions; and that while we only possess the knowledge which is acquired in the first four grades of wisdom, we ought not to doubt of the things that appear to be true in what regards the conduct of life, nor esteem them as so certain that we cannot change our opinions regarding them, even though constrained by the evidence of reason.

From ignorance of this truth, or, if there was any one to whom it was known, from neglect of it, the majority of those who in these later ages aspired to be philosophers, blindly followed Aristotle, so that they frequently corrupted the sense of his writings, and attributed to him various opinions which he would not recognise as his own were he now to return to the world; and those who did not follow him, among whom are to be found many of the greatest minds, did yet not escape being imbued with his opinions in their youth, as these form the staple of instruction in the schools; and thus their minds were so preoccupied that they could not rise to the knowledge of true principles. And though I hold all the philosophers in esteem, and am unwilling to incur odium by my censure, I can adduce a proof of my assertion, which I do not think any of them will gainsay, which is, that they all laid down as a principle what they did not perfectly know. For example, I know none of them who did not suppose that there was gravity in terrestrial bodies; but although experience shows us very clearly that bodies we call heavy descend towards the center of the earth, we do not, therefore, know the nature of gravity, that is, the cause or principle in virtue of which bodies descend, and we must derive our knowledge of it from some other source. The same may be said of a vacuum and atoms, of heat and cold, of dryness and humidity, and of salt, sulphur, and mercury, and the other things of this sort which some have adopted as their principles. But no conclusion deduced from a principle which is not clear can be evident, even although the deduction be formally valid; and hence it follows that no reasonings based on such principles could lead them to the certain knowledge of any one thing, nor consequently advance them one step in the search after wisdom. And if they did discover any truth, this was due to one or other of the four means above mentioned. Notwithstanding this, I am in no degree desirous to lessen the honour which each of them can justly claim; I am only constrained to say, for the consolation of those who have not given their attention to study, that just as in travelling, when we turn our back upon the place to which we were going, we recede the farther from it in proportion as we proceed in the new direction for a greater length of time and with greater speed, so that, though we may be afterwards brought back to the right way, we cannot nevertheless arrive at the destined place as soon as if we had not moved backwards at all; so in philosophy, when we make use of false principles, we depart the farther from the knowledge of truth and wisdom exactly in proportion to the care with which we cultivate them, and apply ourselves to the deduction of diverse consequences from them, thinking that we are philosophizing well, while we are only departing the farther from the truth; from which it must be inferred that they who have learned the least of all that has been hitherto distinguished by the name of philosophy are the most fitted for the apprehension of truth.

After making those matters clear, I should, in the next place, have desired to set forth the grounds for holding that the true principles by which we may reach that highest degree of wisdom wherein consists the sovereign good of human life, are those I have proposed in this work; and two considerations alone are sufficient to establish this—the first of which is, that these principles are very clear, and the second, that we can deduce all other truths from them; for it is only these two conditions that are required in true principles. But I easily prove that they are very clear; firstly, by a reference to the manner in which I found them, namely, by rejecting all propositions that were in the least doubtful, for it is certain that such as could not be rejected by this test when they were attentively considered, are the most evident and clear which the human mind can know. Thus by considering that he who strives to doubt of all is unable nevertheless to doubt that he is while he doubts, and that what reasons thus, in not being able to doubt of itself and doubting nevertheless of everything else, is not that which we call our body, but what we name our mind or thought, I have taken the existence of this thought for the first principle, from which I very clearly deduced the following truths, namely, that there is a God who is the author of all that is in the world, and who, being the source of all truth, cannot have created our understanding of such a nature as to be deceived in the judgments it forms of the things of which it possesses a very clear and distinct perception. Those are all the principles of which I avail myself touching immaterial or metaphysical objects, from which I most clearly deduce these other principles of physical or corporeal things, namely, that there are bodies extended in length, breadth, and depth, which are of diverse figures and are moved in a variety of ways. Such are in sum the principles from which I deduce all other truths. The second circumstance that proves the clearness of these principles is, that they have been known in all ages, and even received as true and indubitable by all men, with the exception only of the existence of God, which has been doubted by some, because they attributed too much to the perceptions of the senses, and God can neither be seen nor touched.

But, though all the truths which I class among my principles were known at all times, and by all men, nevertheless, there has been no one up to the present, who, so far as I know, has adopted them as principles of philosophy: in other words, as such that we can deduce from them the knowledge of whatever else is in the world. It accordingly now remains for me to prove that they are such; and it appears to me that I cannot better establish this than by the test of experience: in other words, by inviting readers to peruse the following work. For, though I have not treated in it of all matters—that being impossible—I think I have so explained all of which I had occasion to treat, that they who read it attentively will have ground for the persuasion that it is unnecessary to seek for any other principles than those I have given, in order to arrive at the most exalted knowledge of which the mind of man is capable; especially if, after the perusal of my writings, they take the trouble to consider how many diverse questions are therein discussed and explained, and, referring to the writings of others, they see how little probability there is in the reasons that are adduced in explanation of the same questions by principles different from mine. And that they may the more easily undertake this, I might have said that those imbued with my doctrines have much less difficulty in comprehending the writings of others, and estimating their true value, than those who have not been so imbued; and this is precisely the opposite of what I before said of such as commenced with the ancient philosophy, namely, that the more they have studied it the less fit are they for rightly apprehending the truth.

I should also have added a word of advice regarding the manner of reading this work, which is, that I should wish the reader at first to go over the whole of it, as he would a romance, without greatly straining his attention, or tarrying at the difficulties he may perhaps meet with in it, with the view simply of knowing in general the matters of which I treat; and that afterwards, if they seem to him to merit a more careful examination, and he feel a desire to know their causes, he may read it a second time, in order to observe the connection of my reasonings; but that he must not then give it up in despair, although he may not everywhere sufficiently discover the connection of the proof, or understand all the reasonings—it being only necessary to mark with a pen the places where the difficulties occur, and continue to read without interruption to the end; then, if he does not grudge to take up the book a third time, I am confident he will find in a fresh perusal the solution of most of the difficulties he will have marked before; and that, if any still remain, their solution will in the end be found in another reading.

I have observed, on examining the natural constitutions of different minds, that there are hardly any so dull or slow of understanding as to be incapable of apprehending good opinions, or even of acquiring all the highest sciences, if they be but conducted along the right road. And this can also be proved by reason; for, as the principles are clear, and as nothing ought to be deduced from them, unless most manifest inferences, no one is so devoid of intelligence as to be unable to comprehend the conclusions that flow from them.

But, besides the entanglement of prejudices, from which no one is entirely exempt, although it is they who have been the most ardent students of the false sciences that receive the greatest detriment from them, it happens very generally that people of ordinary capacity neglect to study from a conviction that they want ability, and that others, who are more ardent, press on too rapidly: whence it comes to pass that they frequently admit principles far from evident, and draw doubtful inferences from them. For this reason, I should wish to assure those who are too distrustful of their own ability that there is nothing in my writings which they may not entirely understand, if they only take the trouble to examine them; and I should wish, at the same time, to warn those of an opposite tendency that even the most superior minds will have need of much time and attention to remark all I designed to embrace therein.

After this, that I might lead men to understand the real design I had in publishing them, I should have wished here to explain the order which it seems to me one ought to follow with the view of instructing himself. In the first place, a man who has merely the vulgar and imperfect knowledge which can be acquired by the four means above explained, ought, before all else, to endeavour to form for himself a code of morals sufficient to regulate the actions of his life, as well for the reason that this does not admit of delay as because it ought to be our first care to live well. In the next place, he ought to study Logic, not that of the schools, for it is only, properly speaking, a dialectic which teaches the mode of expounding to others what we already know, or even of speaking much, without judgment, of what we do not know, by which means it corrupts rather than increases good sense—but the logic which teaches the right conduct of the reason with the view of discovering the truths of which we are ignorant; and, because it greatly depends on usage, it is desirable he should exercise himself for a length of time in practising its rules on easy and simple questions, as those of the mathematics. Then, when he has acquired some skill in discovering the truth in these questions, he should commence to apply himself in earnest to true philosophy, of which the first part is Metaphysics, containing the principles of knowledge, among which is the explication of the principal attributes of God, of the immateriality of the soul, and of all the clear and simple notions that are in us; the second is Physics, in which, after finding the true principles of material things, we examine, in general, how the whole universe has been framed; in the next place, we consider, in particular, the nature of the earth, and of all the bodies that are most generally found upon it, as air, water, fire, the loadstone and other minerals. In the next place, it is necessary also to examine singly the nature of plants, of animals, and above all of man, in order that we may thereafter be able to discover the other sciences that are useful to us. Thus, all Philosophy is like a tree, of which Metaphysics is the root, Physics the trunk, and all the other sciences the branches that grow out of this trunk, which are reduced to three principal, namely, Medicine, Mechanics, and Ethics. By the science of Morals, I understand the highest and most perfect which, presupposing an entire knowledge of the other sciences, is the last degree of wisdom.

But as it is not from the roots or the trunks of trees

that we gather the fruit, but only from the extremities of their branches, so the principal utility of philosophy depends on the separate uses of its parts, which we can only learn last of all. But, though I am ignorant of almost all these, the zeal I have always felt in endeavouring to be of service to the public, was the reason why I published, some ten or twelve years ago, certain Essays on the doctrines I thought I had acquired. The first part of these Essays was a "Discourse on the Method of rightly conducting the Reason, and seeking Truth in the Sciences," in which I gave a summary of the principal rules of logic, and also of an imperfect ethic, which a person may follow provisionally so long as he does not know any better. The other parts were three treatises: the first of Dioptrics, the second of Meteors, and the third of Geometry. In the Dioptrics, I designed to show that we might proceed far enough in philosophy as to arrive, by its means, at the knowledge of the arts that are useful to life, because the invention of the telescope, of which I there gave an explanation, is one of the most difficult that has ever been made. In the treatise of Meteors, I desired to exhibit the difference that subsists between the philosophy I cultivate and that taught in the schools, in which the same matters are usually discussed. In fine, in the Geometry, I professed to demonstrate that I had discovered many things that were before unknown, and thus afford ground for believing that we may still discover many others, with the view of thus stimulating all to the investigation of truth. Since that period, anticipating the difficulty which many would experience in apprehending the foundations of the Metaphysics, I endeavoured to explain the chief points of them in a book of

Meditations, which is not in itself large, but the size of which has been increased, and the matter greatly illustrated, by the Objections which several very learned persons sent to me on occasion of it, and by the Replies which I made to them. At length, after it appeared to me that those preceding treatises had sufficiently prepared the minds of my readers for the *Principles of Philosophy,* I also published it; and I have divided this work into four parts, the first of which contains the principles of human knowledge, and which may be called the First Philosophy, or Metaphysics. That this part, accordingly, may be properly understood, it will be necessary to read beforehand the book of Meditations I wrote on the same subject. The other three parts contain all that is most general in Physics, namely, the explication of the first laws or principles of nature, and the way in which the heavens, the fixed stars, the planets, comets, and generally the whole universe, were composed; in the next place, the explication, in particular, of the nature of this earth, the air, water, fire, the magnet, which are the bodies we most commonly find everywhere around it, and of all the qualities we observe in these bodies, as light, heat, gravity, and the like. In this way, it seems to me, I have commenced the orderly explanation of the whole of philosophy, without omitting any of the matters that ought to precede the last which I discussed.

But to bring this undertaking to its conclusion, I ought hereafter to explain, in the same manner, the nature of the other more particular bodies that are on the earth, namely, minerals, plants, animals, and especially man; finally, to treat thereafter with accuracy of Medicine, Ethics, and Mechanics. I should require to do this in order to give to the world a complete body of philosophy; and I do not yet feel myself so old,—I do not so much distrust my strength, nor do I find myself so far removed from the knowledge of what remains, as that I should not dare to undertake to complete this design, provided I were in a position to make all the experiments which I should require for the basis and verification of my reasonings. But seeing that would demand a great expenditure, to which the resources of a private individual like myself would not be adequate, unless aided by the public, and as I have no ground to expect this aid, I believe that I ought for the future to content myself with studying for my own instruction, and posterity will excuse me if I fail hereafter to labour for them.

Meanwhile, that it may be seen wherein I think I have already promoted the general good, I will here mention the fruits that may be gathered from my Principles. The first is the satisfaction which the mind will experience on finding in the work many truths before unknown; for although frequently truth does not so greatly affect our imagination as falsity and fiction, because it seems less wonderful and is more simple, yet the gratification it affords is always more durable and solid. The second fruit is, that in studying these principles we will become accustomed by degrees to judge better of all the things we come in contact with, and thus be made wiser, in which respect the effect will be quite the opposite of the common philosophy, for we may easily remark in those we call pedants that it renders them less capable of rightly exercising their reason than they would have been if they had never known it. The third is, that the truths which they contain, being highly clear and certain, will take away all ground of dispute, and thus dispose men's minds to gentleness and concord; whereas the contrary is the effect of the controversies of the schools, which, as they insensibly render those who are exercised in them more wrangling and opinionative, are perhaps the prime cause of the heresies and dissensions that now harass the world. The last and chief fruit of these Principles is, that one will be able, by cultivating them, to discover many truths I myself have not unfolded, and thus passing by degrees from one to another, to acquire in course of time a perfect knowledge of the whole of philosophy, and to rise to the highest degree of wisdom. For just as all the arts, though in their beginnings they are rude and imperfect, are yet gradually perfected by practice, from their containing at first something true, and whose effect experience evinces; so in philosophy, when we have true principles, we cannot fail by following them to meet sometimes with other truths; and we could not better prove the falsity of those of Aristotle, than by saying that men made no progress in knowledge by their means during the many ages they prosecuted them.

I well know that there are some men so precipitate and accustomed to use so little circumspection in what they do, that, even with the most solid foundations, they could not rear a firm superstructure; and as it is usually those who are the readiest to make books, they would in a short time mar all that I have done, and introduce uncertainty and doubt into my manner of philosophizing, from which I have carefully endeavoured to banish them, if people were to receive their writings as mine, or as representing my opinions. I had, not long ago, some experience of this in one of those who were believed desirous of following me the most closely,* and one too of whom I had somewhere said that I had such confidence in his genius as to believe that he adhered to no opinions which I should not be ready to avow as mine; for he last year published a book entitled "Fundamenta Physicæ," in which, although he seems to have written nothing on the subject of Physics and Medicine which he did not take from my writings, as well from those I have published as from another still imperfect on the nature of animals, which fell into his hands; nevertheless, because he has copied them badly, and changed the order, and denied certain metaphysical truths upon which all Physics ought to be based, I am obliged wholly to disavow his work, and here to request readers not to attribute to me any opinion unless they find it expressly stated in my own writings, and to receive no opinion as true, whether in my writings or elsewhere, unless they see that it is very clearly deduced from true principles.

I well know, likewise, that many ages may elapse ere all the truths deducible from these principles are evolved out of them, as well because the greater number of such as remain to be discovered depend on certain particular experiments that never occur by chance, but which require to be investigated with care and expense by men of the highest intelligence, as because it will hardly happen that the same persons who have the sagacity to make a right use of them, will possess also the means of making them, and also because the majority of the best minds have formed so low an estimate

---

* Regius; see *La Vie de M. Descartes, réduite en abregé* (Baillet). Liv. vii., chap. vii.—T.

of philosophy in general, from the imperfections they have remarked in the kind in vogue up to the present time, that they cannot apply themselves to the search after truth.

But, in conclusion, if the difference discernible between the principles in question and those of every other system, and the great array of truths deducible from them, lead them to discern the importance of continuing the search after these truths, and to observe the degree of wisdom, the perfection and felicity of life, to which they are fitted to conduct us, I venture to believe that there will not be found one who is not ready to labour hard in so profitable a study, or at least to favour and aid with all his might those who shall devote themselves to it with success.

The height of my wishes is, that posterity may sometime behold the happy issue of it, etc.

TO THE MOST SERENE PRINCESS,
ELIZABETH,
ELDEST DAUGHTER OF FREDERICK, KING OF BOHEMIA, COUNT PALATINE, AND ELECTOR OF THE SACRED ROMAN EMPIRE.

MADAM,—The greatest advantage I have derived from the writings which I have already published, has arisen from my having, through means of them, become known to your Highness, and thus been privileged to hold occasional converse with one in whom so many rare and estimable qualities are united, as to lead me to believe I should do service to the public by proposing them as an example to posterity. It would ill become me to flatter, or to give expression to anything of which I had no certain knowledge, especially in the first pages of a work in which I aim at laying down the principles of truth. And the generous modesty that is conspicuous in all your actions, assures me that the frank and simple judgment of a man who only writes what he believes will be more agreeable to you than the ornate laudations of those who have studied the art of compliment. For this reason, I will give insertion to nothing in this letter for which I have not the certainty both of experience and reason; and in the exordium, as in the rest of the work, I will write only as becomes a philosopher. There is a vast difference between real and apparent virtues; and there is also a great discrepancy between those real virtues that proceed from an accurate knowledge of the truth, and such as are accompanied with ignorance or error. The virtues I call apparent are only, properly speaking, vices, which, as they are less frequent than the vices that are opposed to them, and are farther removed from them than the intermediate virtues, are usually held in higher esteem than those virtues. Thus, because those who fear dangers too much are more numerous than they who fear them too little, temerity is frequently opposed to the vice of timidity, and taken for a virtue, and is commonly more highly esteemed than true fortitude. Thus, also, the prodigal are in ordinary more praised than the liberal; and none more easily acquire a great reputation for piety than the superstitious and hypocritical. With regard to true virtues, these do not all proceed from true knowledge, for there are some that likewise spring from defect or error; thus, simplicity is frequently the source of goodness, fear of devotion, and despair of courage. The virtues that are thus accompanied with some imperfections differ from each other, and have received diverse appellations. But those pure and perfect virtues that arise from the knowledge of good alone are all of the same nature, and may be comprised under the single term wisdom. For, whoever owns the firm and constant resolution of always using his reason as well as lies in his power, and in all his actions of doing what he judges to be best, is truly wise, as far as his nature permits; and by this alone he is just, courageous, temperate, and possesses all the other virtues, but so well balanced as that none of them appears more prominent than another: and for this reason, although they are much more perfect than the virtues that blaze forth through the mixture of some defect, yet, because the crowd thus observes them less, they are not usually extolled so highly. Besides, of the two things that are requisite for the wisdom thus described, namely, the perception of the understanding and the disposition of the will, it is only that which lies in the will which all men can possess equally, inasmuch as the understanding of some is inferior to that of others. But although those who have only an inferior understanding may be as perfectly wise as their nature permits, and may render themselves highly acceptable to God by their virtue, provided they preserve always a firm and constant resolution to do all that they shall judge to be right, and to omit nothing that may lead them to the knowledge of the duties of which they are ignorant; nevertheless, those who preserve a constant resolution of performing the right, and are especially careful in instructing themselves, and who possess also a highly perspicacious intellect, arrive doubtless at a higher degree of wisdom than others; and I see that these three particulars are found in great perfection in your Highness. For, in the first place, your desire of self-instruction is manifest, from the circumstance that neither the amusements of the court, nor the accustomed mode of educating ladies, which ordinarily condemns them to ignorance, have been sufficient to prevent you from studying with much care all that is best in the arts and sciences; and the incomparable perspicacity of your intellect is evinced by this, that you penetrated the secrets of the sciences and acquired an accurate knowledge of them in a very short period. But of the vigour of your intellect I have a still stronger proof, and one peculiar to myself, in that I have never yet met any one who understood so gener-

ally and so well as yourself all that is contained in my writings. For there are several, even among men of the highest intellect and learning, who find them very obscure. And I remark, in almost all those who are versant in Metaphysics, that they are wholly disinclined from Geometry; and, on the other hand, that the cultivators of Geometry have no ability for the investigations of the First Philosophy: insomuch that I can say with truth I know but one mind, and that is your own, to which both studies are alike congenial, and which I therefore, with propriety, designate incomparable. But what most of all enhances my admiration is, that so accurate and varied an acquaintance with the whole circle of the sciences is not found in some aged doctor who has employed many years in contemplation, but in a Princess still young, and whose countenance and years would more fitly represent one of the Graces than a Muse or the sage Minerva. In conclusion, I not only remark in your Highness all that is requisite on the part of the mind to perfect and sublime wisdom, but also all that can be required on the part of the will or the manners, in which benignity and gentleness are so conjoined with majesty that, though fortune has attacked you with continued injustice, it has failed either to irritate or crush you. And this constrains me to such veneration that I not only think this work due to you, since it treats of philosophy which is the study of wisdom, but likewise feel not more zeal for my reputation as a philosopher than pleasure in subscribing myself,—
    Of your most Serene Highness,
        The most devoted servant,
                DESCARTES.

THE PRINCIPLES OF PHILOSOPHY.

PART I.

OF THE PRINCIPLES OF HUMAN KNOWLEDGE.

I. THAT in order to seek truth, it is necessary once in the course of our life, to doubt, as far as possible, of all things.

As we were at one time children, and as we formed various judgments regarding the objects presented to our senses, when as yet we had not the entire use of our reason, numerous prejudices stand in the way of our arriving at the knowledge of truth; and of these it seems impossible for us to rid ourselves, unless we undertake, once in our lifetime, to doubt of all those things in which we may discover even the smallest suspicion of uncertainty.

II. That we ought also to consider as false all that is doubtful.

Moreover, it will be useful likewise to esteem as false the things of which we shall be able to doubt, that we may with greater clearness discover what possesses most certainty and is the easiest to know.

III. That we ought not meanwhile to make use of doubt in the conduct of life.

In the meantime, it is to be observed that we are to avail ourselves of this general doubt only while engaged in the contemplation of truth. For, as far as concerns the conduct of life, we are very frequently obliged to follow opinions merely probable, or even sometimes, though of two courses of action we may not perceive more probability in the one than in the other, to choose one or other, seeing the opportunity of acting would not unfrequently pass away before we could free ourselves from our doubts.

IV. Why we may doubt of sensible things.

Accordingly, since we now only design to apply ourselves to the investigation of truth, we will doubt, first, whether of all the things that have ever fallen under our senses, or which we have ever imagined, any one really exist; in the first place, because we know by experience that the senses sometimes err, and it would be imprudent to trust too much to what has even once deceived us; secondly, because in dreams we perpetually seem to perceive or imagine innumerable objects which have no existence. And to one who has thus resolved upon a general doubt, there appear no marks by which he can with certainty distinguish sleep from the waking state.

V. Why we may also doubt of mathematical demonstrations.

We will also doubt of the other things we have before held as most certain, even of the demonstrations of mathematics, and of their principles which we have hitherto deemed self-evident; in the first place, because we have sometimes seen men fall into error in such matters, and admit as absolutely certain and self evident what to us appeared false, but chiefly because we have learnt that God who created us is all-powerful; for we do not yet know whether perhaps it was his will to create us so that we are always deceived, even in the things we think we know best: since this does not appear more impossible than our being occasionally deceived, which, however, as observation teaches us, is the case. And if we suppose that an all-powerful God is not the author of our being, and that we exist of ourselves or by some other means, still, the less powerful we suppose our author to be, the greater reason will we have for believing that we are not so perfect as that we may not be continually deceived.

VI. That we possess a free-will, by which we can withhold our assent from what is doubtful, and thus avoid error.

But meanwhile, whoever in the end may be the author of our being, and however powerful and deceitful he may be, we are nevertheless conscious of a freedom, by which we can refrain from admitting to a place in our belief aught that is not manifestly certain and undoubted, and thus guard against ever being deceived.

VII. That we cannot doubt of our existence while we doubt, and that this is the first knowledge we acquire when we philosophize in order.

While we thus reject all of which we can entertain the smallest doubt, and even imagine that it is false, we easily indeed suppose that there is neither God, nor sky, nor bodies, and that we ourselves even have neither hands nor feet, nor, finally, a body; but we cannot in the same way suppose that we are not while we doubt of the truth of these things; for there is a repugnance in conceiving that what thinks does not exist at the very time when it thinks. Accordingly, the knowledge, *I think, therefore I am,* is the first and most certain that occurs to one who philosophizes orderly.

VIII. That we hence discover the distinction between the mind and the body, or between a thinking and corporeal thing.

And this is the best mode of discovering the nature of the mind, and its distinctness from the body: for examining what we are, while supposing, as we now do, that there is nothing really existing apart from our thought, we clearly perceive that neither extension, nor figure, nor local motion,* nor anything similar that can be attributed to body, pertains to our nature, and nothing save thought alone; and, consequently, that the notion we have of our mind precedes that of any corporeal thing, and is more certain, seeing we still doubt whether there is any body in existence, while we already perceive that we think.

IX. What thought (*cogitatio*) is.

By the word thought, I understand all that which so takes place in us that we of ourselves are immediately conscious of it; and, accordingly, not only to understand (*intelligere, entendre*), to will (*velle*), to imagine (*imaginari*), but even to perceive (*sentire, sentir*), are here the same as to think (*cogitare, penser*). For if I say, I see, or, I walk, therefore I am; and if I understand by vision or walking the act of my eyes or of my limbs, which is the work of the body, the conclusion is not absolutely certain, because, as is often the case in dreams, I may think that I see or walk, although I do not open my eyes or move from my place, and even, perhaps, although I have no body: but, if I mean the sensation itself, or consciousness of seeing or walking, the knowledge is manifestly certain, because

* Instead of "local motion," the French has "existence in any place."

it is then referred to the mind, which alone perceives or is conscious that it sees or walks.*

X. *That the notions which are simplest and self-evident, are obscured by logical definitions; and that such are not to be reckoned among the cognitions acquired by study, [but as born with us].*

I do not here explain several other terms which I have used, or design to use in the sequel, because their meaning seems to me sufficiently self-evident. And I frequently remarked that philosophers erred in attempting to explain, by logical definitions, such truths as are most simple and self-evident; for they thus only rendered them more obscure. And when I said that the proposition, *I think, therefore I am,* is of all others the first and most certain which occurs to one philosophizing orderly, I did not therefore deny that it was necessary to know what thought, existence, and certitude are, and the truth that, in order to think it is necessary to be, and the like; but, because these are the most simple notions, and such as of themselves afford the knowledge of nothing existing, I did not judge it proper there to enumerate them.

XI. *How we can know our mind more clearly than our body.*

But now that it may be discerned how the knowledge we have of the mind not only precedes, and has greater certainty, but is even clearer, than that we have of the body, it must be remarked, as a matter that is highly manifest by the natural light, that to nothing no affections or qualities belong; and, accordingly, that where we observe certain affections, there

* In the French, "which alone has the power of perceiving, or of being conscious in any other way whatever."

a thing or substance to which these pertain, is necessarily found. The same light also shows us that we know a thing or substance more clearly in proportion as we discover in it a greater number of qualities. Now, it is manifest that we remark a greater number of qualities in our mind than in any other thing; for there is no occasion on which we know anything whatever when we are not at the same time led with much greater certainty to the knowledge of our own mind. For example, if I judge that there is an earth because I touch or see it, on the same ground, and with still greater reason, I must be persuaded that my mind exists; for it may be, perhaps, that I think I touch the earth while there is one in existence; but it is not possible that I should so judge, and my mind which thus judges not exist; and the same holds good of whatever object is presented to our mind.

XII. How it happens that every one does not come equally to know this.

Those who have not philosophized in order have had other opinions on this subject, because they never distinguished with sufficient care the mind from the body. For, although they had no difficulty in believing that they themselves existed, and that they had a higher assurance of this than of any other thing, nevertheless, as they did not observe that by *themselves,* they ought here to understand their *minds* alone [when the question related to metaphysical certainty]; and since, on the contrary, they rather meant their bodies which they saw with their eyes, touched with their hands, and to which they erroneously attributed the faculty of perception, they were prevented from distinctly apprehending the nature of the mind.

XIII. In what sense the knowledge of other things depends upon the knowledge of God.

But when the mind, which thus knows itself but is still in doubt as to all other things, looks around on all sides, with a view to the farther extension of its knowledge, it first of all discovers within itself the ideas of many things; and while it simply contemplates them, and neither affirms nor denies that there is anything beyond itself corresponding to them, it is in no danger of erring. The mind also discovers certain common notions out of which it frames various demonstrations that carry conviction to such a degree as to render doubt of their truth impossible, so long as we give attention to them. For example, the mind has within itself ideas of numbers and figures, and it has likewise among its common notions the principle *that if equals be added to equals the wholes will be equal,* and the like; from which it is easy to demonstrate that the three angles of a triangle are equal to two right angles, etc. Now, so long as we attend to the premises from which this conclusion and others similar to it were deduced, we feel assured of their truth; but, as the mind cannot always think of these with attention, when it has the remembrance of a conclusion without recollecting the order of its deduction, and is uncertain whether the author of its being has created it of a nature that is liable to be deceived, even in what appears most evident, it perceives that there is just ground to distrust the truth of such conclusions, and that it cannot possess any certain knowledge until it has discovered its author.

XIV. That we may validly infer the existence of

God from necessary existence being comprised in the concept we have of him.

When the mind afterwards reviews the different ideas that are in it, it discovers what is by far the chief among them—that of a Being omniscient, all-powerful, and absolutely perfect; and it observes that in this idea there is contained not only possible and contingent existence, as in the ideas of all other things which it clearly perceives, but existence absolutely necessary and eternal. And just as because, for example, the equality of its three angles to two right angles is necessarily comprised in the idea of a triangle, the mind is firmly persuaded that the three angles of a triangle are equal to two right angles; so, from its perceiving necessary and eternal existence to be comprised in the idea which it has of an all-perfect Being, it ought manifestly to conclude that this all-perfect Being exists.

XV. That necessary existence is not in the same way comprised in the notions which we have of other things, but merely contingent existence.

The mind will be still more certain of the truth of this conclusion, if it consider that it has no idea of any other thing in which it can discover that necessary existence is contained; for, from this circumstance alone, it will discern that the idea of an all-perfect Being has not been framed by itself, and that it does not represent a chimera, but a true and immutable nature, which must exist since it can only be conceived as necessarily existing.

XVI. That prejudices hinder many from clearly knowing the necessity of the existence of God.

Our mind would have no difficulty in assenting to

this truth, if it were, first of all, wholly free from prejudices; but as we have been accustomed to distinguish, in all other things, essence from existence, and to imagine at will many ideas of things which neither are nor have been, it easily happens, when we do not steadily fix our thoughts on the contemplation of the all-perfect Being, that a doubt arises as to whether the idea we have of him is not one of those which we frame at pleasure, or at least of that class to whose essence existence does not pertain.

XVII. That the greater objective (representative) perfection there is in our idea of a thing, the greater also must be the perfection of its cause.

When we further reflect on the various ideas that are in us, it is easy to perceive that there is not much difference among them, when we consider them simply as certain modes of thinking, but that they are widely different, considered in reference to the objects they represent; and that their causes must be so much the more perfect according to the degree of objective perfection contained in them.* For there is no difference between this and the case of a person who has the idea of a machine, in the construction of which great skill is displayed, in which circumstances we have a right to inquire how he came by this idea, whether, for example, he somewhere saw such a machine constructed by another, or whether he was so accurately taught the mechanical sciences, or is endowed with such force of genius, that he was able of himself to invent it, without having elsewhere seen anything like it; for all the ingenuity which is contained in the idea

* "as what they represent of their object has more perfection."
—*French.*

objectively only, or as it were in a picture, must exist at least in its first and chief cause, whatever that may be, not only objectively or representatively, but in truth formally or eminently.

XVIII. That the existence of God may be again inferred from the above.

Thus, because we discover in our minds the idea of God, or of an all-perfect Being, we have a right to inquire into the source whence we derive it; and we will discover that the perfections it represents are so immense as to render it quite certain that we could only derive it from an all-perfect Being; that is, from a God really existing. For it is not only manifest by the natural light that nothing cannot be the cause of anything whatever, and that the more perfect cannot arise from the less perfect, so as to be thereby produced as by its efficient and total cause, but also that it is impossible we can have the idea or representation of anything whatever, unless there be somewhere, either in us or out of us, an original which comprises, in reality, all the perfections that are thus represented to us; but, as we do not in any way find in ourselves those absolute perfections of which we have the idea, we must conclude that they exist in some nature different from ours, that is, in God, or at least that they were once in him; and it most manifestly follows [from their infinity] that they are still there.

XIX. That, although we may not comprehend the nature of God, there is yet nothing which we know so clearly as his perfections.

This will appear sufficiently certain and manifest to those who have been accustomed to contemplate the idea of God, and to turn their thoughts to his infinite perfections; for, although we may not comprehend them, because it is of the nature of the infinite not to be comprehended by what is finite, we nevertheless conceive them more clearly and distinctly than material objects, for this reason, that, being simple, and unobscured by limits,* they occupy our mind more fully.

XX. That we are not the cause of ourselves, but that this is God, and consequently that there is a God.

But, because every one has not observed this, and because, when we have an idea of any machine in which great skill is displayed, we usually know with sufficient accuracy the manner in which we obtained it, and as we cannot even recollect when the idea we have of a God was communicated to us by him, seeing it was always in our minds, it is still necessary that we should continue our review, and make inquiry after our author, possessing, as we do, the idea of the infinite perfections of a God: for it is in the highest degree evident by the natural light, that that which knows something more perfect than itself, is not the source of its own being, since it would thus have given to itself all the perfections which it knows; and that, consequently, it could draw its origin from no other being than from him who possesses in himself all those perfections, that is, from God.

XXI. That the duration alone of our life is sufficient to demonstrate the existence of God.

* After *limits,* "what of them we do conceive is much less confused. There is, besides, no speculation more calculated to aid in perfecting our understanding, and which is more important than this, inasmuch as the consideration of an object that has no limits to its perfections fills us with satisfaction and assurance."—*French.*

The truth of this demonstration will clearly appear, provided we consider the nature of time, or the duration of things; for this is of such a kind that its parts are not mutually dependent, and never co-existent; and, accordingly, from the fact that we now are, it does not necessarily follow that we shall be a moment afterwards, unless some cause, viz., that which first produced us, shall, as it were, continually reproduce us, that is, conserve us. For we easily understand that there is no power in us by which we can conserve ourselves, and that the being who has so much power as to conserve us out of himself, must also by so much the greater reason conserve himself, or rather stand in need of being conserved by no one whatever, and, in fine, be God.

XXII. That in knowing the existence of God, in the manner here explained, we likewise know all his attributes, as far as they can be known by the natural light alone.

There is the great advantage in proving the existence of God in this way, viz., by his idea, that we at the same time know what he is, as far as the weakness of our nature allows; for, reflecting on the idea we have of him which is born with us, we perceive that he is eternal, omniscient, omnipotent, the source of all goodness and truth, creator of all things, and that, in fine, he has in himself all that in which we can clearly discover any infinite perfection or good that is not limited by any imperfection.

XXIII. That God is not corporeal, and does not perceive by means of senses as we do, or will the evil of sin.

For there are indeed many things in the world that

are to a certain extent imperfect or limited, though possessing also some perfection; and it is accordingly impossible that any such can be in God. Thus, looking to corporeal nature,* since divisibility is included in local extension, and this indicates imperfection, it is certain that God is not body. And although in men it is to some degree a perfection to be capable of perceiving by means of the senses, nevertheless since in every sense there is passivity† which indicates dependency, we must conclude that God is in no manner possessed of senses, and that he only understands and wills, not, however, like us, by acts in any way distinct, but always by an act that is one, identical, and the simplest possible, understands, wills, and operates all, that is, all things that in reality exist; for he does not will the evil of sin, seeing this is but the negation of being.

XXIV. *That in passing from the knowledge of God to the knowledge of the creatures, it is necessary to remember that our understanding is finite, and the power of God infinite.*

But as we know that God alone is the true cause of all that is or can be, we will doubtless follow the best way of philosophizing, if, from the knowledge we have of God himself, we pass to the explication of the things which he has created, and essay to deduce it from the notions that are naturally in our minds, for we will thus obtain the most perfect science, that is, the knowledge of effects through their causes. But

---

* In the French, "since extension constitutes the nature of body."

† In the French, "because our perceptions arise from impressions made upon us from another source," *i. e.*, than ourselves.

that we may be able to make this attempt with sufficient security from error, we must use the precaution to bear in mind as much as possible that God, who is the author of things, is infinite, while we are wholly finite.

XXV. That we must believe all that God has revealed, although it may surpass the reach of our faculties.

Thus, if perhaps God reveal to us or others, matters concerning himself which surpass the natural powers of our mind, such as the mysteries of the incarnation and of the trinity, we will not refuse to believe them, although we may not clearly understand them; nor will we be in any way surprised to find in the immensity of his nature, or even in what he has created, many things that exceed our comprehension.

XXVI. That it is not needful to enter into disputes* regarding the infinite, but merely to hold all that in which we can find no limits as indefinite, such as the extension of the world, the divisibility of the parts of matter, the number of the stars, etc.

We will thus never embarrass ourselves by disputes about the infinite, seeing it would be absurd for us who are finite to undertake to determine anything regarding it, and thus as it were to limit it by endeavouring to comprehend it. We will accordingly give ourselves no concern to reply to those who demand whether the half of an infinite line is also infinite, and whether an infinite number is even or odd, and the like, because it is only such as imagine their minds to be infinite who seem bound to entertain questions of this sort. And, for our part, looking to all those things in which in cer-

* "to essay to comprehend the infinite."—*French.*

tain senses, we discover no limits, we will not, therefore, affirm that they are infinite, but will regard them simply as indefinite. Thus, because we cannot imagine extension so great that we cannot still conceive greater, we will say that the magnitude of possible things is indefinite, and because a body cannot be divided into parts so small that each of these may not be conceived as again divided into others still smaller, let us regard quantity as divisible into parts whose number is indefinite; and as we cannot imagine so many stars that it would seem impossible for God to create more, let us suppose that their number is indefinite, and so in other instances.

XXVII. What difference there is between the indefinite and the infinite.

And we will call those things indefinite rather than infinite, with the view of reserving to God alone the appellation of infinite; in the first place, because not only do we discover in him alone no limits on any side, but also because we positively conceive that he admits of none; and in the second place, because we do not in the same way positively conceive that other things are in every part unlimited, but merely negatively admit that their limits, if they have any, cannot be discovered by us.

XXVIII. That we must examine, not the final, but the efficient, causes of created things.

Likewise, finally, we will not seek reasons of natural things from the end which God or nature proposed to himself in their creation (*i. e.*, final causes),* for we

* " We will not stop to consider the ends which God proposed to himself in the creation of the world, and we will entirely reject from our philosophy the search of final causes."—*French.*

ought not to presume so far as to think that we are sharers in the counsels of Deity, but, considering him as the efficient cause of all things, let us endeavour to discover by the natural light* which he has planted in us, applied to those of his attributes of which he has been willing we should have some knowledge, what must be concluded regarding those effects we perceive by our senses; bearing in mind, however, what has been already said, that we must only confide in this natural light so long as nothing contrary to its dictates is revealed by God himself.†

XXIX. That God is not the cause of our errors.

The first attribute of God which here falls to be considered, is that he is absolutely veracious and the source of all light, so that it is plainly repugnant for him to deceive us, or to be properly and positively the cause of the errors to which we are consciously subject; for although the address to deceive seems to be some mark of subtlety of mind among men, yet without doubt the will to deceive only proceeds from malice or from fear and weakness, and consequently cannot be attributed to God.

XXX. That consequently all which we clearly perceive is true, and that we are thus delivered from the doubts above proposed.

Whence it follows, that the light of nature, or faculty of knowledge given us by God, can never compass any object which is not true, in as far as it attains to a knowledge of it, that is, in as far as the object is clearly and distinctly apprehended. For God would

* " Faculty of reasoning."—*French*.

† The last clause, beginning "bearing in mind," **is omitted in the French**.

have merited the appellation of a deceiver if he had given us this faculty perverted, and such as might lead us to take falsity for truth [when we used it aright]. Thus the highest doubt is removed, which arose from our ignorance on the point as to whether perhaps our nature was such that we might be deceived even in those things that appear to us the most evident. The same principle ought also to be of avail against all the other grounds of doubting that have been already enumerated. For mathematical truths ought now to be above suspicion, since these are of the clearest. And if we perceive anything by our senses, whether while awake or asleep, we will easily discover the truth provided we separate what there is of clear and distinct in the knowledge from what is obscure and confused. There is no need that I should here say more on this subject, since it has already received ample treatment in the metaphysical Meditations; and what follows will serve to explain it still more accurately.

XXXI. *That our errors are, in respect of God, merely negations, but, in respect of ourselves, privations.*

But as it happens that we frequently fall into error, although God is no deceiver, if we desire to inquire into the origin and cause of our errors, with a view to guard against them, it is necessary to observe that they depend less on our understanding than on our will, and that they have no need of the actual concourse of God, in order to their production; so that, when considered in reference to God, they are merely negations, but in reference to ourselves, privations.

XXXII. *That there are only two modes of think-*

ing in us, viz., the perception of the understanding and the action of the will.

For all the modes of thinking of which we are conscious may be referred to two general classes, the one of which is the perception or operation of the understanding, and the other the volition or operation of the will. Thus, to perceive by the senses (*sentire*), to imagine, and to conceive things purely intelligible,[8] are only different modes of perceiving (*percipiendi*); but to desire, to be averse from, to affirm, to deny, to doubt, are different modes of willing.

XXXIII. That we never err unless when we judge of something which we do not sufficiently apprehend.

When we apprehend anything we are in no danger of error, if we refrain from judging of it in any way; and even when we have formed a judgment regarding it, we would never fall into error, provided we gave our assent only to what we clearly and distinctly perceived; but the reason why we are usually deceived, is that we judge without possessing an exact knowledge of that of which we judge.

XXXIV. That the will as well as the understanding is required for judging.

I admit that the understanding is necessary for judging, there being no room to suppose that we can judge of that which we in no way apprehend; but the will also is required in order to our assenting to what we have in any degree perceived. It is not necessary, however, at least to form any judgment whatever, that we have an entire and perfect apprehension of a thing; for we may assent to many things of which we have only a very obscure and confused knowledge.

XXXV. That the will is of greater extension than

the understanding, and is thus the source of our errors.

Further, the perception of the intellect extends only to the few things that are presented to it, and is always very limited: the will, on the other hand, may, in a certain sense, be said to be infinite, because we observe nothing that can be the object of the will of any other, even of the unlimited will of God, to which ours cannot also extend, so that we easily carry it beyond the objects we clearly perceive; and when we do this, it is not wonderful that we happen to be deceived.

XXXVI. That our errors cannot be imputed to God.

But although God has not given us an omniscient understanding, he is not on this account to be considered in any wise the author of our errors, for it is of the nature of created intellect to be finite, and of finite intellect not to embrace all things.

XXXVII. That the chief perfection of man is his being able to act freely or by will, and that it is this which renders him worthy of praise or blame.

That the will should be the more extensive is in harmony with its nature; and it is a high perfection in man to be able to act by means of it, that is, freely; and thus in a peculiar way to be the master of his own actions, and merit praise or blame. For self-acting machines are not commended because they perform with exactness all the movements for which they were adapted, seeing their motions are carried on necessarily; but the maker of them is praised on account of the exactness with which they were framed, because he did not act of necessity, but freely; and, on the same principle, we must attribute to ourselves something more on this account, that when we embrace truth, we do so not of necessity, but freely.

XXXVIII. That error is a defect in our mode of acting, not in our nature; and that the faults of their subjects may be frequently attributed to other masters, but never to God.

It is true, that as often as we err, there is some defect in our mode of action or in the use of our liberty, but not in our nature, because this is always the same, whether our judgments be true or false. And although God could have given to us such perspicacity of intellect that we should never have erred, we have, notwithstanding, no right to demand this of him; for, although with us he who was able to prevent evil and did not is held guilty of it, God is not in the same way to be reckoned responsible for our errors because he had the power to prevent them, inasmuch as the dominion which some men possess over others has been instituted for the purpose of enabling them to hinder those under them from doing evil, whereas the dominion which God exercises over the universe is perfectly absolute and free. For this reason we ought to thank him for the goods he has given us, and not complain that he has not blessed us with all which we know it was in his power to impart.

XXXIX. That the liberty of our will is self-evident.

Finally, it is so manifest that we possess a free will, capable of giving or withholding its assent, that this truth must be reckoned among the first and most common notions which are born with us. This, indeed, has already very clearly appeared, for when essaying to doubt of all things, we went so far as to suppose even that he who created us employed his limitless power in deceiving us in every way, we were conscious nevertheless of being free to abstain from believing what was not in every respect certain and undoubted. But that of which we are unable to doubt at such a time is as self-evident and clear as any thing we can ever know.

XL. That it is likewise certain that God has fore-ordained all things.

But because what we have already discovered of God, gives us the assurance that his power is so immense that we would sin in thinking ourselves capable of ever doing anything which he had not ordained beforehand, we should soon be embarrassed in great difficulties if we undertook to harmonise the pre-ordination of God with the freedom of our will, and endeavoured to comprehend both truths at once.

XLI. How the freedom of our will may be reconciled with the Divine pre-ordination.

But, in place of this, we will be free from these embarrassments if we recollect that our mind is limited, while the power of God, by which he not only knew from all eternity what is or can be, but also willed and pre-ordained it, is infinite. It thus happens that we possess sufficient intelligence to know clearly and distinctly that this power is in God, but not enough to comprehend how he leaves the free actions of men indeterminate; and, on the other hand, we have such consciousness of the liberty and indifference which exists in ourselves, that there is nothing we more clearly or perfectly comprehend: [so that the omnipotence of God ought not to keep us from believing it]. For it would be absurd to doubt of that of which we are fully conscious, and which we experience as existing in ourselves, because we do not comprehend another matter which, from its very nature, we know to be incomprehensible.

XLII. How, although we never will to err, it is nevertheless by our will that we do err.

But now since we know that all our errors depend upon our will, and as no one wishes to deceive himself, it may seem wonderful that there is any error in our judgments at all. It is necessary to remark, however, that there is a great difference between willing to be deceived, and willing to yield assent to opinions in which it happens that error is found. For though there is no one who expressly wishes to fall into error. we will yet hardly find any one who is not ready to assent to things in which, unknown to himself, error lurks; and it even frequently happens that it is the desire itself of following after truth that leads those not fully aware of the order in which it ought to be sought for, to pass judgment on matters of which they have no adequate knowledge, and thus to fall into error.

XLIII. That we shall never err if we give our assent only to what we clearly and distinctly perceive.

But it is certain we will never admit falsity for truth, so long as we judge only of that which we clearly and distinctly perceive; because, as God is no deceiver, the faculty of knowledge which he has given us cannot be fallacious, nor, for the same reason, the faculty of will, when we do not extend it beyond the objects we clearly know. And even although this truth could not be established by reasoning, the minds of all have been so impressed by nature as spontaneously to assent to whatever is clearly perceived, and to experience an impossibility to doubt of its truth.

XLIV. That we uniformly judge improperly when we assent to what we do not clearly perceive, although our judgment may chance to be true; and that it is frequently our memory which deceives us by leading us to believe that certain things were formerly sufficiently understood by us.

It is likewise certain that, when we approve of any reason which we do not apprehend, we are either deceived, or, if we stumble on the truth, it is only by chance, and thus we can never possess the assurance that we are not in error. I confess it seldom happens that we judge of a thing when we have observed we do not apprehend it, because it is a dictate of the natural light never to judge of what we do not know. But we most frequently err in this, that we presume upon a past knowledge of much to which we give our assent, as to something treasured up in the memory, and perfectly known to us; whereas, in truth, we have no such knowledge.

XLV. What constitutes clear and distinct perception.

There are indeed a great many persons who, through their whole lifetime, never perceive anything in a way necessary for judging of it properly; for the knowledge upon which we can establish a certain and indubitable judgment must be not only clear, but also distinct. I call that clear which is present and manifest to the mind giving attention to it, just as we are said clearly to see objects when, being present to the eye looking on, they stimulate it with sufficient force, and it is disposed to regard them; but the distinct is that which is so precise and different from all other objects as to comprehend in itself only what is clear.*

XLVI. It is shown, from the example of pain, that a perception may be clear without being distinct, but that it cannot be distinct unless it is clear.

For example, when any one feels intense pain, the knowledge which he has of this pain is very clear, but it is not always distinct; for men usually confound it with the obscure judgment they form regarding its nature, and think that there is in the suffering part something similar to the sensation of pain of which they are alone conscious. And thus perception may be clear without being distinct, but it can never be distinct without likewise being clear.

XLVII. That, to correct the prejudices of our early years, we must consider what is clear in each of our simple† notions.

And, indeed, in our early years, the mind was so immersed in the body, that, although it perceived many things with sufficient clearness, it yet knew nothing distinctly; and since even at that time we exercised our judgment in many matters, numerous prejudices were thus contracted, which, by the majority, are never afterwards laid aside. But that we may now be in a position to get rid of these, I will here briefly enumerate all the simple notions of which our thoughts are composed, and distinguish in each what is clear from what is obscure, or fitted to lead into error.

XLVIII. That all the objects of our knowledge are

---

* "what appears manifestly to him who considers it as he ought."—*French.*

† "first."—*French.*

to be regarded either (1) as things or the affections of things: or (2) as eternal truths; with the enumeration of things.

Whatever objects fall under our knowledge we consider either as things or the affections of things,* or as eternal truths possessing no existence beyond our thought. Of the first class the most general are substance, duration, order, number, and perhaps also some others, which notions apply to all the kinds of things. I do not, however, recognise more than two highest kinds (*summa genera*) of things; the first of intellectual things, or such as have the power of thinking, including mind or thinking substance and its properties; the second, of material things, embracing extended substance, or body and its properties. Perception, volition, and all modes as well of knowing as of willing, are related to thinking substance; on the other hand, to extended substance we refer magnitude, or extension in length, breadth, and depth, figure, motion, situation, divisibility of parts themselves, and the like. There are, however, besides these, certain things of which we have an internal experience that ought not to be referred either to the mind of itself, or to the body alone, but to the close and intimate union between them, as will hereafter be shown in its place. Of this class are the appetites of hunger and thirst, etc., and also the emotions or passions of the mind which are not exclusively mental affections, as the emotions of anger, joy, sadness, love, etc.; and, finally, all the sen-

* Things and the affections of things are (in the French) equivalent to "what has some (*i. e.* a *real*) existence," as opposed to the class of "eternal truths," which have merely an *ideal* existence.

sations, as of pain, titillation, light and colours, sounds, smells, tastes, heat, hardness, and the other tactile qualities.

XLIX. That the eternal truths cannot be thus enumerated, but that this is not necessary.

What I have already enumerated we are to regard as things, or the qualities or modes of things. We now come to speak of eternal truths. When we apprehend that it is impossible a thing can arise from nothing, this proposition, *ex nihilo nihil fit,* is not considered as somewhat existing, or as the mode of a thing, but as an eternal truth having its seat in our mind, and is called a common notion or axiom. Of this class are the following:—It is impossible the same thing can at once be and not be; what is done cannot be undone; he who thinks must exist while he thinks; and innumerable others, the whole of which it is indeed difficult to enumerate, but this is not necessary, since, if blinded by no prejudices, we cannot fail to know them when the occasion of thinking them occurs.

L. That these truths are clearly perceived, but not equally by all men, on account of prejudices.

And, indeed, with regard to these common notions, it is not to be doubted that they can be clearly and distinctly known, for otherwise they would not merit this appellation: as, in truth, some of them are not, with respect to all men, equally deserving of the name, because they are not equally admitted by all: not, however, from this reason, as I think, that the faculty of knowledge of one man extends farther than that of another, but rather because these common notions are opposed to the prejudices of some, who, on this account, are not able readily to embrace them, even although others, who are free from those prejudices, apprehend them with the greatest clearness.

LI. *What substance is, and that the term is not applicable to God and the creatures in the same sense.*

But with regard to what we consider as things or the modes of things, it is worth while to examine each of them by itself. By substance we can conceive nothing else than a thing which exists in such a way as to stand in need of nothing beyond itself in order to its existence. And, in truth, there can be conceived but one substance which is absolutely independent, and that is God. We perceive that all other things can exist only by help of the concourse of God. And, accordingly, the term substance does not apply to God and the creatures *univocally,* to adopt a term familiar in the schools; that is, no signification of this word can be distinctly understood which is common to God and them.

LII. *That the term is applicable univocally to the mind and the body, and how substance itself is known.*

Created substances, however, whether corporeal or thinking, may be conceived under this common concept; for these are things which, in order to their existence, stand in need of nothing but the concourse of God. But yet substance cannot be first discovered merely from its being a thing which exists independently, for existence by itself is not observed by us. We easily, however, discover substance itself from any attribute of it, by this common notion, that of nothing there are no attributes, properties, or qualities: for, from perceiving that some attribute is present, we infer that some existing thing or substance to which it may be attributed is also of necessity present.

LIII. That of every substance there is one principal attribute, as thinking of the mind, extension of the body.

But, although any attribute is sufficient to lead us to the knowledge of substance, there is, however, one principal property of every substance, which constitutes its nature or essence, and upon which all the others depend. Thus, extension in length, breadth, and depth, constitutes the nature of corporeal substance; and thought the nature of thinking substance. For every other thing that can be attributed to body, presupposes extension, and is only some mode of an extended thing; as all the properties we discover in the mind are only diverse modes of thinking. Thus, for example, we cannot conceive figure unless in something extended, nor motion unless in extended space, nor imagination, sensation, or will, unless in a thinking thing. But, on the other hand, we can conceive extension without figure or motion, and thought without imagination or sensation, and so of the others; as is clear to any one who attends to these matters.

LIV. How we may have clear and distinct notions of the substance which thinks, of that which is corporeal, and of God.

And thus we may easily have two clear and distinct notions or ideas, the one of created substance, which thinks, the other of corporeal substance, provided we carefully distinguish all the attributes of thought from those of extension. We may also have a clear and distinct idea of an uncreated and independent thinking substance, that is, of God, provided we do not suppose that this idea adequately represents to us all that is in God, and do not mix up with it anything fictitious, but attend simply to the characters that are comprised in the notion we have of him, and which we clearly know to belong to the nature of an absolutely perfect Being. For no one can deny that there is in us such an idea of God, without groundlessly supposing that there is no knowledge of God at all in the human mind.

LV. *How duration, order, and number may be also distinctly conceived.*

We will also have most distinct conceptions of duration, order, and number, if, in place of mixing up with our notions of them that which properly belongs to the concept of substance, we merely think that the duration of a thing is a mode under which we conceive this thing, in so far as it continues to exist; and, in like manner, that order and number are not in reality different from things disposed in order and numbered, but only modes under which we diversely consider these things.

LVI. *What are modes, qualities, attributes.*

And, indeed, we here understand by modes the same with what we elsewhere designate attributes or qualities. But when we consider substance as affected or varied by them, we use the term modes; when from this variation it may be denominated of such a kind, we adopt the term qualities [to designate the different modes which cause it to be so named]; and, finally, when we simply regard these modes as in the substance, we call them attributes. Accordingly, since God must be conceived as superior to change, it is not proper to say that there are modes or qualities in him, but simply attributes; and even in created things that which is found in them always in the same mode, as existence and duration in the thing which exists and endures, ought to be called attribute and not mode or quality.

LVII. That some attributes exist in the things to which they are attributed, and others only in our thought; and what duration and time are.

Of these attributes or modes there are some which exist in the things themselves, and others that have only an existence in our thought; thus, for example, time, which we distinguish from duration taken in its generality, and call the measure of motion, is only a certain mode under which we think duration itself, for we do not indeed conceive the duration of things that are moved to be different from the duration of things that are not moved: as is evident from this, that if two bodies are in motion for an hour, the one moving quickly and the other slowly, we do not reckon more time in the one than in the other, although there may be much more motion in the one of the bodies than in the other. But that we may comprehend the duration of all things under a common measure, we compare their duration with that of the greatest and most regular motions that give rise to years and days, and which we call time; hence what is so designated is nothing superadded to duration, taken in its generality, but a mode of thinking.

LVIII. That number and all universals are only modes of thought.

In the same way number, when it is not considered as in created things, but merely in the abstract or in general, is only a mode of thinking; and the same is true of all those general ideas we call universals.

LIX. How universals are formed; and what are the

five common, viz., genus, species, difference, property, and accident.

Universals arise merely from our making use of one and the same idea in thinking of all individual objects between which there subsists a certain likeness; and when we comprehend all the objects represented by this idea under one name, this term likewise becomes universal. For example, when we see two stones, and do not regard their nature farther than to remark that there are two of them, we form the idea of a certain number, which we call the binary; and when we afterwards see two birds or two trees, and merely take notice of them so far as to observe that there are two of them, we again take up the same idea as before, which is, accordingly, universal; and we likewise give to this number the same universal appellation of binary. In the same way, when we consider a figure of three sides, we form a certain idea, which we call the idea of a triangle, and we afterwards make use of it as the universal to represent to our mind all other figures of three sides. But when we remark more particularly that of figures of three sides, some have a right angle and others not, we form the universal idea of a right-angled triangle, which being related to the preceding as more general, may be called species; and the right angle the universal difference by which right-angled triangles are distinguished from all others; and farther, because the square of the side which sustains the right angle is equal to the squares of the other two sides, and because this property belongs only to this species of triangles, we may call it the universal property of the species. Finally, if we suppose that of these triangles some are moved and others not, this will be their universal accident; and, accordingly, we commonly reckon five universals, viz., genus, species, difference, property, accident.

LX. Of distinctions; and first of the real.

But number in things themselves arises from the distinction there is between them: and distinction is threefold, viz., real, modal, and of reason. The real properly subsists between two or more substances; and it is sufficient to assure us that two substances are really mutually distinct, if only we are able clearly and distinctly to conceive the one of them without the other. For the knowledge we have of God renders it certain that he can effect all that of which we have a distinct idea: wherefore, since we have now, for example, the idea of an extended and corporeal substance, though we as yet do not know with certainty whether any such thing is really existent, nevertheless, merely because we have the idea of it, we may be assured that such may exist; and, if it really exists, that every part which we can determine by thought must be really distinct from the other parts of the same substance. In the same way, since every one is conscious that he thinks, and that he in thought can exclude from himself every other substance, whether thinking or extended, it is certain that each of us thus considered is really distinct from every other thinking and corporeal substance. And although we suppose that God united a body to a soul so closely that it was impossible to form a more intimate union, and thus made a composite whole, the two substances would remain really distinct, notwithstanding this union; for with whatever tie God connected them, he was not able to rid himself of the power he possessed of separating them, or of conserving the one apart from the other, and the things which God can separate or conserve separately are really distinct.

LXI. Of the modal distinction.

There are two kinds of modal distinctions, viz., that between the mode properly so-called and the substance of which it is a mode, and that between two modes of the same substance. Of the former we have an example in this, that we can clearly apprehend substance apart from the mode which we say differs from it; while, on the other hand, we cannot conceive this mode without conceiving the substance itself. There is, for example, a modal distinction between figure or motion and corporeal substance in which both exist; there is a similar distinction between affirmation or recollection and the mind. Of the latter kind we have an illustration in our ability to recognise the one of two modes apart from the other, as figure apart from motion, and motion apart from figure; though we cannot think of either the one or the other without thinking of the common substance in which they adhere. If, for example, a stone is moved, and is withal square, we can, indeed, conceive its square figure without its motion, and reciprocally its motion without its square figure; but we can conceive neither this motion nor this figure apart from the substance of the stone. As for the distinction according to which the mode of one substance is different from another substance, or from the mode of another substance, as the motion of one body is different from another body or from the mind, or as motion is different from doubt, it seems to me that it should be called real rather than modal, because these modes cannot be clearly conceived apart from the really distinct substances of which they are the modes.

LXII. Of the distinction of reason (logical distinction).

Finally, the distinction of reason is that between a substance and some one of its attributes, without which it is impossible, however, we can have a distinct conception of the substance itself; or between two such attributes of a common substance, the one of which we essay to think without the other. This distinction is manifest from our inability to form a clear and distinct idea of such substance, if we separate from it such attribute; or to have a clear perception of the one of two such attributes if we separate it from the other. For example, because any substance which ceases to endure ceases also to exist, duration is not distinct from substance except in thought (*ratione*); and in general all the modes of thinking which we consider as in objects differ only in thought, as well from the objects of which they are thought as from each other in a common object.* It occurs, indeed, to me that I have elsewhere classed this kind of distinction with the modal (viz., towards the end of the Reply to the First Objections to the Meditations on the First Philosophy); but there it was only necessary to treat of these distinctions generally, and it was sufficient for my purpose at that time simply to distinguish both of them from the real.

LXIII. How thought and extension may be dis-

* "and generally all the attributes that lead us to entertain different thoughts of the same thing, such as, for example, the extension of body and its property of divisibility, do not differ from the body which is to us the object of them, or from each other, unless as we sometimes confusedly think the one without thinking the other.—*French.*

tinctly known, as constituting, the one the nature of mind, the other that of body.

Thought and extension may be regarded as constituting the natures of intelligent and corporeal substance; and then they must not be otherwise conceived than as the thinking and extended substances themselves, that is, as mind and body, which in this way are conceived with the greatest clearness and distinctness. Moreover, we more easily conceive extended or thinking substance than substance by itself, or with the omission of its thinking or extension. For there is some difficulty in abstracting the notion of substance from the notions of thinking and extension, which, in truth, are only diverse in thought itself (*i. e.*, logically different); and a concept is not more distinct because it comprehends fewer properties, but because we accurately distinguish what is comprehended in it from all other notions.

LXIV. How these may likewise be distinctly conceived as modes of substance.

Thought and extension may be also considered as modes of substance; in as far, namely, as the same mind may have many different thoughts, and the same body, with its size unchanged, may be extended in several diverse ways, at one time more in length and less in breadth or depth, and at another time more in breadth and less in length; and then they are modally distinguished from substance, and can be conceived not less clearly and distinctly, provided they be not regarded as substances or things separated from others, but simply as modes of things. For by regarding them as in the substances of which they are the modes, we distinguish them from these substances, and take them for what in truth they are: whereas, on the other hand, if we wish to consider them apart from the substances in which they are, we should by this itself regard them as self-subsisting things, and thus confound the ideas of mode and substance.

LXV. How we may likewise know their modes.

In the same way we will best apprehend the diverse modes of thought, as intellection, imagination, recollection, volition, etc., and also the diverse modes of extension, or those that belong to extension, as all figures, the situation of parts and their motions, provided we consider them simply as modes of the things in which they are; and motion as far as it is concerned, provided we think merely of locomotion, without seeking to know the force that produces it, and which nevertheless I will essay to explain in its own place.

LXVI. How our sensations, affections, and appetites may be clearly known, although we are frequently wrong in our judgments regarding them.

There remain our sensations, affections, and appetites, of which we may also have a clear knowledge, if we take care to comprehend in the judgments we form of them only that which is precisely contained in our perception of them, and of which we are immediately conscious. There is, however, great difficulty in observing this, at least in respect of sensations; because we have all, without exception, from our youth judged that all the things we perceived by our senses had an existence beyond our thought, and that they were entirely similar to the sensations, that is, perceptions, we had of them. Thus when, for example, we saw a certain colour, we thought we saw something occupying a place out of us, and which was entirely similar to hat idea of colour we were then conscious of; and from the habit of judging in this way, we seemed to see this so clearly and distinctly that we esteemed it (*i. e.*, the externality of the colour) certain and indubitable.

LXVII. That we are frequently deceived in our judgments regarding pain itself.

The same prejudice has place in all our other sensations, even in those of titillation and pain. For though we are not in the habit of believing that there exist out of us objects that resemble titillation and pain, we do not nevertheless consider these sensations as in the mind alone, or in our perception, but as in the hand, or foot, or some other part of our body. There is no reason, however, to constrain us to believe that the pain, for example, which we feel, as it were, in the foot is something out of the mind existing in the foot, or that the light which we see, as it were, in the sun exists in the sun as it is in us. Both these beliefs are prejudices of our early years, as will clearly appear in the sequel.

LXVIII. How in these things what we clearly conceive is to be distinguished from that in which we may be deceived.

But that we may distinguish what is clear in our sensations from what is obscure, we ought most carefully to observe that we possess a clear and distinct knowledge of pain, colour, and other things of this sort, when we consider them simply as sensations or thoughts; but that, when they are judged to be certain things subsisting beyond our mind, we are wholly unable to form any conception of them. Indeed, when any one tells us that he sees colour in a body or feels pain in one of his limbs, this is exactly the same as if he said that he there saw or felt something of the nature of which he was entirely ignorant, or that he did not know what he saw or felt. For although, when less attentively examining his thoughts, a person may easily persuade himself that he has some knowledge of it, since he supposes that there is something resembling that sensation of colour or of pain of which he is conscious; yet, if he reflects on what the sensation of colour or pain represents to him as existing in a coloured body or in a wounded member, he will find that of such he has absolutely no knowledge.

LXIX. That magnitude, figure, etc., are known far differently from colour, pain, etc.

What we have said above will be more manifest, especially if we consider that size in the body perceived, figure, motion (at least local, for philosophers by fancying other kinds of motion have rendered its nature less intelligible to themselves), the situation of parts, duration, number, and those other properties which, as we have already said, we clearly perceive in all bodies, are known by us in a way altogether different from that in which we know what colour is in the same body, or pain, smell, taste, or any other of those properties which I have said above must be referred to the senses. For although when we see a body we are not less assured of its existence from its appearing figured than from its appearing coloured,* we yet know with far greater clearness its property of figure than its colour.

LXX. That we may judge of sensible things in two

* " by the colour we perceive on occasion of it."—*French.*

ways, by the one of which we avoid error, by the other fall into it.

It is thus manifest that to say we perceive colours in objects is in reality equivalent to saying we perceive something in objects and are yet ignorant of what it is, except as that which determines in us a certain highly vivid and clear sensation, which we call the sensation of colours. There is, however, very great diversity in the manner of judging: for so long as we simply judge that there is an unknown something in objects (that is, in things such as they are, from which the sensation reached us), so far are we from falling into error that, on the contrary, we thus rather provide against it, for we are less apt to judge rashly of a thing which we observe we do not know. But when we think we perceive colours in objects, although we are in reality ignorant of what we then denominate colour, and are unable to conceive any resemblance between the colour we suppose to be in objects, and that of which we are conscious in sensation, yet because we do not observe this, or because there are in objects several properties, as size, figure, number, etc., which, as we clearly know, exist, or may exist in them as they are perceived by our senses or conceived by our understanding, we easily glide into the error of holding that what is called colour in objects is something entirely resembling the colour we perceive, and thereafter of supposing that we have a clear perception of what is in no way perceived by us.

LXXI. *That the chief cause of our errors is to be found in the prejudices of our childhood.*

And here we may notice the first and chief cause of our errors. In early life the mind was so closely bound to the body that it attended to nothing beyond the thoughts by which it perceived the objects that made impression on the body: nor as yet did it refer these thoughts to anything existing beyond itself, but simply felt pain when the body was hurt, or pleasure when anything beneficial to the body occurred, or if the body was so highly affected that it was neither greatly benefited nor hurt, the mind experienced the sensations we call tastes, smells, sounds, heat, cold, light, colours, and the like, which in truth are representative of nothing existing out of our mind, and which vary according to the diversities of the parts and modes in which the body is affected.* The mind at the same time also perceived magnitudes, figures, motions, and the like, which were not presented to it as sensations but as things or the modes of things existing, or at least capable of existing out of thought, although it did not yet observe this difference between these two kinds of perceptions. And afterwards when the machine of the body, which has been so fabricated by nature that it can of its own inherent power move itself in various ways, by turning itself at random on every side, followed after what was useful and avoided what was detrimental; the mind, which was closely connected with it, reflecting on the objects it pursued or avoided, remarked, for the first time, that they existed out of itself, and not only attributed to them magnitudes, figures, motions, and the like, which it apprehended either as things or as the modes of things,

* "which vary according to the diversities of the movements that pass from all parts of our body to the part of the brain to which it (the mind) is closely joined and united."— *French.*

but, in addition, attributed to them tastes, odours, and the other ideas of that sort, the sensations of which were caused by itself;* and as it only considered other objects in so far as they were useful to the body, in which it was immersed, it judged that there was greater or less reality in each object, according as the impressions it caused on the body were more or less powerful. Hence arose the belief that there was more substance or body in rocks and metals than in air or water, because the mind perceived in them more hardness and weight. Moreover, the air was thought to be merely nothing so long as we experienced no agitation of it by the wind, or did not feel it hot or cold. And because the stars gave hardly more light than the slender flames of candles, we supposed that each star was but of this size. Again, since the mind did not observe that the earth moved on its axis, or that its superficies was curved like that of a globe, it was on that account more ready to judge the earth immovable and its surface flat. And our mind has been imbued from our infancy with a thousand other prejudices of the same sort which afterwards in our youth we forgot we had accepted without sufficient examination, and admitted as possessed of the highest truth and clearness, as if they had been known by means of our senses, or implanted in us by nature.

LXXII. *That the second cause of our errors is that we cannot forget these prejudices.*

And although now in our mature years, when the mind, being no longer wholly subject to the body, is not in the habit of referring all things to it, but also

* "which it perceived on occasion of them" (*i. e.*, of external objects).—*French.*

seeks to discover the truth of things considered in themselves, we observe the falsehood of a great many of the judgments we had before formed; yet we experience a difficulty in expunging them from our memory, and, so long as they remain there, they give rise to various errors. Thus, for example, since from our earliest years we imagined the stars to be of very small size, we find it highly difficult to rid ourselves of this imagination, although assured by plain astronomical reasons that they are of the greatest,—so prevailing is the power of preconceived opinion.

LXXIII. The third cause is, that we become fatigued by attending to those objects which are not present to the senses; and that we are thus accustomed to judge of these not from present perception but from pre-conceived opinion.

Besides, our mind cannot attend to any object without at length experiencing some pain and fatigue; and of all objects it has the greatest difficulty in attending to those which are present neither to the senses nor to the imagination: whether for the reason that this is natural to it from its union with the body, or because in our early years, being occupied merely with perceptions and imaginations, it has become more familiar with, and acquired greater facility in thinking in those modes than in any other. Hence it also happens that many are unable to conceive any substance except what is imaginable and corporeal, and even sensible. For they are ignorant of the circumstance, that those objects alone are imaginable which consist in extension, motion, and figure, while there are many others besides these that are intelligible; and they persuade themselves that nothing can subsist but body, and, finally, that there is no body which is not sensible. And since in truth we perceive no object such as it is by sense alone [but only by our reason exercised upon sensible objects], as will hereafter be clearly shown, it thus happens that the majority during life perceive nothing unless in a confused way.

LXXIV. The fourth source of our errors is, that we attach our thoughts to words which do not express them with accuracy.

Finally, since for the use of speech we attach all our conceptions to words by which to express them, and commit to memory our thoughts in connection with these terms, and as we afterwards find it more easy to recall the words than the things signified by them, we can scarcely conceive anything with such distinctness as to separate entirely what we conceive from the words that were selected to express it. On this account the majority attend to words rather than to things; and thus very frequently assent to terms without attaching to them any meaning, either because they think they once understood them, or imagine they received them from others by whom they were correctly understood. This, however, is not the place to treat of this matter in detail, seeing the nature of the human body has not yet been expounded, nor the existence even of body established; enough, nevertheless, appears to have been said to enable one to distinguish such of our conceptions as are clear and distinct from those that are obscure and confused.

LXXV. Summary of what must be observed in order to philosophize correctly.

Wherefore if we would philosophize in earnest, and give ourselves to the search after all the truths we are capable of knowing, we must, in the first place, lay aside our prejudices; in other words, we must take care scrupulously to withhold our assent from the opinions we have formerly admitted, until upon new examination we discover that they are true. We must, in the next place, make an orderly review of the notions we have in our minds, and hold as true all and only those which we will clearly and distinctly apprehend. In this way we will observe, first of all, that we exist in so far as it is our nature to think, and at the same time that there is a God upon whom we depend; and after considering his attributes we will be able to investigate the truth of all other things, since God is the cause of them. Besides the notions we have of God and of our mind, we will likewise find that we possess the knowledge of many propositions which are eternally true, as, for example, that nothing cannot be the cause of anything, etc. We will farther discover in our minds the knowledge of a corporeal or extended nature that may be moved, divided, etc., and also of certain sensations that affect us, as of pain, colours, tastes, etc., although we do not yet know the cause of our being so affected; and, comparing what we have now learned, by examining those things in their order, with our former confused knowledge of them, we will acquire the habit of forming clear and distinct conceptions of all the objects we are capable of knowing. In these few precepts seem to me to be comprised the most general and important principles of human knowledge.

LXXVI. That we ought to prefer the Divine authority to our perception;* but that, apart from things

* " reasonings."—*French.*

revealed, we ought to assent to nothing that we do not clearly apprehend.

Above all, we must impress on our memory the infallible rule, that what God has revealed is incomparably more certain than anything else; and that we ought to submit our belief to the Divine authority rather than to our own judgment, even although perhaps the light of reason should, with the greatest clearness and evidence, appear to suggest to us something contrary to what is revealed. But in things regarding which there is no revelation, it is by no means consistent with the character of a philosopher to accept as true what he has not ascertained to be such, and to trust more to the senses, in other words, to the inconsiderate judgments of childhood than to the dictates of mature reason.

PART II.

OF THE PRINCIPLES OF MATERIAL THINGS.

I. THE grounds on which the existence of material things may be known with certainty.

Although we are all sufficiently persuaded of the existence of material things, yet, since this was before called in question by us, and since we reckoned the persuasion of their existence as among the prejudices of our childhood, it is now necessary for us to investigate the grounds on which this truth may be known with certainty. In the first place, then, it cannot be doubted that every perception we have comes to us from some object different from our mind; for it is not in our power to cause ourselves to experience one perception rather than another, the perception being entirely dependent on the object which affects our senses. It may, indeed, be matter of inquiry whether that object be God, or something different from God; but because we perceive, or rather, stimulated by sense, clearly and distinctly apprehend, certain matter extended in length, breadth, and thickness, the various parts of which have different figures and motions, and give rise to the sensation we have of colours, smells, pain, etc., God would, without question, deserve to be regarded as a deceiver, if he directly and of himself presented to our mind the idea of this extended matter, or merely caused it to be presented to us by some object which possessed neither extension, figure, nor motion. For we clearly conceive this matter as entirely distinct from God, and from ourselves, or our mind; and appear even clearly to discern that the idea of it is formed in us on occasion of objects existing out of our minds, to which it is in every respect similar. But since God cannot deceive us, for this is repugnant to his nature, as has been already remarked, we must unhesitatingly conclude that there exists a certain object extended in length, breadth, and thickness, and possessing all those properties which we clearly apprehend to belong to what is extended. And this extended substance is what we call body or matter.

II. How we likewise know that the human body is closely connected with the mind.

We ought also to conclude that a certain body is more closely united to our mind than any other, because we clearly observe that pain and other sensations affect us without our foreseeing them; and these, the mind is conscious, do not arise from itself alone, nor pertain to it, in so far as it is a thing which thinks, but only in so far as it is united to another thing extended and movable, which is called the human body. But this is not the place to treat in detail of this matter.

III. That the perceptions of the senses do not teach us what is in reality in things, but what is beneficial or hurtful to the composite whole of mind and body.

It will be sufficient to remark that the perceptions of the senses are merely to be referred to this intimate union of the human body and mind, and that they usually make us aware of what, in external objects, may be useful or adverse to this union, but do not present to us these objects as they are in themselves, unless occasionally and by accident. For, after this observation, we will without difficulty lay aside the prejudices of the senses, and will have recourse to our understanding alone on this question by reflecting carefully on the ideas implanted in it by nature.

IV. That the nature of body consists not in weight hardness, colour and the like, but in extension alone.

In this way we will discern that the nature of matter or body, considered in general, does not consist in its being hard, or ponderous, or coloured, or that which affects our senses in any other way, but simply in its being a substance extended in length, breadth, and depth. For with respect to hardness, we know nothing of it by sense farther than that the parts of hard bodies resist the motion of our hands on coming into contact with them; but if every time our hands moved towards any part, all the bodies in that place receded as quickly as our hands approached, we should never feel hardness; and yet we have no reason to believe that bodies which might thus recede would on this account lose that which makes them bodies. The nature of body does not, therefore, consist in hardness. In the same way, it may be shown that weight, colour, and all the other qualities of this sort, which are perceived in corporeal matter, may be taken from it, itself meanwhile remaining entire: it thus follows that the nature of body depends on none of these.

V. That the truth regarding the nature of body is obscured by the opinions respecting rarefaction and a vacuum with which we are pre-occupied.

There still remain two causes to prevent its being fully admitted that the true nature of body consists in extension alone. The first is the prevalent opinion, that most bodies admit of being so rarefied and condensed that, when rarefied, they have greater extension than when condensed; and some even have subtilized to such a degree as to make a distinction between the substance of body and its quantity, and between quantity itself and extension. The second cause is this, that where we conceive only extension in length, breadth, and depth, we are not in the habit of saying that body is there, but only space and further void space, which the generality believe to be a mere negation.

VI. In what way rarefaction takes place.

But with regard to rarefaction and condensation, whoever gives his attention to his own thoughts, and admits nothing of which he is not clearly conscious, will not suppose that there is anything in those processes further than a change of figure in the body rarefied or condensed: so that, in other words, rare bodies are those between the parts of which there are numerous distances filled with other bodies; and dense bodies, on the other hand, those whose parts approaching each other, either diminish these distances or take them wholly away, in the latter of which cases the body is rendered absolutely dense. The body, however, when condensed, has not, therefore, less extension than when the parts embrace a greater space, owing to their removal from each other, and their dispersion into branches. For we ought not to attribute to it the extension of the pores or distances which its parts do not occupy when it is rarefied, but to the other bodies that fill these interstices; just as when we see a sponge full of water or any other liquid, we do not suppose that each part of the sponge has cn this account greater extension than when compressed and dry, but only that its pores are wider, and therefore that the body is diffused over a larger space.

VII. That rarefaction cannot be intelligibly explained unless in the way here proposed.

And indeed I am unable to discover the force of the reasons which have induced some to say that rarefaction is the result of the augmentation of the quantity of body, rather than to explain it on the principle exemplified in the case of a sponge. For although when air or water is rarefied we do not see any of the pores that are rendered large, or the new body that is added to occupy them, it is yet less agreeable to reason to suppose something that is unintelligible for the purpose of giving a verbal and merely apparent explanation of the rarefaction of bodies, than to conclude, because of their rarefaction, that there are pores or distances between the parts which are increased in size, and filled with some new body. Nor ought we to refrain from assenting to this explanation, because we perceive this new body by none of our senses, for there is no reason which obliges us to believe that we should perceive by our senses all the bodies in existence. And we see that it is very easy to explain rarefaction in this manner, but impossible in any other; for, in fine, there would be, as appears to me, a manifest contradiction in supposing that any body was increased by a quantity or extension which it had not before, without the addition to it of a new extended substance, in other words, of another body, because it is impossible to conceive any addition of extension or quantity to a thing without supposing the addition of a substance having quantity or extension, as will more clearly appear from what follows.

VIII. *That quantity and number differ only in thought (ratione) from that which has quantity and is numbered.*

For quantity differs from extended substance, and number from what is numbered, not in reality but merely in our thought; so that, for example, we may consider the whole nature of a corporeal substance which is comprised in a space of ten feet, although we do not attend to this measure of ten feet, for the obvious reason that the thing conceived is of the same nature in any part of that space as in the whole; and, on the other hand, we can conceive the number ten, as also a continuous quantity of ten feet, without thinking of this determinate substance, because the concept of the number ten is manifestly the same whether we consider a number of ten feet or ten of anything else; and we can conceive a continuous quantity of ten feet without thinking of this or that determinate substance, although we cannot conceive it without some extended substance of which it is the quantity. It is in reality, however, impossible that any, even the least part, of such quantity or extension, can be taken away, without the retrenchment at the same time of as much of the substance, nor, on the other hand, can we lessen the substance, without at the same time taking as much from the quantity or extension.

IX. *That corporeal substance, when distinguished from its quantity, is confusedly conceived as something incorporeal.*

Although perhaps some express themselves otherwise on this matter, I am nevertheless convinced that they do not think differently from what I have now said: for when they distinguish (corporeal) substance from extension or quantity, they either mean nothing by the word (corporeal) substance, or they form in their minds merely a confused idea of incorporeal substance, which they falsely attribute to corporeal, and leave to extension the true idea of this corporeal substance; which extension they call an accident, but with such impropriety as to make it easy to discover that their words are not in harmony with their thoughts.

X. What space or internal place is.

Space or internal place, and the corporeal substance which is comprised in it, are not different in reality, but merely in the mode in which they are wont to be conceived by us. For, in truth, the same extension in length, breadth, and depth, which constitutes space, constitutes body; and the difference between them lies only in this, that in body we consider extension as particular, and conceive it to change with the body; whereas in space we attribute to extension a generic unity, so that after taking from a certain space the body which occupied it, we do not suppose that we have at the same time removed the extension of the space, because it appears to us that the same extension remains there so long as it is of the same magnitude and figure, and preserves the same situation in respect to certain bodies around it, by means of which we determine this space.

XI. How space is not in reality different from corporeal substance.

And indeed it will be easy to discern that it is the same extension which constitutes the nature of body as of space, and that these two things are mutually diverse only as the nature of the genus and species differs from that of the individual, provided we reflect on the idea we have of any body, taking a stone for example, and reject all that is not essential to the nature of body. In the first place, then, hardness may be rejected, because if the stone were liquefied or reduced to powder, it would no longer possess hardness, and yet would not cease to be a body; colour also may be thrown out of account, because we have frequently seen stones so transparent as to have no colour; again, we may reject weight, because we have the case of fire, which, though very light, is still a body; and, finally, we may reject cold, heat, and all the other qualities of this sort, either because they are not considered as in the stone, or because, with the change of these qualities, the stone is not supposed to have lost the nature of body. After this examination we will find that nothing remains in the idea of body, except that it is something extended in length, breadth, and depth; and this something is comprised in our idea of space, not only of that which is full of body, but even of what is called void space.

XII. *How space differs from body in our mode of conceiving it.*

There is, however, some difference between them in the mode of conception; for if we remove a stone from the space or place in which it was, we conceive that its extension also is taken away, because we regard this as particular, and inseparable from the stone itself: but meanwhile we suppose that the same extension of place in which this stone was remains, although the place of the stone be occupied by wood, water, air, or by any other body, or be even supposed vacant, because we now consider extension in general, and think that the same is common to stones, wood, water, air, and other bodies, and even to a vacuum itself, if there is any such thing, provided it be of the same magnitude and figure as before, and preserve the same situation among the external bodies which determine this space.

XIII. What external place is.

The reason of which is, that the words place and space signify nothing really different from body which is said to be in place, but merely designate its magnitude, figure, and situation among other bodies. For it is necessary, in order to determine this situation, to regard certain other bodies which we consider as immovable; and, according as we look to different bodies, we may see that the same thing at the same time does and does not change place. For example, when a vessel is being carried out to sea, a person sitting at the stern may be said to remain always in one place, if we look to the parts of the vessel, since with respect to these he preserves the same situation; and on the other hand, if regard be had to the neighbouring shores, the same person will seem to be perpetually changing place, seeing he is constantly receding from one shore and approaching another. And besides, if we suppose that the earth moves, and that it makes precisely as much way from west to east as the vessel from east to west, we will again say that the person at the stern does not change his place, because this place will be determined by certain immovable points which we imagine to be in the heavens. But if at length we are persuaded that there are no points really immovable in the universe, as will hereafter be shown to be probable, we will thence conclude that nothing has a permanent place unless in so far as it is fixed by our thought.

XIV. Wherein place and space differ.

The terms place and space, however, differ in signification, because place more expressly designates situation than magnitude or figure, while, on the other hand, we think of the latter when we speak of space. For we frequently say that a thing succeeds to the place of another, although it be not exactly of the same magnitude or figure; but we do not therefore admit that it occupies the same space as the other; and when the situation is changed we say that the place also is changed, although there are the same magnitude and figure as before: so that when we say that a thing is in a particular place, we mean merely that it is situated in a determinate way in respect of certain other objects; and when we add that it occupies such a space or place, we understand besides that it is of such determinate magnitude and figure as exactly to fill this space.

XV. How external place is rightly taken for the superficies of the surrounding body.

And thus we never indeed distinguish space from extension in length, breadth, and depth; we sometimes, however, consider place as in the thing placed, and at other times as out of it. Internal place indeed differs in no way from space; but external place may be taken for the superficies that immediately surrounds the thing placed. It ought to be remarked that by superficies we do not here understand any part of the surrounding body, but only the boundary between the surrounding and surrounded bodies, which is nothing more than a mode; or at least that we speak of superficies in general which is no part of one body rather than another, but is always considered the same, provided it retain the same magnitude and figure. For although the whole surrounding body with its superficies were changed, it would not be supposed that the body which was surrounded by it had therefore changed its place, if it meanwhile preserved the same situation with respect to the other bodies that are regarded as immovable. Thus, if we suppose that a boat is carried in one direction by the current of a stream, and impelled by the wind in the opposite with an equal force, so that its situation with respect to the banks is not changed, we will readily admit that it remains in the same place, although the whole superficies which surrounds it is incessantly changing.

XVI. That a vacuum or space in which there is absolutely no body is repugnant to reason.

With regard to a vacuum, in the philosophical sense of the term, that is, a space in which there is no substance, it is evident that such does not exist, seeing the extension of space or internal place is not different from that of body. For since from this alone, that a body has extension in length, breadth, and depth, we have reason to conclude that it is a substance, it being absolutely contradictory that nothing should possess extension, we ought to form a similar inference regarding the space which is supposed void, viz., that since there is extension in it there is necessarily also substance.

XVII. That a vacuum in the ordinary use of the term does not exclude all body.

And, in truth, by the term vacuum in its common

use, we do not mean a place or space in which there is absolutely nothing, but only a place in which there is none of those things we presume ought to be there. Thus, because a pitcher is made to hold water, it is said to be empty when it is merely filled with air; or if there are no fish in a fish-pond, we say there is nothing in it, although it be full of water; thus a vessel is said to be empty, when, in place of the merchandise which it was designed to carry, it is loaded with sand only, to enable it to resist the violence of the wind; and, finally, it is in the same sense that we say space is void when it contains nothing sensible, although it contain created and self-subsisting matter; for we are not in the habit of considering the bodies near us, unless in so far as they cause in our organs of sense, impressions strong enough to enable us to perceive them. And if, in place of keeping in mind what ought to be understood by these terms a vacuum and nothing, we afterwards suppose that in the space we called a vacuum, there is not only no sensible object, but no object at all, we will fall into the same error as if, because a pitcher in which there is nothing but air, is, in common speech, said to be empty, we were therefore to judge that the air contained in it is not a substance (*res subsistens*).

XVIII. How the prejudice of an absolute vacuum is to be corrected.

We have almost all fallen into this error from the earliest age, for, observing that there is no necessary connection between a vessel and the body it contains, we thought that God at least could take from a vessel the body which occupied it, without it being necessary that any other should be put in the place of the one removed. But that we may be able now to correct this false opinion, it is necessary to remark that there is in truth no connection between the vessel and the particular body which it contains, but that there is an absolutely necessary connection between the concave figure of the vessel and the extension considered generally which must be comprised in this cavity; so that it is not more contradictory to conceive a mountain without a valley than such a cavity without the extension it contains, or this extension apart from an extended substance, for, as we have often said, of nothing there can be no extension. And accordingly, if it be asked what would happen were God to remove from a vessel all the body contained in it, without permitting another body to occupy its place, the answer must be that the sides of the vessel would thus come into proximity with each other. For two bodies must touch each other when there is nothing between them, and it is manifestly contradictory for two bodies to be apart, in other words, that there should be a distance between them, and this distance yet be nothing; for all distance is a mode of extension, and cannot therefore exist without an extended substance.

XIX. That this confirms what was said of rarefaction.

After we have thus remarked that the nature of corporeal substance consists only in its being an extended thing, and that its extension is not different from that which we attribute to space, however empty, it is easy to discover the impossibility of any one of its parts in any way whatsoever occupying more space at one time than at another, and thus of being otherwise rarefied than in the way explained above; and it is easy to perceive also that there cannot be more matter or body in a vessel when it is filled with lead or gold, or any other body however heavy and hard, than when it but contains air and is supposed to be empty: for the quantity of the parts of which a body is composed does not depend on their weight or hardness, but only on the extension, which is always equal in the same vase.

XX. *That from this the non-existence of atoms may likewise be demonstrated.*

We likewise discover that there cannot exist any atoms or parts of matter that are of their own nature indivisible. For however small we suppose these parts to be, yet because they are necessarily extended, we are always able in thought to divide any one of them into two or more smaller parts, and may accordingly admit their divisibility. For there is nothing we can divide in thought which we do not thereby recognize to be divisible; and, therefore, were we to judge it indivisible our judgment would not be in harmony with the knowledge we have of the thing; and although we should even suppose that God had reduced any particle of matter to a smallness so extreme that it did not admit of being further divided, it would nevertheless be improperly styled indivisible, for though God had rendered the particle so small that it was not in the power of any creature to divide it, he could not however deprive himself of the ability to do so, since it is absolutely impossible for him to lessen his own omnipotence, as was before observed. Wherefore, absolutely speaking, the smallest extended particle is always divisible, since it is such of its very nature.

XXI. *It is thus also demonstrated that the extension of the world is indefinite.*

We further discover that this world or the whole (*universitas*) of corporeal substance, is extended without limit, for wherever we fix a limit, we still not only imagine beyond it spaces indefinitely extended, but perceive these to be truly imaginable, in other words, to be in reality such as we imagine them; so that they contain in them corporeal substance indefinitely extended, for, as has been already shown at length, the idea of extension which we conceive in any space whatever is plainly identical with the idea of corporeal substance.

XXII. It also follows that the matter of the heavens and earth is the same, and that there cannot be a plurality of worlds.

And it may also be easily inferred from all this that the earth and heavens are made of the same matter; and that even although there were an infinity of worlds, they would all be composed of this matter; from which it follows that a plurality of worlds is impossible, because we clearly conceive that the matter whose nature consists only in its being an extended substance, already wholly occupies all the imaginable spaces where these other worlds could alone be, and we cannot find in ourselves the idea of any other matter.

XXIII. That all the variety of matter, or the diversity of its forms, depends on motion.

There is therefore but one kind of matter in the whole universe, and this we know only by its being extended. All the properties we distinctly perceive to belong to it are reducible to its capacity of being divided and moved according to its parts; and accordingly it is capable of all those affections which we perceive can arise from the motion of its parts. For the partition of matter in thought makes no change in it; but all variation of it, or diversity of form, depends on motion. The philosophers even seem universally to have observed this, for they said that nature was the principle of motion and rest, and by nature they understood that by which all corporeal things become such as they are found in experience.

XXIV. *What motion is, taking the term in its common use.*

But motion (viz., local, for I can conceive no other kind of motion, and therefore I do not think we ought to suppose there is any other in nature), in the ordinary sense of the term, is nothing more than the *action by which a body passes from one place to another.* And just as we have remarked above that the same thing may be said to change and not to change place at the same time, so also we may say that the same thing is at the same time moved and not moved. Thus, for example, a person seated in a vessel which is setting sail, thinks he is in motion if he look to the shore that he has left, and consider it as fixed; but not if he regard the ship itself, among the parts of which he preserves always the same situation. Moreover, because we are accustomed to suppose that there is no motion without action, and that in rest there is the cessation of action, the person thus seated is more properly said to be at rest than in motion, seeing he is not conscious of being in action.

XXV. *What motion is properly so called.*

But if, instead of occupying ourselves with that which has no foundation, unless in ordinary usage, we desire to know what ought to be understood by motion according to the truth of the thing, we may say, in order to give it a determinate nature, that it is *the transporting of one part of matter or of one body from the vicinity of those bodies that are in immediate contact with it, or which we regard as at rest,*[9] *to the vicinity of other bodies.* By a body as a part of matter, I understand all that which is transferred together, although it be perhaps composed of several parts, which in themselves have other motions; and I say that it is the transporting and not the force or action which transports, with the view of showing that motion is always in the movable thing, not in that which moves; for it seems to me that we are not accustomed to distinguish these two things with sufficient accuracy. Farther, I understand that it is a mode of the movable thing, and not a substance, just as figure is a property of the thing figured, and repose of that which is at rest.

PART III.

OF THE VISIBLE WORLD.

I. That we cannot think too highly of the works of God.

Having now ascertained certain principles of material things, which were sought, not by the prejudices of the senses, but by the light of reason, and which thus possess so great evidence that we cannot doubt of their truth, it remains for us to consider whether from these alone we can deduce the explication of all the phenomena of nature. We will commence with those phenomena that are of the greatest generality, and upon which the others depend, as, for example, with the general structure of this whole visible world. But in order to our philosophizing aright regarding this, two things are first of all to be observed. The first is, that we should ever bear in mind the infinity of the power and goodness of God, that we may not fear falling into error by imagining his works to be too great, beautiful, and perfect, but that we may, on the contrary, take care lest, by supposing limits to them of which we have no certain knowledge, we appear to think less highly than we ought of the power of God.

II. That we ought to beware lest, in our presumption, we imagine that the ends which God proposed to himself in the creation of the world are understood by us.

The second is, that we should beware of presuming

too highly of ourselves, as it seems we should do if we supposed certain limits to the world, without being assured of their existence either by natural reasons or by divine revelation, as if the power of our thought extended beyond what God has in reality made; but likewise still more if we persuaded ourselves that all things were created by God for us only, or if we merely supposed that we could comprehend by the power of our intellect the ends which God proposed to himself in creating the universe.

III. In what sense it may be said that all things were created for the sake of man.

For although, as far as regards morals, it may be a pious thought to believe that God made all things for us, seeing we may thus be incited to greater gratitude and love toward him; and although it is even in some sense true, because there is no created thing of which we cannot make some use, if it be only that of exercising our mind in considering it, and honouring God on account of it, it is yet by no means probable that all things were created for us in this way that God had no other end in their creation; and this supposition would be plainly ridiculous and inept in physical reasoning, for we do not doubt but that many things exist, or formerly existed and have now ceased to be, which were never seen or known by man, and were never of use to him.

PART IV.

OF THE EARTH.

CLXXXVIII. *Of what is to be borrowed from disquisitions on animals and man to advance the knowledge of material objects.*

I should add nothing farther to this the Fourth Part of the Principles of Philosophy, did I purpose carrying out my original design of writing a Fifth and Sixth Part, the one treating of things possessed of life, that is, animals and plants, and the other of man. But because I have not yet acquired sufficient knowledge of all the matters of which I should desire to treat in these two last parts, and do not know whether I shall ever have sufficient leisure to finish them, I will here subjoin a few things regarding the objects of our senses, that I may not, for the sake of the latter, delay too long the publication of the former parts, or of what may be desiderated in them, which I might have reserved for explanation in those others: for I have hitherto described this earth, and generally the whole visible world, as if it were merely a machine in which there was nothing at all to consider except the figures and motions of its parts, whereas our senses present to us many other things, for example colours, smells, sounds, and the like, of which, if I did not speak at all, it would be thought I had omitted the explication of the majority of the objects that are in nature.

CLXXXIX. What perception (*sensus*) is, and how we perceive.

We must know, therefore, that although the human soul is united to the whole body, it has, nevertheless, its principal seat in the brain, where alone it not only understands and imagines, but also perceives; and this by the medium of the nerves, which are extended like threads from the brain to all the other members, with which they are so connected that we can hardly touch any one of them without moving the extremities of some of the nerves spread over it; and this motion passes to the other extremities of those nerves which are collected in the brain round the seat of the soul,[*] as I have already explained with sufficient minuteness in the fourth chapter of the Dioptrics. But the movements which are thus excited in the brain by the nerves variously affect the soul or mind, which is intimately conjoined with the brain, according to the diversity of the motions themselves. And the diverse affections of the mind or thoughts that immediately arise from these motions, are called perceptions of the senses (*sensuum perceptiones*), or, as we commonly speak, sensations (*sensus*).

CXC. Of the distinction of the senses; and, first, of the internal, that is, of the affections of the mind (passions), and the natural appetites.

The varieties of these sensations depend, firstly, on the diversity of the nerves themselves, and, secondly, of the movements that are made in each nerve. We have not, however, as many different senses as there are nerves. We can distinguish but seven principal

---

[*] " common sense."—*French.*

classes of nerves, of which two belong to the internal, and the other five to the external senses. The nerves which extend to the stomach, the œsophagus, the fauces, and the other internal parts that are subservient to our natural wants, constitute one of our internal senses. This is called the natural appetite (*appetitus naturalis*). The other internal sense, which embraces all the emotions (*commotiones*) of the mind or passions, and affections, as joy, sadness, love, hate, and the like, depends upon the nerves which extend to the heart and the parts about the heart, and are exceedingly small; for, by way of example, when the blood happens to be pure and well tempered, so that it dilates in the heart more readily and strongly than usual, this so enlarges and moves the small nerves scattered around the orifices, that there is thence a corresponding movement in the brain, which affects the mind with a certain natural feeling of joy; and as often as these same nerves are moved in the same way, although this is by other causes, they excite in our mind the same feeling (*sensus, sentiment*). Thus, the imagination of the enjoyment of a good does not contain in itself the feeling of joy, but it causes the animal spirits to pass from the brain to the muscles in which these nerves are inserted; and thus dilating the orifices of the heart, it also causes these small nerves to move in the way appointed by nature to afford the sensation of joy. Thus, when we receive news, the mind first of all judges of it, and if the news be good, it rejoices with that intellectual joy (*gaudium intellectuale*) which is independent of any emotion (*commotio*) of the body, and which the Stoics did not deny to their wise man [although they supposed him exempt from all passion]. But as soon as this joy passes from the understanding to the imagination, the spirits flow from the brain to the muscles that are about the heart, and there excite the motion of the small nerves, by means of which another motion is caused in the brain, which affects the mind with the sensation of animal joy (*laetitia animalis*). On the same principle, when the blood is so thick that it flows but sparingly into the ventricles of the heart, and is not there sufficiently dilated, it excites in the same nerves a motion quite different from the preceding, which, communicated to the brain, gives to the mind the sensation of sadness, although the mind itself is perhaps ignorant of the cause of its sadness. And all the other causes which move these nerves in the same way may also give to the mind the same sensation. But the other movements of the same nerves produce other effects, as the feelings of love, hate, fear, anger, etc., as far as they are merely affections or passions of the mind; in other words, as far as they are confused thoughts which the mind has not from itself alone, but from its being closely joined to the body, from which it receives impressions; for there is the widest difference between these passions and the distinct thoughts which we have of what ought to be loved, or chosen, or shunned, etc., [although these are often enough found together]. The natural appetites, as hunger, thirst, and the others, are likewise sensations excited in the mind by means of the nerves of the stomach, fauces, and other parts, and are entirely different from the will which we have to eat, drink, [and to do all that which we think proper for the conservation of our body] ; but, because this will or appetition almost always accompanies them, they are therefore named appetites.

CXCI. Of the external senses; and first of touch.

We commonly reckon the external senses five in number, because there are as many different kinds of objects which move the nerves and their organs, and an equal number of kinds of confused thoughts excited in the soul by these emotions. In the first place, the nerves terminating in the skin of the whole body can be touched through this medium by any terrene objects whatever, and moved by these wholes, in one way by their hardness, in another by their gravity, in a third by their heat, in a fourth by their humidity, etc.—and in as many diverse modes as they are either moved or hindered from their ordinary motion, to that extent are diverse sensations excited in the mind, from which a corresponding number of tactile qualities derive their appellations. Besides this, when these nerves are moved a little more powerfully than usual, but not nevertheless to the degree by which our body is in any way hurt, there thus arises a sensation of titillation, which is naturally agreeable to the mind, because it testifies to it of the powers of the body with which it is joined, [in that the latter can suffer the action causing this titillation, without being hurt]. But if this action be strong enough to hurt our body in any way, this gives to our mind the sensation of pain. And we thus see why corporeal pleasure and pain, although sensations of quite an opposite character, arise nevertheless from causes nearly alike.

CXCII. Of taste.

In the second place, the other nerves scattered over the tongue and the parts in its vicinity are diversely moved by the particles of the same bodies, separated from each other and floating in the saliva in the mouth, and thus cause sensations of diverse tastes according to the diversity of figure in these particles.*

CXCIII. Of smell.

Thirdly, two nerves also or appendages of the brain, for they do not go beyond the limits of the skull, are moved by the particles of terrestrial bodies, separated and flying in the air, not indeed by all particles indifferently, but by those only that are sufficiently subtle and penetrating to enter the pores of the bone we call the spongy, when drawn into the nostrils, and thus to reach the nerves. From the different motions of these particles arise the sensations of the different smells.

CXCIV. Of hearing.

Fourthly, there are two nerves within the ears, so attached to three small bones that are mutually sustaining, and the first of which rests on the small membrane that covers the cavity we call the tympanum of the ear, that all the diverse vibrations which the surrounding air communicates to this membrane are transmitted to the mind by these nerves, and these vibrations give rise, according to their diversity, to the sensations of the different sounds.

CXCV. Of sight.

Finally, the extremities of the optic nerves, composing the coat in the eyes called the retina, are not moved by the air nor by any terrestrial object, but only by the globules of the second element,[10] whence we have the sense of light and colours: as I have already at suffi-

---

* In the French this section begins, "Taste, after touch the grossest of the senses," etc.

cient length explained in the Dioptrics and treatise of Meteors.*

CXCVI. That the soul perceives only in so far as it is in the brain.

It is clearly established, however, that the soul does not perceive in so far as it is in each member of the body, but only in so far as it is in the brain, where the nerves by their movements convey to it the diverse actions of the external objects that touch the parts of the body in which they are inserted. For, in the first place, there are various maladies, which, though they affect the brain alone, yet bring disorder upon, or deprive us altogether of the use of, our senses, just as sleep, which affects the brain only, and yet takes from us daily during a great part of our time the faculty of perception, which afterwards in our waking state is restored to us. The second proof is, that though there be no disease in the brain, [or in the members in which the organs of the external senses are], it is nevertheless sufficient to take away sensation from the part of the body where the nerves terminate, if only the movement of one of the nerves that extend from the brain to these members be obstructed in any part of the distance that is between the two. And the last proof is, that we sometimes feel pain as if in certain of our members, the cause of which, however, is not in these members where it is felt, but somewhere nearer the brain, through which the nerves pass that give to the mind the sensation of it. I could establish this fact by innumerable experiments; I will

---

* In the French this section begins, "Finally, sight is the most subtle of all the senses," etc.

here, however, merely refer to one of them. A girl suffering from a bad ulcer in the hand, had her eyes bandaged whenever the surgeon came to visit her, not being able to bear the sight of the dressing of the sore; and, the gangrene having spread, after the expiry of a few days the arm was amputated from the elbow [without the girl's knowledge]; linen cloths tied one above the other were substituted in place of the part amputated, so that she remained for some time without knowing that the operation had been performed, and meanwhile she complained of feeling various pains, sometimes in one finger of the hand that was cut off, and sometimes in another. The only explanation of this is, that the nerves which before stretched downwards from the brain to the hand, and then terminated in the arm close to the elbow, were there moved in the same way as they required to be moved before in the hand for the purpose of impressing on the mind residing in the brain the sensation of pain in this or that finger. [And this clearly shows that the pain of the hand is not felt by the mind in so far as it is in the hand, but in so far as it is in the brain.]

CXCVII. *That the nature of the mind is such that from the motion alone of body the various sensations can be excited in it.*

In the next place, it can be proved that our mind is of such a nature that the motions of the body alone are sufficient to excite in it all sorts of thoughts, without it being necessary that these should in any way resemble the motions which give rise to them, and especially that these motions can excite in it those confused thoughts called sensations (*sensus, sensationes*). For we see that words, whether uttered by the voice or merely written, excite in our minds all kinds of thoughts and emotions. On the same paper, with the same pen and ink, by merely moving the point of the pen over the paper in a particular way, we can trace letters that will raise in the minds of our readers the thoughts of combats, tempests, or the furies, and the passions of indignation and sorrow; in place of which, if the pen be moved in another way hardly different from the former, this slight change will cause thoughts widely different from the above, such as those of repose, peace, pleasantness, and the quite opposite passions of love and joy. Some one will perhaps object that writing and speech do not immediately excite in the mind any passions, or imaginations of things different from the letters and sounds, but afford simply the knowledge of these, on occasion of which the mind, understanding the signification of the words, afterwards excites in itself the imaginations and passions that correspond to the words. But what will be said of the sensations of pain and titillation? The motion merely of a sword cutting a part of our skin causes pain, [but does not on that account make us aware of the motion or figure of the sword]. And it is certain that this sensation of pain is not less different from the motion that causes it, or from that of the part of our body which the sword cuts, than are the sensations we have of colour, sound, odour, or taste. On this ground we may conclude that our mind is of such a nature that the motions alone of certain bodies can also easily excite in it all the other sensations, as the motion of a sword excites in it the sensation of pain.

CXCVIII. That by our senses we know nothing of

external objects beyond their figure [or situation], magnitude, and motion.

Besides, we observe no such difference between the nerves as to lead us to judge that one set of them convey to the brain from the organs of the external senses anything different from another, or that anything at all reaches the brain besides the local motion of the nerves themselves. And we see that local motion alone causes in us not only the sensation of titillation and of pain, but also of light and sounds. For if we receive a blow on the eye of sufficient force to cause the vibration of the stroke to reach the retina, we see numerous sparks of fire, which, nevertheless, are not out of our eye; and when we stop our ear with our finger, we hear a humming sound, the cause of which can only proceed from the agitation of the air that is shut up within it. Finally, we frequently observe that heat [hardness, weight], and the other sensible qualities, as far as they are in objects, and also the forms of those bodies that are purely material, as, for example, the forms of fire, are produced in them by the motion of certain other bodies, and that these in their turn likewise produce other motions in other bodies. And we can easily conceive how the motion of one body may be caused by that of another, and diversified by the size, figure, and situation of its parts, but we are wholly unable to conceive how these same things (viz., size, figure, and motion), can produce something else of a nature entirely different from themselves, as, for example, those substantial forms and real qualities which many philosophers suppose to be in bodies; nor likewise can we conceive how these qualities or forms possess force to cause motions in other bodies. But since we know, from the nature of our soul, that the diverse motions of body are sufficient to produce in it all the sensations which it has, and since we learn from experience that several of its sensations are in reality caused by such motions, while we do not discover that anything besides these motions ever passes from the organs of the external senses to the brain, we have reason to conclude that we in no way likewise apprehend that in external objects, which we call light, colour, smell, taste, sound, heat or cold, and the other tactile qualities, or that which we call their substantial forms, unless as the various dispositions of these objects which have the power of moving our nerves in various ways.*

CXCIX. *That there is no phenomenon of nature whose explanation has been omitted in this treatise.*

And thus it may be gathered, from an enumeration that is easily made, that there is no phenomenon of nature whose explanation has been omitted in this treatise; for beyond what is perceived by the senses, there is nothing that can be considered a phenomenon of nature. But leaving out of account motion, magnitude, figure, [and the situation of the parts of each body], which I have explained as they exist in body, we perceive nothing out of us by our senses except light, colours, smells, tastes, sounds, and the tactile qualities; and these I have recently shown to be nothing more, at least so far as they are known to us, than certain dispositions of the objects, consisting in magnitude, figure, and motion.

CC. *That this treatise contains no principles which*

---

* "the diverse figures, situations, magnitudes, and motions of their parts."—*French.*

are not universally received; and that this philosophy is not new, but of all others the most ancient and common.

But I am desirous also that it should be observed that, though I have here endeavoured to give an explanation of the whole nature of material things, I have nevertheless made use of no principle which was not received and approved by Aristotle, and by the other philosophers of all ages; so that this philosophy, so far from being new, is of all others the most ancient and common: for I have in truth merely considered the figure, motion, and magnitude of bodies, and examined what must follow from their mutual concourse on the principles of mechanics, which are confirmed by certain and daily experience. But no one ever doubted that bodies are moved, and that they are of various sizes and figures, according to the diversity of which their motions also vary, and that from mutual collision those somewhat greater than others are divided into many smaller, and thus change figure. We have experience of the truth of this, not merely by a single sense, but by several, as touch, sight, and hearing: we also distinctly imagine and understand it. This cannot be said of any of the other things that fall under our senses, as colours, sounds, and the like; for each of these affects but one of our senses, and merely impresses upon our imagination a confused image of itself, affording our understanding no distinct knowledge of what it is.

CCI. That sensible bodies are composed of insensible particles.

But I allow many particles in each body that are perceived by none of our senses, and this will not perhaps be approved of by those who take the senses for the measure of the knowable. [We greatly wrong human reason, however, as appears to me, if we suppose that it does not go beyond the eye-sight]; for no one can doubt that there are bodies so small as not to be perceptible by any of our senses, provided he only consider what is each moment added to those bodies that are being increased little by little, and what is taken from those that are diminished in the same way. A tree increases daily, and it is impossible to conceive how it becomes greater than it was before, unless we at the same time conceive that some body is added to it. But who ever observed by the senses those small bodies that are in one day added to a tree while growing? Among the philosophers at least, those who hold that quantity is indefinitely divisible, ought to admit that in the division the parts may become so small as to be wholly imperceptible. And indeed it ought not to be a matter of surprise, that we are unable to perceive very minute bodies; for the nerves that must be moved by objects to cause perception are not themselves very minute, but are like small cords, being composed of a quantity of smaller fibres, and thus the most minute bodies are not capable of moving them. Nor do I think that any one who makes use of his reason will deny that we philosophize with much greater truth when we judge of what takes place in those small bodies which are imperceptible from their minuteness only, after the analogy of what we see occurring in those we do perceive, [and in this way explain all that is in nature, as I have essayed to do in this treatise], than when we give an explanation of the same things by inventing I know not what novelties, that have no rela-

PART IV. 207

tion to the things we actually perceive, [as first matter, substantial forms, and all that grand array of qualities which many are in the habit of supposing, each of which is more difficult to comprehend than all that is professed to be explained by means of them].

CCII. That the philosophy of Democritus is not less different from ours than from the common.*

But it may be said that Democritus also supposed certain corpuscles that were of various figures, sizes, and motions, from the heaping together and mutual concourse of which all sensible bodies arose; and, nevertheless, his mode of philosophizing is commonly rejected by all. To this I reply that the philosophy of Democritus was never rejected by any one, because he allowed the existence of bodies smaller than those we perceive, and attributed to them diverse sizes, figures, and motions, for no one can doubt that there are in reality such, as we have already shown; but it was rejected, in the first place, because he supposed that these corpuscles were indivisible, on which ground I also reject it; in the second place, because he imagined there was a vacuum about them, which I show to be impossible; thirdly, because he attributed gravity to these bodies, of which I deny the existence in any body, in so far as a body is considered by itself, because it is a quality that depends on the relations of situation and motion which several bodies bear to each other; and, finally, because he has not explained in particular how all things arose from the concourse of corpuscles alone, or, if he gave this explanation with regard to a few of them, his whole reasoning was far from being coherent,

---

* "that of Aristotle or the others."—*French.*

[or such as would warrant us in extending the same explanation to the whole of nature]. This, at least, is the verdict we must give regarding his philosophy, if we may judge of his opinions from what has been handed down to us in writing. I leave it to others to determine whether the philosophy I profess possesses a valid coherency, [and whether on its principles we can make the requisite number of deductions; and, inasmuch as the consideration of figure, magnitude, and motion has been admitted by Aristotle and by all the others, as well as by Democritus, and since I reject all that the latter has supposed, with this single exception, while I reject generally all that has been supposed by the others, it is plain that this mode of philosophizing has no more affinity with that of Democritus than of any other particular sect].

CCIII. *How we may arrive at the knowledge of the figures, [magnitudes], and motions of the insensible particles of bodies.*

But, since I assign determinate figures, magnitudes, and motions to the insensible particles of bodies, as if I had seen them, whereas I admit that they do not fall under the senses, some one will perhaps demand how I have come by my knowledge of them. [To this I reply, that I first considered in general all the clear and distinct notions of material things that are to be found in our understanding, and that, finding no others except those of figures, magnitudes, and motions, and of the rules according to which these three things can be diversified by each other, which rules are the principles of geometry and mechanics, I judged that all the knowledge man can have of nature must of necessity be drawn from this source; because all the other notions we have of sensible things, as confused and obscure, can be of no avail in affording us the knowledge of anything out of ourselves, but must serve rather to impede it]. Thereupon, taking as my ground of inference the simplest and best known of the principles that have been implanted in our minds by nature, I considered the chief differences that could possibly subsist between the magnitudes, and figures, and situations of bodies insensible on account of their smallness alone, and what sensible effects could be produced by their various modes of coming into contact; and afterwards, when I found like effects in the bodies that we perceive by our senses, I judged that they could have been thus produced, especially since no other mode of explaining them could be devised. And in this matter the example of several bodies made by art was of great service to me: for I recognize no difference between these and natural bodies beyond this, that the effects of machines depend for the most part on the agency of certain instruments, which, as they must bear some proportion to the hands of those who make them, are always so large that their figures and motions can be seen; in place of which, the effects of natural bodies almost always depend upon certain organs so minute as to escape our senses. And it is certain that all the rules of mechanics belong also to physics, of which it is a part or species, [so that all that is artificial is withal natural]: for it is not less natural for a clock, made of the requisite number of wheels, to mark the hours, than for a tree, which has sprung from this or that seed, to produce the fruit peculiar to it. Accordingly, just as those who are familiar with automata, when they are informed of the use of a machine, and see some of its parts, easily infer from these the way in which the others, that are not seen by them, are made; so from considering the sensible effects and parts of natural bodies, I have essayed to determine the character of their causes and insensible parts.

CCIV. *That, touching the things which our senses do not perceive, it is sufficient to explain how they can be,* [*and that this is all that Aristotle has essayed*].

But here some one will perhaps reply, that although I have supposed causes which could produce all natural objects, we ought not on this account to conclude that they were produced by these causes; for, just as the same artisan can make two clocks, which, though they both equally well indicate the time, and are not different in outward appearance, have nevertheless nothing resembling in the composition of their wheels; so doubtless the Supreme Maker of things has an infinity of diverse means at his disposal, by each of which he could have made all the things of this world to appear as we see them, without it being possible for the human mind to know which of all these means he chose to employ. I most freely concede this; and I believe that I have done all that was required, if the causes I have assigned are such that their effects accurately correspond to all the phenomena of nature, without determining whether it is by these or by others that they are actually produced. And it will be sufficient for the use of life to know the causes thus imagined, for medicine, mechanics, and in general all the arts to which the knowledge of physics is of service, have for their end only those effects that are sensible, and that are accordingly to be reckoned among the phenomena of nature.* And lest it should be supposed that Aristotle did, or professed to do, anything more than this, it ought to be remembered that he himself expressly says, at the commencement of the seventh chapter of the first book of the Meteorologics, that, with regard to things which are not manifest to the senses, he thinks to adduce sufficient reasons and demonstrations of them, if he only shows that they may be such as he explains them.†

CCV. That nevertheless there is a moral certainty that all the things of this world are such as has been here shown they may be.

But nevertheless, that I may not wrong the truth by supposing it less certain than it is, I will here distinguish two kinds of certitude. The first is called moral, that is, a certainty sufficient for the conduct of life, though, if we look to the absolute power of God, what is morally certain may be false. [Thus, those who never visited Rome do not doubt that it is a city of Italy, though it might be that all from whom they got their information were deceived]. Again, if any one, wishing to decipher a letter written in Latin characters that are not placed in regular order, bethinks

---

* " have for their end only to apply certain sensible bodies to each other in such a way that, in the course of natural causes, certain sensible effects may be produced; and we will be able to accomplish this quite as well by considering the series of certain causes thus imagined, although false, as if they were the true, since this series is supposed similar as far as regards sensible effects."—*French.*

†'Επεὶ δὲ περὶ τῶν ἀφανῶν τῇ αἰσθήσει νομίζομεν ἱκανῶς ἀποδεδεῖχθαι κατὰ τὸν λόγον, ἐὰν εἰς τὸ δυνατὸν ἀναγάγωμεν, ἔκ τε τῶν νῦν φαινομένων ὑπολάβοι τις ἂν ὧδε περὶ τούτων μάλιστα συμβαίνειν. Μετεωρ a. 7.—T.

himself of reading a B wherever an A is found, and a C wherever there is a B, and thus of substituting in place of each letter the one which follows it in the order of the alphabet, and if by this means he finds that there are certain Latin words composed of these, he will not doubt that the true meaning of the writing is contained in these words, although he may discover this only by conjecture, and although it is possible that the writer of it did not arrange the letters on this principle of alphabetical order, but on some other, and thus concealed another meaning in it: for this is so improbable [especially when the cipher contains a number of words] as to seem incredible. But they who observe how many things regarding the magnet, fire, and the fabric of the whole world, are here deduced from a very small number of principles, though they deemed that I had taken them up at random and without grounds, will yet perhaps acknowledge that it could hardly happen that so many things should cohere if these principles were false.

CCVI. *That we possess even more than a moral certainty of it.*

Besides, there are some, even among natural, things which we judge to be absolutely certain. [Absolute certainty arises when we judge that it is impossible a thing can be otherwise than as we think it]. This certainty is founded on the metaphysical ground, that, as God is supremely good and the source of all truth, the faculty of distinguishing truth from error which he gave us, cannot be fallacious so long as we use it aright, and distinctly perceive anything by it. Of this character are the demonstrations of mathematics. the knowledge that material things exist, and the clear reasonings that are formed regarding them. The results I have given in this treatise will perhaps be admitted to a place in the class of truths that are absolutely certain, if it be considered that they are deduced in a continuous series from the first and most elementary principles of human knowledge; especially if it be sufficiently understood that we can perceive no external objects unless some local motion be caused by them in our nerves, and that such motion cannot be caused by the fixed stars, owing to their great distance from us, unless a motion be also produced in them and in the whole heavens lying between them and us: for these points being admitted, all the others, at least the more general doctrines which I have advanced regarding the world or earth [*e. g.*, the fluidity of the heavens, Part III., §. XLVI.], will appear to be almost the only possible explanations of the phenomena they present.

CCVII. That, however, I submit all my opinions to the authority of the church.

Nevertheless, lest I should presume too far, I affirm nothing, but submit all these my opinions to the authority of the church and the judgment of the more sage; and I desire no one to believe anything I may have said, unless he is constrained to admit it by the force and evidence of reason.

APPENDIX.

(From the Reply to the Second Objections—Latin, 1670. pp. 85-91. French, Garnier. Tom. II., pp. 74-84.)

REASONS WHICH ESTABLISH THE EXISTENCE OF GOD, AND THE DISTINCTION BETWEEN THE MIND AND BODY OF MAN, DISPOSED IN GEOMETRICAL ORDER.

DEFINITIONS.

I. By the term *thought* (*cogitatio, pensée*), I comprehend all that is in us, so that we are immediately conscious of it. Thus, all the operations of the will, intellect, imagination, and senses, are thoughts. But I have used the word *immediately* expressly to exclude whatever follows or depends upon our thoughts; for example, voluntary motion has, in truth, thought for its source (principle), but yet it is not itself thought. [Thus, walking is not a thought, but the perception or knowledge we have of our walking is.]

II. By the word *idea* I understand that form of any thought, by the immediate perception of which I am conscious of that same thought; so that I can express nothing in words, when I understand what I say, without making it certain, by this alone, that I possess the idea of the thing that is signified by these words. And thus I give the appellation idea not to the images alone that are depicted in the phantasy; on the contrary, I do not here apply this name to them, in so far as they are in the corporeal phantasy, that is to say, in so far as they are depicted in certain parts of the brain, but only in so far as they inform the mind itself, when turned towards that part of the brain.

III. By the *objective reality of an idea* I understand the entity or being of the thing represented by the idea, in so far as this entity is in the idea; and, in the same manner, it may be called either an objective perfection, or objective artifice, etc. (*artificium objectivum*). For all that we conceive to be in the objects of the ideas is objectively [or by representation] in the ideas themselves.

IV. The same things are said to be *formally* in the objects of the ideas when they are in them such as we conceive them; and they are said to be in the objects *eminently* when they are not indeed such as we conceive them, but are so great that they can supply this defect by their excellence.

V. Everything in which there immediately resides, as in a subject, or by which there exists any object we perceive, that is, any property, or quality, or attribute of which we have in us a real idea, is called *substance*. For we have no other idea of substance, accurately taken, except that it is a thing in which exists formally or eminently this property or quality which we perceive, or which is objectively in some one of our ideas, since we are taught by the natural light that nothing can have no real attribute.

VI. The substance in which thought immediately resides is here called *mind* (*mens, esprit*). I here speak, however, of *mens* rather than of *anima,* for the latter is equivocal, being frequently applied to denote a corporeal object.

VII. The substance which is the immediate subject of local extension, and of the accidents that presuppose this extension, as figure, situation, local motion, etc., is called *body*. But whether the substance which is called mind be the same with that which is called body, or whether they are two diverse substances, is a question to be hereafter considered.

VIII. The substance which we understand to be supremely perfect, and in which we conceive nothing that involves any defect, or limitation of perfection, is called *God*.

IX. When we say that some attribute is contained in the nature or concept of a thing, this is the same as if we said that the attribute is true of the thing, or that it may be affirmed of the thing itself.

X. Two substances are said to be really distinct, when each of them may exist without the other.

POSTULATES.

1st. I request that my readers consider how feeble are the reasons that have hitherto led them to repose faith in their

APPENDIX.

senses, and how uncertain are all the judgments which they afterwards founded on them; and that they will revolve this consideration in their mind so long and so frequently, that, in fine, they may acquire the habit of no longer trusting so confidently in their senses; for I hold that this is necessary to render one capable of apprehending metaphysical truths.

2d. That they consider their own mind, and all those of its attributes of which they shall find they cannot doubt, though they may have supposed that all they ever received by the senses was entirely false, and that they do not leave off considering it until they have acquired the habit of conceiving it distinctly, and of believing that it is more easy to know than any corporeal object.

3d. That they diligently examine such propositions as are self-evident, which they will find within themselves, as the following:—That the same thing cannot at once be and not be; that nothing cannot be the efficient cause of anything, and the like;—and thus exercise that clearness of understanding that has been given them by nature, but which the perceptions of the senses are wont greatly to disturb and obscure—exercise it, I say, pure and delivered from the objects of sense; for in this way the truth of the following axioms will appear very evident to them.

4th. That they examine the ideas of those natures which contain in them an assemblage of several attributes, such as the nature of the triangle, that of the square, or of some other figure; as also the nature of mind, the nature of body, and above all that of God, or of a being supremely perfect. And I request them to observe that it may with truth be affirmed that all these things are in objects, which we clearly conceive to be contained in them: for example, because that, in the nature of the rectilineal triangle, this property is found contained—viz., that its three angles are equal to two right angles, and that in the nature of body or of an extended thing, divisibility is comprised (for we do not conceive any extended thing so small that we cannot divide it, at least in thought)—it is true that the three angles of a rectilineal triangle are equal to two right angles, and that all body is divisible.

5th. That they dwell much and long on the contemplation

of the supremely perfect Being, and, among other things, consider that in the ideas of all other natures, possible existence is indeed contained, but that in the idea of God is contained not only possible but absolutely necessary existence. For, from this alone, and without any reasoning, they will discover that God exists: and it will be no less evident in itself than that two is an equal and three an unequal number, with other truths of this sort. For there are certain truths that are thus manifest to some without proof, which are not comprehended by others without a process of reasoning.

6th. That carefully considering all the examples of clear and distinct perception, and all of obscure and confused, of which I spoke in my Meditations, they accustom themselves to distinguish things that are clearly known from those that are obscure, for this is better learnt by example than by rules; and I think that I have there opened up, or at least in some degree touched upon, all examples of this kind.

7th. That readers adverting to the circumstance that they never discovered any falsity in things which they clearly conceived, and that, on the contrary, they never found, unless by chance, any truth in things which they conceived but obscurely, consider it to be wholly irrational, if, on acount only of certain prejudices of the senses, or hypotheses which contain what is unknown, they call in doubt what is clearly and distinctly conceived by the pure understanding; for they will thus readily admit the following axioms to be true and indubitable, though I confess that several of them might have been much better unfolded, and ought rather to have been proposed as theorems than as axioms, if I had desired to be more exact.

AXIOMS OR COMMON NOTIONS.

I. Nothing exists of which it cannot be inquired what is the cause of its existing; for this can even be asked respecting God; not that there is need of any cause in order to his existence, but because the very immensity of his nature is the cause or reason why there is no need of any cause of his existence.

II. The present time is not dependent on that which immediately preceded it; for this reason, there is not need of a less cause for conserving a thing than for at first producing it.

III. Any thing or any perfection of a thing actually existent cannot have *nothing*, or a thing non-existent, for the cause of its existence.

IV. All the reality or perfection which is in a thing is found formally or eminently in its first and total cause.

V. Whence it follows likewise, that the objective reality of our ideas requires a cause in which this same reality is contained, not simply objectively, but formally or eminently. And it is to be observed that this axiom must of necessity be admitted, as upon it alone depends the knowledge of all things, whether sensible or insensible. For whence do we know, for example, that the sky exists? Is it because we see it? But this vision does not affect the mind unless in so far as it is an idea, and an idea inhering in the mind itself, and not an image depicted on the phantasy; and, by reason of this idea, we cannot judge that the sky exists unless we suppose that every idea must have a cause of its objective reality which is really existent; and this cause we judge to be the sky itself, and so in the other instances.

VI. There are diverse degrees of reality, that is, of entity [or perfection]: for substance has more reality than accident or mode, and infinite substance than finite; it is for this reason also that there is more objective reality in the idea of substance than in that of accident, and in the idea of infinite than in the idea of finite substance.

VII. The will of a thinking being is carried voluntarily and freely, for that is of the essence of will, but nevertheless infallibly, to the good that is clearly known to it; and, therefore, if it discover any perfections which it does not possess, it will instantly confer them on itself if they are in its power; [for it will perceive that to possess them is a greater good than to want them.]

VIII. That which can accomplish the greater or more difficult, can also accomplish the less or the more easy.

IX. It is a greater and more difficult thing to create or conserve a substance than to create or conserve its attributes or properties; but this creation of a thing is not greater or more difficult than its conservation, as has been already said.

X. In the idea or concept of a thing existence is contained, because we are unable to conceive anything unless under the form of a thing which exists; but with this difference that, in the concept of a limited thing, possible or contingent existence is alone contained, and in the concept of a being sovereignly perfect, perfect and necessary existence is comprised.

PROPOSITION I.

The existence of God is known from the consideration of his nature alone.

DEMONSTRATION.

To say that an attribute is contained in the nature or in the concept of a thing, is the same as to say that this attribute is true of this thing, and that it may be affirmed to be in it. (Definition IX.)

But necessary existence is contained in the nature or in the concept of God (by Axiom X.)

Hence it may with truth be said that necessary existence is in God, or that God exists.

And this syllogism is the same as that of which I made use in my reply to the sixth article of these objections; and its conclusion may be known without proof by those who are free from all prejudice, as has been said in Postulate V. But because it is not so easy to reach so great perspicacity of mind, we shall essay to establish the same thing by other modes.

PROPOSITION II.

The existence of God is demonstrated, *a posteriori*, from this alone, that his idea is in us.

DEMONSTRATION.

The objective reality of each of our ideas requires a cause in which this same reality is contained, not simply objectively, but formally or eminently (by Axiom V.)

But we have in us the idea of God (by Definitions II and VIII), and of this idea the objective reality is not contained in us, either formally or eminently (by Axiom VI), nor can it be contained in any other except in God himself (by Definition VIII).

Therefore this idea of God which is in us demands God for its cause, and consequently God exists (by Axiom III).

PROPOSITION III.

The existence of God is also demonstrated from this, that we ourselves, who possess the idea of him, exist.

DEMONSTRATION.

If I possessed the power of conserving myself, I should likewise have the power of conferring, *a fortiori*, on myself, all the perfections that are awanting to me (by Axioms VIII and IX), for these perfections are only attributes of substance whereas I myself am a substance.

But I have not the power of conferring on myself these perfections, for otherwise I should already possess them (by Axiom VII).

Hence, I have not the power of self-conservation.

Further, I cannot exist without being conserved, so long as I exist, either by myself, supposing I possess the power, or by another who has this power (by Axioms I and II).

But I exist, and yet I have not the power of self-conservation, as I have recently proved. Hence I am conserved by another.

Further, that by which I am conserved has in itself formally or eminently all that is in me (by Axiom IV).

But I have in me the perception of many perfections that are awanting to me, and that also of the idea of God (by Definitions II and VIII). Hence the perception of these same perfections is in him by whom I am conserved.

Finally, that same being by whom I am conserved cannot have the perception of any perfections that are awanting to him, that is to say, which he has not in himself formally or eminently (by Axiom VII); for having the power of conserving me, as has been recently said, he should have, *a fortiori*, the power of conferring these perfections on himself, if they were awanting to him (by Axioms VIII and IX).

But he has the perception of all the perfections which I discover to be wanting to me, and which I conceive can be in God alone, as I recently proved:

Hence he has all these in himself, formally or eminently, and thus he is God.

COROLLARY.

God has created the sky and the earth and all that is therein contained; and besides this he can make all the things which we clearly conceive in the manner in which we conceive them.

DEMONSTRATION.

All these things clearly follow from the preceding proposition. For in it we have proved the existence of God, from its being necessary that some one should exist in whom are contained formally or eminently all the perfections of which there is in us any idea.

But we have in us the idea of a power so great, that by the being alone in whom it resides, the sky and the earth, etc., must have been created, and also that by the same being all the other things which we conceive as possible can be produced.

Hence, in proving the existence of God, we have also proved with it all these things.

PROPOSITION IV.

The mind and body are really distinct.

DEMONSTRATION.

All that we clearly conceive can be made by God in the manner in which we conceive it (by foregoing Corollary).

But we clearly conceive mind, that is, a substance which thinks, without body, that is to say, without an extended substance (by Postulate II); and, on the other hand, we as clearly conceive body without mind (as every one admits).

Hence, at least, by the omnipotence of God, the mind can exist without the body, and the body without the mind.

Now, substances which can exist independently of each other, are really distinct (by Definition X).

But the mind and the body are substances (by Definitions V, VI, and VII), which can exist independently of each other, as I have recently proved:

Hence the mind and the body are really distinct.

And it must be observed that I have here made use of the omnipotence of God in order to found my proof on it, not that there is need of any extraordinary power in order to separate the mind from the body, but for this reason, that, as I have treated of God only in the foregoing propositions, I could not draw my proof from any other source than from him: and it matters very little by what power two things are separated in order to discover that they are really distinct.

NOTES.

I. TO PERCEIVE—PERCEPTION—p. 10.

THE term *perception* (*perceptio*) has a much wider signification in the writings of Descartes and the Cartesians than in the literature of the schools of philosophy in our times. Perception is, at present, used to denote the immediate knowledge we obtain through sense, or even still further restricted to the apprehension of what have been called the *primary qualities* of matter; with the Cartesians, and the older philosophers generally, the word is employed in the same sense in which we use *consciousness*, to denote an act of mind by which we merely apprehend or take note of the object of thought or consciousness, considered as distinguished from any affirmation or negation (judgment) regarding it. Accordingly, in Cartesian literature *perception* is synonymous with *cognition*, when, in the narrower sense of the term, it is said to consist in the *apprehension of a thing, or in the immediate consciousness of that which is known*, as opposed to judgment and reasoning. It thus includes both the representative knowledge of imagination (and with the Cartesians, of sense), and the mediate or representative knowledge given in a notion or concept; for we cannot, either in imagination or conception, represent without being conscious of the representation, *i. e.,* without perceiving or immediately apprehending it. *Percipere* in Cartesian literature is thus, with greater or less propriety, considered as equivalent to *cognoscere, intelligere* (in the narrower sense of these terms), *rem menti propositam concipere, intueri; cogitatione sibi representare; rerum ideas intueri; res per ideas videre; rem per intellectus ideam intueri, cernere; rei ideam in intellectu habere. Perceptio* is properly synonymous with *perceptio simplex, apprehensio seu apprehensio simplex (q. prehensio objecti ab intellectu) intellectio simplex, visio simplex, cognitio,* and less properly with *conceptus, notio, idea rei.* In logical language, the character of perception is expressed by saying that the act has for its object a *thema simplex, i. e.,* in the language of Descartes, either substance or attribute, as opposed to the *thema conjunctum seu compositum,* or *notionum complexio per affirmationem et negationem, i. e., enunciatio,* or, in the language of Descartes, a truth.—Prin. of Phil., P. I., § 48. Claubergius, Op. P. I., pp. 334, 503. (Ed. 1691.) Flenderus, Log. Cont. Claub. Ill. §§ 1.5. (4th Ed.)

To illustrate more particularly the nature and sphere of perception, as the term is used in the Cartesian school, it is necessary to attend to the division of the phænomena of consciousness, adopted by Descartes, and current among his followers. Descartes divides all our thoughts (*cogitationes*)—and with him thought is the general name for each mode or phænomenon of consciousness—into two grand classes, viz., the Activities and Passivities of mind (*actiones et passiones sive affectus animae*), the distinguishing element of these two classes being, that in the former case the mind of itself determines its own modification; in the latter it is determined to it, by some action, to wit, foreign from the will. The *first* class embraces all the acts of the Will, or the *volitions,* (*volitiones sive operationes voluntatis*), inasmuch as all such modifications of mind are considered by him as determinable, and actually determined, by the power of free choice or will, *i. e.,* by the mind itself; and under volition (*i. e.,* to use the language of his followers, *latio quaedam animi tendens ad objectum in idea propositum*) he comprehends judgment and will proper (*velle et nolle*), according as the object is regarded under the notions of the *true* and the *false,* or of the *good* and the *bad.* To the *second* class he refers all the Cognitive acts of the mind, considered merely as apprehensive of their objects (*perceptiones sive operationes intellectus*), inasmuch as our apprehensions are not made arbitrarily, or at the pleasure of our will, but determined by their objects, and are thus, in a sense, *passions* or passivities. In this way all the acts, whether of sense, memory, imagination, or the pure intellect, are but different modes of perceiving; for in each we only know as we are conscious of, or apprehend, the object of the act. Further, as each mental modification has a reality for us only in so far as we actually apprehend or are conscious of it, it is plain that, in every actual mode of mind, there is involved *a consciousness,* or, in the Cartesian language, *a perception;* and thus we are said to perceive not only when in sense we apprehend by idea or representation *extension* or *figure*—the qualities of somewhat lying beyond ourselves, or the representative object in imagination, but likewise when we are conscious of the forth-putting of an act of will or of being affected by joy or hope. More particularly as, according to the Cartesian doctrine, the consciousness of a modification of mind, a volition, for example, is, though in thought (*ratione*) separable, not really distinct from this modification itself, all modes of mind whatsoever, as participating of consciousness, are, in a sense, *perceptions;* for this implies nothing more than that they exist in consciousness. In this sense *perception* is not contrasted with, but comprehends *volition,* though extending further. As some modifications of mind, however, though only manifesting themselves through knowledge, are yet not apprehension simply or even knowledge, but to use his own phrase, have other forms, as volition, we may consider them in reference to these other characters; and as, on the Cartesian doctrine, these characters are negative of each other, we thus obtain classes not only in opposition, but in fundamental contrast. These distinguishing characteristics are, as we have seen, the qualities of activity and of passivity, which thus afford *two* grand divisions of the mental modifications, called respectively volitions and perceptions.

That perception was only logically discriminated from its object on the doctrine of Descartes, will be manifest from what follows:—

"I observe (he says) that whatever is done, or recently happens, is generally called by the philosophers *passion,* in respect of the subject to which it happens, and *action* in respect of that which causes it to take place, so that, although agent and patient are often very diverse, *action and passion nevertheless remain one and the same thing, having these two names by reason of the two different subjects to which it can be referred."*—De Pass. P. I. Art. 1.

"Our perceptions are of two species: some have the mind for their cause, and others the body. Those that have the mind for their cause are the perceptions of our volitions, and of all our imaginations that depend on it; *for it is certain that we cannot will anything without perceiving by the same means that we will it;* and, although in respect of our mind it may be an action to will a thing, we may say that it is also in it a passion to perceive that it wills; nevertheless, *because this perception and volition are only in reality the same thing,* the denomination is always made from the more noble, and thus we are not accustomed to call it a passion, but simply an action."—Ibid. Art. 19. Con. on the Note in general. Art. 17. Prin. of Phil., P. I., § 32. Med. III., page 45. Ep., P. II., CXV., quoted below. Hamilton's Reid. Note D, pp. 876, 877. Compare note II, *Idea.*

Under the head of *perception* it may be necessary to remark farther that the term perception (*perceptio*) is not used in reference to sense without the adjunct *sensus* or *sensuum*—the terms in this relation being *sensus, sensatio, idea,* and the verb *sentire* not *percipere*.

II. IDEA—p. 10.

The meaning attached to the term *idea* in the writings of Descartes is by no means uniform or constant. The first grand distinction in the signification of the word arises from its application by Descartes to denote indifferently a *material* or a *mental* modification; and this in relation to sense and imagination. Considered with respect to these faculties, *idea* is sometimes applied to designate the impression on the brain or material organism generally, to which the idea proper or mental modification is attached, and at other times to mark the mental modification itself, regarded as the object of the faculty. As instances of the former application of the word, we may adduce the following passages:—"*Ideam* quam formant hi spiritus."—Tract. de Homine, § 84. "Glandula *ideas* objectorum, quae in aliorum sensuum organa agunt, aeque facile recipere possit."—Ibid, § 85. "*Ideas* quas sensus externi in phantasiam mittunt."—Diopt. cap. iv. § 6. To obviate the ambiguity incidental to this twofold and quite opposite use of the term, De la Forge, an eminent Cartesian, denominated the movement in the organism *species,* or *corporeal species,* reserving idea for the modification of the mind alone.—Traité de l'Esprit de l'Homme, chap. x. p. 99. Hamilton's Reid, p. 834.

Descartes himself, indeed, in the course of the controversies to which his speculations gave rise, became aware of the necessity of distinguishing in expression the material from the mental idea; and in order to this he seems occasionally disposed to refuse the appellation idea to the material modification, while he more frequently uses the term image (*imago*), than idea in this relation. One of these passages I shall quote, not only in proof of this, but also as establishing the fact of the reality and distinctness of the material and mental modifications. "I do not simply (he says) call by the name *idea* the images that are depicted in the phantasy; on the contrary, I do not call them by this name in so far as they are in the corporeal phantasy; but I designate generally by the term idea *all that is in our mind when we conceive a thing in whatever manner we may conceive it."*—Lett. lxxv., Garnier, tom. iv. p. 319.

It should be observed, however, that by idea in the sense of corporeal species, Descartes did not mean a picture, likeness, or image of the object existing in the brain, but simply a certain organic movement, or agitation of the nerves, determined by the object and communicated to the brain, the seat of the *sensus communis.* This purely material modification had, on the one hand, not necessarily any resemblance to the object which was the cause of it, and therefore was not representative of it; nor, on the other, should it be supposed that it in any way resembled, far less was identical with, the (mental) idea connected with it, since notwithstanding certain loose statements, there is sufficient ground to hold that, on the doctrine of Descartes, the corporeal impression was no object of perception or consciousness at all. As these are points of essential importance towards a right comprehension of the philosophy of Descartes, I may be allowed to enter somewhat into detail; and first of all, I shall refer to the passages in which he has distinctly laid down the doctrines here attributed to him.

"That the ideas which the external senses send into the phantasy, are not images of the objects; or at least that there is no need of their being like them.

"It must be observed, besides, that the mind does not stand in need of images sent from objects to the brain in order to perceive (as is the generally received opinion of the philosophers); or at least that the nature of these images is to be conceived far otherwise than is commonly done. For, as philosophers consider in them nothing beyond their resemblance to the objects they represent, they are unable to show how these images can be formed by the objects, and received into the organs of the external senses, and finally transmitted by the nerves to the brain. And they had no ground to suppose there were such images, beyond observing that our thought can be efficaciously excited by a picture to conceive the object pictured; from which it appeared to them that the mind must be, in the same way, excited to apprehend the objects which affect the senses, by means of certain small images delineated in our head. Whereas we ought to consider that there are many things besides images that can excite our thoughts; as, for example, words and signs which in no way resemble the things they signify. And if, that we may depart as little as possible from the commonly received opinions, we may be allowed to concede that the objects we perceive are really depicted in the brain, we must at least remark that no image is ever absolutely like to the object it represents; for in that case there would be no distinction between the object and its image; but that a partial likeness (*rudem similitudinem*) is sufficient, and that frequently even the perfection of images consists in their not resembling the objects as far as they might. Thus, we see that engravings formed merely by the placing of ink here and there on paper, represent to us forests, cities, men, and even battles and tempests; and yet of the innumerable qualities of these objects which they exhibit to our thought, there is none except the figure of which they really bear the likeness. And it is to be remarked that even this likeness is very imperfect, since on a plane surface they represent to us bodies variously rising and sinking; and even that according to the rules of perspective, they frequently represent circles better by ovals than by other circles, and squares by rhombi than by other squares, and so on in other instances; so that in order to the absolute perfection of the image, and the accurate delineation of the object, the former more frequently requires to be unlike the latter."—Diopt. cap. iv. § 6 C. § 7. Prin. of Phil., p. iv. §§ 197, 198.

" Whoever has well comprised (says Descartes in contravention of the doctrine of Regius, *that all our common notions owe their origin to observation and tradition*), the extent and limits of our senses, and what precisely by their means can reach our faculty of thinking, must admit that no idea or objects are represented to us by them *such as we form them by thought;* so that there is nothing in our ideas that is not natural to the mind or to the faculty of thinking which it possesses, if we but except certain circumstances that pertain only to experience; for example, it is experience alone that leads us to judge that such and such ideas, which are now present to the mind, are related to certain objects that are out of us; *not in truth that those things transmitted them into our mind by the organs of the senses such as we perceive them; but because they transmitted something which gave occasion to our mind, by the natural faculty it possesses, to form them at that time rather than at another.* For, as our author himself avers in article 19, in accordance with the doctrine of my Principles, nothing can come from external objects to our mind by the medium of the senses, *except certain corporeal movements; but neither these movements themselves nor the figures arising from them, are conceived by us such as they are in the organs of sense,* as I have amply explained in the Dioptrics: whence it follows that even the ideas of motion and figures are naturally in us. And much more the ideas of pain, colours, sounds, and of other similar things, must be natural to us, to the end *that our mind, on occasion of certain corporeal movements, with which they have no resemblance, may be able to represent them to itself."*—Remarks on the Programme of Regius, Ep. P. i. xcix, (Ed. 1668), or tom. iv. Lett. xxxviii. of Garnier's Ed.

" Finally, I hold that all those (ideas) which involve no negation or affirmation, are innate in us, *for the organs of the senses convey nothing to us of the same character as the idea which is formed on occasion of them,* and thus the idea must have been previously in us."—Ep. P. ii. lv., or Garnier's Ed. tom. iv. Lett. lxix.

" Whence do we know that the sky exists? Is it because we see it? But this vision does not affect the mind unless in so far as it is an *idea, and an idea inhering in the mind itself, and not an image depicted on the phantasy."*—App. Ax. 5. p. 219.

" I hold that there is no other difference between the mind and its ideas than between a piece of wax and the diverse figures of which it is capable. And since the receiving diverse figures is not properly an action in the wax, but a passion; so it seems to me to be also a passion in the mind that it receives this or that idea; and I consider that except its volitions it has no actions, but that its ideas are induced upon it, partly by objects affecting the senses, partly by the impressions that are in the brain, and partly also by the dispositions which have gone before in the mind itself, and by the movements of its will."—Ep. P. i. cxv.

" The mind always receives these (its *perceptions*) from the things represented by them."—De Pass. Part i. Art. 17.

Among Cartesians, compare De la Forge, De l'Esprit de l'Homme, cap. x. Geulinx, Dictata in Prin. Phil. P. iv. § 189. Malebranche, Recherche de la Vérité, Liv. ii.; De l'Imagination, chap. v. § 1; also Liv. i. Des Sens, chap. x. § 5.

I am aware that some maintain that Descartes held the material impression to be an object of consciousness, an opinion to which both Reid and Stewart incline (see Reid's Essays on the Intellectual Powers; Essay ii., chap. viii.; Stewart's Dissertation, note N. p. 245; Elements, Part i. chap. i., note, p. 45, ed. 1850.) That such is not the doctrine of Descartes, is manifest from the passages already cited. It may be necessary, however, in order to a fuller consideration of the question, to refer to those doubtful statements which at first sight appear to give some countenance to the supposition.

I shall, first of all, quote and give references to what seem the strongest of the ambiguous passages. "I easily understand," he says, "that if some body exists with which my mind is so united as to be able, as it were, to consider it when it chooses, it may thus imagine corporeal objects, so that this mode of thinking differs from pure intellection only in this respect, that the mind in conceiving, turns in some way upon itself, and considers some one of the ideas it possesses within itself; but, in imagining, it turns toward the body, and contemplates in it some object conformed to the idea which it either conceived of itself or apprehended by sense."—Med. vi., page 86.

"The former, or corporeal species which must be in the brain in order to imagination, are not thoughts; but the operation of the mind imagining or *turning towards these species,* is a thought."—Ep. p. ii. liv. (De Pass. p. i., art. 35. Appendix, Def. ii., p. 215).

These and similar passages might seem, at first sight, to countenance the supposition, that Descartes admitted a knowledge of the corporeal species or organic impression. Such an interpretation is, however, rash and untenable, were there no other ground for rejecting it, save the various contradictions of the principles of the philosophy of which it is supposed to form a part, for these are so many and so manifest, that we could hardly suppose such a thinker as Descartes to have allowed them to escape his notice. Before showing that the passages in themselves do not really warrant the interpretation here referred to, I shall point out its general inconsistency, not only with the main principle, but with certain particular doctrines of Cartesianism, and these the most important and distinctive.

In the first place, then, had Descartes admitted a knowledge of the material impression, either in sense or imagination, and, be it observed, an *immediate* knowledge is the only supposable, he must have allowed an immediate consciousness of matter, for the corporeal species is a material object. But this would have been to contradict the fundamental principle of his philosophy, according to which, mind, on account of its absolute diversity from body, is supposed to be able to hold no immediate converse with matter, but only to be cognisant of it by means of its own modifications, determined hyperphysically on occasion of certain affections of the body with which it is conjoined. And thus, if the mind be immediately cognisant of the corporeal species, what occupies the prominent and distinctive place in Cartesianism,—viz., the host of mental ideas representative of the outward object, becomes forthwith the superfluity and excrescence of the system; for if the mind can take immediate cognisance of the corporeal species, *i. e.* of matter, why postulate a mental representation in order to the perception of the outward object?

But in the second place, whether the material impression be an object of consciousness or not, Descartes must still be held to allow the existence of a mental modification or idea. The species, therefore, on the hypothesis that it is an object of consciousness, is either really *identical* with the mental idea, or it is *different* from it. To take the former supposition, or that of the identity of the material and mental modifications, it will follow that mind and matter are no longer distinguishable, are no longer diverse substances, seeing their modifications coincide—a tenet no less at variance with the entire course of the speculations of Descartes, than is the doctrine from which it flows with the numerous explicit statements, in which he declares the total diversity of the material and mental ideas, as modifications of substances in themselves distinct. But the organic impression, if not identical with, must be diverse from, the mental idea. Now as, on the hypothesis in question, the material idea is perceived, and as the mental is likewise an object of perception, there must be in each of the faculties of sense and imagination a two-fold object. For such a doctrine, there is not the shadow of a ground in all the writings of Descartes.

But, in the third place, let it be supposed that Descartes did not allow the existence of mental ideas at all, and therefore only a single object in perception, and that the organic impression, even with this gratuitous allowance a palpable contradiction in the doctrine of the philosopher would arise. The organic impression, in order to constitute the representative idea of the object, must *represent* the object, not *suggest it* or represent it *materially* (*materialiter*), as a natural sign, for the object could not be simply suggested to the mind or thus represented, without appearing in a mental modification or idea, which is contrary to the hypothesis. But an object that is material, and at the same time representative, must, **if it** represent by itself, represent *intentionally (intentionaliter)*; in other words, it must resemble the object it represents, or be the image or likeness of it. It is the property of mind alone to be capable of representing something different from itself, or even quite opposed, in a modification not at all resembling the thing represented; as, for example, an extended object in an unextended modification. But the resemblance of the material idea to the outward object, is a doctrine explicitly denied by Descartes.—(*Vide* Remarks on Programme of Regius, quoted above, Prin. of Phil., p. iv., §§ 197, 198.)

But finally, the whole hypothesis makes Descartes contradict not only his own doctrine of representation, but destroy the general conditions of any representative doctrine whatever; for, as the only ground on which a doctrine of representation can be supposed necessary, is that the mind is not immediately percipient of the outward object, if Descartes at the same time holds that the representation, itself material and an object external to the mind, because existing in the brain, is perceived. he must allow to the mind, at first hand, that power on the denial of the existence of which the assertion of the need of a representative object is founded.

These considerations are, I think, sufficient to show, that it is at least highly improbable, that Descartes meant in the passages quoted to allow to the mind a consciousness of the organic impression in sense and imagination. To have done so, would have been to fill his philosophy with anomalies and contradictions of the most palpable kind.

But let us attend shortly to the passages themselves, to discover whether they render such an interpretation of them imperative. In the passages quoted, the mind is said to turn itself towards the species, and these again are said to inform (*informare*) the mind.

With regard to the first phrase, *conversion towards the species,* it will be found, by a reference to the passages in which it occurs, that it is always used as descriptive of the acts of sense and imagination, when these are spoken of in contrast to the act of the pure intellect, or that faculty whose exercise is independent of all organic impression; and then the contrast indicated is in the *origin* or *source* of the *ideas,* or objects of these faculties, those of sense and imagination having their (remote) source in body,—those of intellect, their (immediate) origin in the mind itself. In this way, all that conversion towards the species indicates, is merely that the mind does not receive certain ideas *directly* from itself but is in some way dependent for at least their actual presence on certain conditions of the bodily organism. And this, it is manifest, does not necessarily imply the consciousness by the mind of the organic impression.

Again, the corporeal species may in its turn be said to *inform* the mind (*informare mentem*), inasmuch as it is to it the mental modification or idea, viewed apart from its hyperphysical origin, is immediately attached, and on occasion of which it is revealed to consciousness; and this on the law of the union of mind and body, as parts of the same whole. In the same sense, Deity is said to inform the mind, in so constituting it as that in the course of the development of its powers, the knowledge of himself should naturally arise.

But, in the second place, the species may, in a literal sense, be said to inform the mind, for the word, in its strict acceptation, merely denotes the giving a particular form or shape to a thing; and in the Cartesian phraseology, the spiritual notions or mental ideas were but the different forms of the mind in which its acts were clothed, limited, and determined.—*Vide* Appendix, Def. ii. p. 215. De la Forge, De l'Esprit, chap. x., p. 131 and *passim*. Claub. Op. p. ii., p. 606.

The doctrine of Descartes on this point seems to be well put by Chauvin, when, after noticing the doctrines of certain of the Peripatetics regarding species, he says:—"There are, however, among more recent philosophers, not a few who retain the nomenclature of *species impressa* and *expressa*. But with them the *species impressa* is nothing more than a certain motion impressed either mediately or immediately, by external objects, on the parts of the body, and thence by the nerves transmitted to the brain, or a certain commotion of the fibres of the brain, proceeding from the agitation of the animal spirits flowing in the brain; which, as they have no resemblance to the objects of nature, are esteemed *representamens* of these things, on no other account *than because the mind on occasion of them* [i. e., *the motions*], *makes the things present to itself,* *and contemplates the same in its own ideas therefrom arising. * * * ** But the *species expressa* is nothing more than that notion of the mind which is expressed on the presence of the *species impressa,* and by attention to and inspection (*intuitione*) of which the thing itself is known."—Lexicon Rationale, Species, (1692). Con. Prin. of Phil., part iv. §§ 189, 197, 198.

But lastly, the whole ambiguity is probably due to the extreme timidity of the philosopher, and his anxious solicitude to bring the results of his own independent reflection into an apparent harmony with the opinions generally received in his time; which led him frequently to clothe his really new doctrines in the current forms of expression.

There is thus, not even on the special ground of the ambiguous passages themselves, any reason to suppose that Descartes ever departed from a doctrine essential to the consistency of his philosophy, viz., the non-consciousness of the organic impression. So much for idea as a material or organic modification.

We must now, however, consider idea in reference to mind, *i. e.,* as an object of consciousness. In this relation the fundamental notion to be attached to the term, as used by Descartes and the Cartesians, is that of a representative thought, or an object of consciousness, in and by the knowledge of which we become aware of something distinct from this object itself. Idea, Descartes says, is to be taken "pro omni re cogitatâ quatenus habet tantum esse objectivum in intellectu."—Diss. de Meth P. iv. note. "Idea est ipsa res cogitatio quatenus est objective in intellectu." Again, idea is "cogitato tanquam rei imago."—*Con.* Med. iii. 45, and Works *passim.* De La Forge, De l'Esprit, chap. x. pp. 128, 131.

It is necessary, however, with a view to an adequate understanding of the Cartesian philosophy, to distinguish the two aspects under which the same idea was viewed by Descartes and his followers. The mental idea, while really one and indivisible, was considered in two logically distinct relations, viz., both as an object and as a medium of knowledge, that is, in reference to the mind knowing and the object known. This distinction is made by Descartes in several passages of the Meditations. Thus, "If ideas are taken in so far only as they are *certain modes of consciousness,* I do not remark any difference or inequality among them, and all seem in the same manner to proceed from myself; but considering them as *images, of which one represents one thing and another a different,* it is evident that a great diversity obtains among them."—Med. iii. p. 48. Preface of Med. p. 10.

This distinction of idea as act and as representative object, pervades the whole body of Cartesian literature. Thus, to take an example, "Every concept or idea," says Clauberg, "has a *twofold* dependence; *the one from the conceiving and thinking intellect,* in as far as it is an *act;* the other from the thing conceived or like, of which, to wit, it is the *representation* or *image,* or whence it is struck out by imitation."—Op. P. ii. p. 607 (Ed. 1691). *Con.* De la Forge, De l'Esprit, chap. x. pp. 128, 131. Flenderus, Logica Contracta Claubergiana (4th ed.) § 5, p. 12.

Idea has thus with the Cartesians a twofold relation or dependence (*realitas, perfectio, esse, dependentia*). In so far as it is an act or mode of the mind (*operatio mentis, intellectus*), idea possesses a *formal* and *proper* being (*esse formale seu proprium*); in so far as it is the representation of the object thought (*imago rei cogitatae*), or in the place of that object (*in vice illius*), it has an *objective* or *vicarious* being (*esse objectivum sive vicarium*). Again, idea, as standing in this double relation or dependence, is said to have a twofold cause, viz., an *efficient* and an *exemplary.* In so far as a mode of consciousness, the idea has its efficient cause in intellect or in the mind itself (*uti operans suae operationis causa*); in so far as representative, the object is the *exemplary* cause, standing in relation to the idea as the archetype to the ectype, the principal to the vicarious.

It is the discrimination of idea as a mental operation or representative object, which affords the logical distinction of *perception* and *idea,* to be met with on all hands in Cartesian literature. "By the term *idea,*" says Descartes himself, "I understand that form of any thought by the immediate *perception* of which I am conscious of that same thought."—Appendix, Def. ii. p. 215.

" I have said," says Arnauld, "that I take *perception* and *idea* for the same thing. It should be observed, however, that this thing, although one, has two relations; the one to the mind which it modifies, the other to the thing perceived, in so far as it is objectively in the mind, and that the word *perception* more distinctly marks the *former* relation, and *idea* the *latter*. Thus, the perception of a square marks more directly my mind as perceiving a square; and the idea of a square marks more directly the square in so far as it is objectively in my mind."—Des Vraies et des Fausses Idées, chap. v. Def. 6. *Con.* De la Forge, De l'Esprit, chap. x. pp. 128, 140.

It should be observed, however, with regard to this distinction of *idea* and *perception,* that with Descartes *perception* is sometimes used where, in accordance with the propriety of language, we should have expected *idea*. Thus he says, "The mind always receives these (its perceptions) from the things *represented* by them." (De Pass., P. i. Art. 17.) On the other hand, we find idea where, in accordance with his general nomenclature, we should have looked for perception. "When I will and fear, because at the same time I perceive that I will and fear, the volition itself and fear are reckoned by me among *ideas.*"—Ob. et Resp. Tertiæ, Ob. v. p. 98 (Ed. 1670).

Looking to ideas as the immediate objects of knowledge or perception, and considering them in relation to the faculties of which they are the objects, they may be classed as ideas of sense, of imagination, and of the pure intellect, in the exercise of each of which powers we are said to be apprehensive or percipient of ideas. But, as the objects of these powers, ideas differ both in their origin, and according to the character of the objects they represent. In the first relation, ideas arise either simply from the mind, as those of the pure intellect, or from the mind on occasion of body, modified by the corporeal species, as those of sense and imagination. Considered as to their origin, the ideas of sense and imagination thus stand in contrast to those of the pure intellect, for in sense and imagination there is always a physical impression or corporeal species as the cause or occasion of the mental idea; whereas the intellect, as deriving its ideas from the mind itself, has no need of a material organ or of corporeal species. The ideas of sense and imagination, while they agree in being the result, though hyperphysically determined, of a physical antecedent in the form of the corporeal species, and thus in both depending on the bodily organism, nevertheless differ in this, that the species to which the idea is attached is in the case of sense immediately dependent on the presence and action of external objects; while in imagination it depends only remotely on external objects, and proximately on the will, the memory, and the action of the animal spirits.

But the chief contrast of ideas arises from the character of the objects they represent. In this relation, on the Cartesian doctrine, ideas fall into two great classes. The first comprehends all ideas of the individual and picturable, in other words, all the objects of sense and imagination; the second contains all our notions of the general, relative, or unpicturable—in other words, the ideas of the pure intellect. (*Con.* Med. vi. pp. 84-89; Prin. of Phil. P. i. §73. Lett. lxxv., vol. iv. p. 318 of Garnier's ed., or vol. vi., L. lxii. duod. ed. De la Forge, De l'Esprit, chap. xviii. pp. 298-302.)—Under sense it should be observed that idea, in the writings of Descartes as well as of others in the Cartesian school, denotes indifferently the apprehension of the primary and the sensations of the secondary qualities of matter. Thus, Descartes speaks of the sensation or idea (*sensus vel idea*) of colour and heat. Malebranche limited idea (*idée*) to the apprehension of the primary, reserving *sentiment* to designate the sensations of the secondary qualities.—As the secondary qualities on their subjective side were held by the Cartesians to be merely modifications of the percipient subject, and not to exist in nature as in consciousness, idea as applied to them (which was not generally the case out of the writings of Descartes), was not representative. *Vide* Prin. of Phil. P. i. §§ 69, 70, 71.

III. OBJECTIVE REALITY—(*realitas objectiva*)—p. 18.

After what has been already said of the twofold relation of idea in the philosophy of Descartes, it is unnecessary to add much by way of explanation of the term *objective reality*. This, as we have said, denotes that aspect of a representative thought in which it is considered in relation to the object represented; hence the object is said to possess objective reality in so far as it exists by representation in thought (*quatenus objicitur intellectui*). This use of the term objective, it will be remarked, is precisely opposed to the more modern (Kantian) acceptation of the same word, and corresponds, to a certain extent, with the counter-term *subjective;* for objective reality (*i. e.,* the reality of representation) is in truth a subjective reality.

It may be of importance to note the *two* relations from which the representative reality of an idea is distinguished in Cartesian literature, with their appropriate designations. In the first place, the representative perfection (being) of an idea, was distinguished from the object of the idea in so far as it possessed an absolute existence, or existence independent of thought. In this relation the object was said to possess *realitas actualis, formalis,* as opposed to *realitas objectiva.* (*Con.* Med. iii. pp. 49; Med. vi. p. 92.) The object as it exists in nature was by other philosophers, and among these by some of the Cartesians, called *ens principale, reale, fundamentale* (*quasi fundamentum ideae*).

In the second place, the representative being of an idea was distinguished from its relation to the mind of which it is the act, and in this aspect idea, so far as act, was said to possess *esse reale, materiale, formale* (*q. forma quaedam mentis,* and this in contrast with *objectivum*), *proprium;* in relation to the object represented, it was said to possess *esse intentionale, formale* (and this in contrast with *materiale*), *objectivum, vicarium;* these are the strictly contrasted appellations. The *esse objectivum* was also called *representativum, cognitum, in mente, tanquam in imagine, per imitationem.* Con. Claub. Op. P. ii. pp. 607-617. Hamilton's Reid, pp. 806, 807.

IV. FROM OR THROUGH THE SENSES—(*vel a sensibus vel per sensus*)—p. 22.

"*From the senses,* that is, from sight, by which I first perceived light, and then by its aid colours, figures, magnitudes, and all similar things; *through the senses,* that is, through hearing, in apprehending the words of men."—Claubergius, in h. loc. Op. P. ii. p. 1182.

V. THOUGHT—(*cogitatio, pensée; cogitare, penser*)—p. 25.

Thought, (*cogitatio, pensée*), is, in the Cartesian phraseology, applied to designate all that takes place within us, of which we are immediately conscious, *i. e.,* all the modifications of the mind or thinking principle. *Thought* is thus but another term for *consciousness,* and embraces all the acts of the will, the intellect, the imagination, and senses.—Med. iii. p. 45; Prin. of Phil. P. i. § 9; Resp. ad. Sec. Object. Def. i. (Appendix p. 215.)

"Thought," says De la Forge, "I take for that perception, consciousness, or internal knowledge which each of us feels immediately by himself when he perceives what he does or what passes in him."—De l'Esprit, chap. iii. p. 14, chap. vi. p. 54. Arnauld, Des Vraies et des Fausses Idées, chap. v. def. i.

"Mens," says Claubergius, "si vult cogitat, si non vult cogitat, si amat cogitat, si odit cogitat, si affirmat cogitat, si negat cogitat, si dubitat cogitat, si demonstrat cogitat, somniando cogitat, vigilando cogitat, sentiendo cogitat, imaginando cogitat, &c., atque ita in qualibet ejus functione cogitatio involvitur."—Op. P. ii. p. 600; P. i. p. 188; Log. P. i. § 102.

Consciousness is thus, in the doctrine of the Cartesians, the general condition of our mental modifications, and in no way really distinct from the activities and passivities of which it is the condition. Though, in a sense already explained (as opposed to *volition*), *perception* is said to be contained under consciousness as its genus, they are yet nearly convertible terms. The difference between the two forms of expression seems to be, that thought, while embracing all the modifications of mind, whether volitions or perceptions, is not distinguished from the former as a *passivity*, while perception is. Thought, as thus denoting a mental modification both in its active and passive relation, marks the opposition and contrast of the modification to its negative, the extended, *i. e.*, matter, while viewed as a *perception* the phænomenon is regarded mainly in reference to its simple existence in consciousness, or as an apprehended property of mind. It seems to be in accordance with this view that the mind is uniformly spoken of as *res cogitans* (not *percipiens*) when opposed to its negative, the unthinking and extended.

VI. INNATE IDEAS—(*ideae innatae*)—p. 46.

By *innate idea,* Descartes meant merely a mental modification which, existing in the mind antecedently to all experience, possesses, however, only a *potential* existence, until, on occasion of experience, it is called forth into *actual* consciousness.

It is worthy of remark, in connection with the question of *innate ideas,* that the chief ground on which Descartes holds that certain of our judgments are prior to experience and native to the mind, is the impossibility of deriving them as *universal* from *individual* corporeal movements, which, if efficient, could give rise to modifications merely *individual.*

It will be seen, however, from the passages quoted below, and from a comparison of them with the passage quoted at pp. 229-231, of these notes, that Descartes held a much wider doctrine of innate ideas than the modern, and one the principle of which could not fail sooner or later to result in the doctrine of Occasional Causes, to explain the connection between the corporeal antecedent, which had no causal power, and the rise of the mental modification into actual consciousness.

The following is the article (xii.) in the Programme of Regius which gave occasion to Descartes to make an explicit statement of his doctrine of *innate ideas.*

" Mens," says Regius, " non indiget ideis, vel notionibus, vel axiomatibus innatis: sed sola ejus facultas cogitandi, ipsi, ad actiones suas peragendas, sufficit." On this Descartes remarks: "In this article he (Regius) appears to differ from me merely in words; for when he says that the mind has no need of ideas, or notions, or axioms that are innate [or naturally impressed upon it], and meanwhile concedes to it a faculty of thinking (that is, a faculty natural to it or innate), he affirms my doctrine in effect, though denying it in word. For I have never either said or thought that the mind has need of innate (natural) ideas, which are anything different from its faculty of thinking; but when I remarked that there were in me certain thoughts which did not proceed from external objects, nor from the determination of my will, but from the faculty of thinking alone which is in me, that I might distinguish the notions or ideas, which are the forms of these thoughts, from others adventitious or factitious, I called them *innate* in the same sense in which we say that generosity is innate in certain families, in others certain diseases, as gout or gravel, not that, therefore, the infants of those families labour under those

NOTES. 243

diseases in the womb of the mother, but because they are born with a certain disposition or faculty of contracting them."

Again, on Art. xiii., he says—"What supposition is more absurd than that all the common notions which are in the mind arise from these corporeal motions, and cannot exist without them? I should wish our author to show me what that corporeal movement is which can form any common notion in our mind; for example,—*that the things which are the same with a third are the same with each other,* or the like. For all those motions are *particular;* but these notions are *universal,* and possess no affinity with motions, nor any relation to them."

"He (Regius) proceeds, in Article xiv., to affirm that the very idea of God which is in us arises not from our faculty of thinking, in which it is innate, but from divine revelation, or tradition, or the observation of things. We shall easily discover the error of this assertion, if we consider that a thing can be said to be from another, either because that other is its proximate and primary cause, or because it is simply the remote and accidental, which, in truth, gives occasion to the primary to produce its own effect at one time rather than at another. Thus, all workmen are the primary and proximate causes of their own works; but they who commission them, or offer payment for the execution of the works, are the accidental and remote causes, because the works would not perhaps have been done without the order. It cannot be doubted but that tradition or the observation of things is the remote cause, inviting us to attend to the idea of God which we possess, and to exhibit it in presence to our thought. But that it is the proximate cause (*effectrix*) of that idea can be alleged only by one who holds that we can know nothing of God beyond the word God, or the corporeal figure exhibited to us by painters in their representations of God. Inasmuch as observation, if it be of sight, presents nothing of its own proper power to the mind except pictures, and pictures whose whole variety is determined solely by that of certain corporeal movements, as our author himself teaches; if it be of hearing, observation presents nothing but words and sounds; if of the other senses, it presents nothing that can be related to God. And, indeed, it is manifest to every one that sight properly and by itself presents nothing except pictures, and hearing nothing but words or sounds; so that all which we think beyond these words or pictures, as the significates of them, are represented to us by ideas coming from no other source than our faculty of thinking, and therefore natural to it; that is always existing in us in power. For to be in any faculty is not to be in act but in power only, because the very word faculty designates nothing but power."—Lett. xxxviii. Garnier's Ed. Tom. iv. Not. in Prog. Latin (1670), p. 175.

On the celebrated question (says De la Forge) as to whether the ideas of the mind are born with it, or acquired, I reply that they are both one and other. They are born with it, not only because it has never received them from the senses, but also because it is created with the faculty of thinking and forming them, which is the proximate and principal cause of them; in the same way that we say gout or gravel is natural to certain families, when the members of them bring with them proximate dispositions to those maladies. But those ideas are acquired, and not natural, if by natural we understand that they are in the substance of the soul as in a conservatory, in the manner in which pictures are disposed in a gallery, that we may consider them as we please; for there is none of them in particular that needs to be actually present to our mind, which, being a thinking substance, can have nothing actually present to it of which it has no knowledge. It is for this reason they are contained in the mind only in *power,* and not in *act.*"—De l'Esprit, chap. x., pp. 143, 144. Con. Clauberg. on Med. iii. Op., P. i., 391.

VII. FORMALLY AND EMINENTLY (*formaliter, eminenter*)—p. 49.

Besides the application of the word *formal* already noticed, viz. (1), in opposition to *objective,* to denote the object as it exists in nature; and (2) as a synonyme for objective in contrast to *material,* to denote the idea so far as it is a representation, there is still another use of the term in the writings of Descartes and in the Cartesian literature. In this *third* application, *formal* is opposed to *eminent,* and refers to the relation of cause and effect. The contrast indicated by these terms in this relation is in regard to the manner in which a cause is said to contain its effect. A cause, as the sum of the perfection or reality of its effect, may contain this reality in either of two ways, and must in one of them. On the one hand, if the perfection of the effect be contained in the cause *in the same mode* in which it exists in the effect, or, if the cause be only possessed, in this respect, of equal perfection with the effect, the reality of the effect is said to be in the cause formally (*formaliter, q. d. secundum eandem formam et rationem*). Thus, the print of the foot has formally the quantity and figure of the foot, and is thus *formally* in its cause. In the same way, any *absolute* perfection is formally in God. On the other hand, if the effect be contained in the cause, not as it is in itself, or according to its intrinsic form, essence, or proper definition, but *in a higher grade or mode of perfection* (*gradu, modo eminentiori*), it is said to be in its cause *eminently.* In this sense the Divine intellect contains the human, since God knows, but without the imperfections incident to the exercise of our faculties of cognition. A cause containing eminently thus contains all the reality of the effect more perfectly than the effect itself. This distinction, borrowed from the schoolmen, has an important application, in the philosophy of Descartes, to the question of the proof of the existence of God through his idea.—*Con.* Med. iii., p. 48, etc. Appendix, def. iv., p. 216; Ax. iv., p. 219 Spinoza, Prin. Phil. Cart., P. i., vol. i., p. 16. (Paulus.) Clauberg. Exercit. vi., p. 613, § 5, 6. (Ed. 1691.) Flender. Log., § 50. Chauvin, Lex. Rat., voc. *Continere.* De Vries, (Anti-Cart.) Exercit. vi., § 4, pp. 55, 56. (Ed. 1695.)

VIII. PURE INTELLECTION (*intellectio pura*)—p. 147.

Intelligence, understanding (*intellectus*), is the general name in Cartesian literature of the powers of cognition in contrast to those of will; and in this sense the term comprehends all the acts, whether of sense, memory, imagination, or of intellect proper. But *intelligence* has, besides its general, a special and restricted signification; and this especially when the qualifying epithet *pure* is joined with it. Pure intellection (*intellectio pura*) denotes not knowledge in general, but the knowledge, whether individual or general, of the mental phænomena, and generally of all those objects we are capable of *thinking* in the narrower sense of the word, but cannot *imagine,* or hold up to our mind in an *image* or *picture.* In a word, with the Cartesians the pure understanding is the faculty of the *unpicturable,* imagination of the *picturable.* Whatever knowledge, therefore, we may be able to reach of mind or of God,—of body in its general relations, or in such of its properties as are either too great or too minute for apprehension by sense,—of those judgments which are native to the mind—falls within the province of the pure intellect.

It should be observed that in this faculty, according to its application, there is knowledge either *without* or *with* ideas —in other words, either an immediate or a mediate knowledge. It is by the pure intellect alone that we take cognisance of our own mind in its phænomena, and these we can immediately, or without idea, apprehend. But of everything distinct from ourselves which we know by the intellect, we can have but a mediate knowledge, or a knowledge by idea. The distinction of the ideas of the imagination and the intellect, is nearly similar to the distinction of thoughts into those of the individual and general, or of *intuitions* (in the older sense of the term), and *notions* or *concepts.—Con.* Note ii., *Idea.* Med. iv. p. 64. Med. vi. pp. 84-86. Prin. of Phil., § 73. Lett. lxxv., Garnier, tom. iv. p. 318 (or lxii. of vol. vi. Ed. 12mo.) Ep. P. i., xxx. Reg. ad Direct. Ing., R. xii. De la Forge, De l'Esprit, chap. xviii, pp. 298-302. Hamilton's Reid, p. 291. Note.

IX. MOTION—p. 191.

The following section of the *Principles* is added to those given in the text, from its bearing logically and historically on the doctrine of Occasional Causes as arising out of Cartesianism:—

" That God is the primary cause of motion; and that he always preserves the same quantity of motion in the universe.

" After having thus adverted to the nature of motion, it is necessary to consider its cause, and that the twofold: firstly, the universal and primary, which is the general cause of all the motions in the world; and secondly, the particular, by which it happens that each of the parts of matter acquires the motion which it had not before. And with respect to the general cause, it seems manifest to me that it is none other than God himself, who, in the beginning, created matter along with motion and rest, and now by his ordinary concourse alone preserves in the whole the same amount of motion and rest that he then placed in it. For although motion is nothing in the matter moved but its mode, it has yet a certain and determinate quantity, which we easily understand may remain always the same in the whole universe, although it changes in each of the parts of it. So that, in truth, we may hold, when a part of matter is moved with double the quickness of another, and that other is twice the size of the former, that there is just precisely as much motion, but no more, in the less body as in the greater; and that in proportion as the motion of any one part is reduced, so is that of some other and equal portion accelerated. We also know that there is perfection in God, not only because he is in himself immutable, but because he operates in the most constant and immutable manner possible: so that with the exception of those mutations which manifest experience, or divine revelation renders certain, and which we perceive or believe are brought about without any change in the Creator, we ought to suppose no other in his works, lest there should thence arise ground for concluding inconstancy in God himself. Whence it follows as most consonant to reason, that merely because God diversely moved the parts of matter when he first created them, and now preserves all that matter, manifestly in the same mode and on the same principle on which he first created it, he also always preserves the same quantity of motion in the matter itself."—Part ii. § 36.

X. SECOND ELEMENT—p. 199.

" Thus we may reckon upon having already discovered two diverse forms in matter, which may be taken for the forms of the first two elements of the visible world. The first is that of the scraping (*raclure*) which must have been separated from the other parts of matter, when they were rounded, and is moved with so much velocity that the force alone of its agitation is sufficient to cause it, in its contact with other bodies, to be broken and divided by them into an infinity of small particles that are of such a figure as always exactly to fill all the holes and small interstices which they find around these bodies. The other is, that of all the rest of the matter whose particles are spherical and very small in comparison of the bodies we see on the earth, but nevertheless possess some determinate quantity, so that they can be divided into others much smaller; and we will still find in addition a third form in some parts of matter, to wit, in those which, on account of their size and figure, cannot be so easily moved as the preceding; and I will endeavour to show that all the bodies of the visible world are composed of these three forms, which are found in matter, as of three diverse elements, to wit, that the sun and the fixed stars have the form of the first of these elements, the heavens that of the second, and the earth with the planets and comets that of the third. For since the sun and the fixed stars emit light, since the heavens transmit it, and since the earth, the planets, and comets reflect it, it appears to me I have ground for these three differences, [luminousness, transparency, and opacity or obscurity, which are the chief we can relate to the sense of sight], in order to distinguish the three elements of the visible world."—Prin. of Phil. Part. iii., § 52. *Con.* Chauvin, Lex. Rat., Art. *Elementum.*